SO-AHX-074

THE AMERICAN IDEAL

'Who are you, indeed, who would talk or sing to
    America?
Have you studied out the land, its idioms and men?
Have you learn'd the physiology, phrenology,
    politics, geography, pride, freedom, friendship,
    of the land? its substratums and objects?
Have you consider'd the organic compact of the
    first day of the first year of Independence,
    sign'd by the Commissioners, ratified by The
    States, and read by Washington at the head of
    the army?
Have you possess'd yourself of the Federal
    Constitution?
Do you see who have left all feudal processes and
    poems behind them, and assumed the poems
    and processes of Democracy?'

VACHEL LINDSAY

THE AMERICAN IDEAL

BY

ARTHUR BRYANT

Essay Index Reprint Series

BOOKS FOR LIBRARIES PRESS
FREEPORT, NEW YORK

First Published 1936
Reprinted 1969

STANDARD BOOK NUMBER:
8369-1251-9

LIBRARY OF CONGRESS CATALOG CARD NUMBER:
77-90617

PRINTED IN THE UNITED STATES OF AMERICA

TO THE
AMERICAN AVIATORS
WITH WHOM
I ONCE SERVED
1917–1918

PREFACE

In another form the studies that appear in this book were given at the request of the Sulgrave Manor Board as the Watson Foundation Lectures in the fall of 1935. I have expanded and recast them to meet the requirements of prose.

Englishmen to their loss are not taught the history of the United States, though they have more to learn from it than from that of any other country. Apart from being an almost incredibly dramatic story of discovery, struggle and expansion, it is the record of the first attempt made on a continental scale to lead the democratic life without the bonds of rank and the scourge of war. And it helps to resolve as nothing else can the bewildering contradictions of modern America. The best clue to a people's character is its own past.

I have therefore told as simply as possible the lives of eight men—among them a Virginian planter, a poor frontier farmer's son, a Boston preacher, the scion of a New York business house, a journalist who in late life essayed diplomacy —who in their different ways have illustrated aspects of American life and thought. Three of them became President of the Republic ; another was an obscure poet who died in early manhood. Yet all had something in common—an ideal which is the unifying theme of this book and which Mr. James Truslow Adams, in his ' Epic of America ' has called the ' American Dream.' I believe that for all America's outward appearance of materialism and ' big business,' this ideal provides the best explanation of her history, and perhaps, despite all the vast changes of the past century, of her future also. I was recently interested to read the same

PREFACE

conclusion in the confessions of a young American, bred out
of the millionaire stock of Wall Street—' that America is
not New York, Boston, Philadelphia or San Francisco,
but a nation of villagers who refuse to be ruled by the big
cities.' The casual visitor to the States, unable to see the
wood for the trees, may miss this phenomenon. History
helps to explain it.

As this work makes no pretence to originality, no biblio-
graphy is given. To those wishing to make a further study
of the subject the following books may be helpful : Henry
S. Randall's ' The Life of Thomas Jefferson ' ; Francis W.
Hirst's ' Life and Letters of Thomas Jefferson ' ; Henry
Adams's ' History of the United States during the Adminis-
trations of Jefferson and Madison ' ; Lord Charnwood's
' Abraham Lincoln ' ; Carl Sandburg's ' The Prairie Years ' ;
Emil Ludwig's ' Lincoln ' ; Oliver Wendell Holmes's ' Ralph
Waldo Emerson ' ; James Elliot Cabot's ' Memoir of Ralph
Waldo Emerson ' ; Van Wyck Brooks's ' Life of Emerson ' ;
Richard Garnett's ' Life of Ralph Waldo Emerson ' ; Augus-
tine Birrell's ' Collected Essays ' ; John Morley's ' Critical
Miscellanies ' ; Henry James's ' Partial Portraits ' ; Matthew
Arnold's ' Discourses in America ' ; Emerson's Essays and
Poems ; Henry A. Beers's ' The Connecticut Wits ' ; Walt
Whitman's ' Leaves of Grass ' ; John Bailey's ' Walt Whitman ' ;
John Burroughs's ' Whitman, a Study,' ' Theodore Roosevelt,
an Autobiography ' ; Theodore Roosevelt's ' The Winning of
the West ' ; Henry F. Pringle's ' Theodore Roosevelt, a Bio-
graphy ' ; Henry Cabot Lodge's ' The Letters of Roosevelt to
Henry Cabot Lodge ' ; William Roscoe Thayer's ' Theo-
dore Roosevelt, an Intimate Biography ' ; Lewis Einstein's
' Roosevelt, His Mind in Action ' ; Lord Charnwood's
' Theodore Roosevelt ' ; Owen Wister's ' Theodore Roose-
velt, The Story of a Friendship ' ; Theodore Roosevelt's
' America and the World War ' ; J. B. Bishop's ' Theodore
Roosevelt and His Time, Shown in his Letters,' ' The Letters
and Friendships of Sir Cecil Spring Rice ' (edited by Stephen
Gwynn) ; Burton J. Hendrick's ' Life and Letters of Walter
H. Page ' ; Richard Rush's ' Residence at the Court of

PREFACE

London '; the Poems of Alan Seeger (with an Introduction by William Archer); Alan Seeger's ' Letters and Diary '; Vachel Lindsay's 'Collected Poems' and ' The Litany of Washington Street '; Stephen Graham's ' Tramping with a Poet in the Rockies '; James Truslow Adams's ' The Epic of America '; Robert E. Spiller's ' The American in England '; Edward Channing's ' History of the United States '; S. E. Morison's ' Oxford History of the United States '; Henry Adams's ' The Education of Henry Adams '; and Herbert Agar's ' The American Presidents.'

I have only to add my personal thanks to Lord Lee of Fareham and the Sulgrave Manor Board for the help they afforded me and the generous confidence they reposed in me ; to the Provost of University College, London, and my friend, Mr. C. O. G. Douie, its secretary, for their hospitality ; to my father and Mr. C. Alport for their kindness in reading the proofs, and to my secretary for the work performed in assisting me to prepare this book for the press.

ARTHUR BRYANT.

PUBLISHERS' NOTE

The Publishers are indebted to Messrs. Macmillan & Co. Ltd. for their kind permission to quote various passages from ' Collected Poems ' by Vachel Lindsay, and also to Messrs. Constable & Co. Ltd. for leave to use quotations from ' Poems ' by Alan Seeger.

CONTENTS

INTRODUCTORY

'THE FAIREST COUNTRY
THAT A MAN MIGHT SEE'

OFTEN during the Middle Ages gazers from the western shores of Europe fancied they could descry against the glories of the sunset the capes and cliffs of a phantom coast. It was christened by many names—Atlantis, Hy-Brazil, Antilia, Avalon. But no sensible man had ever supposed it really existed. The educated few believed that the Atlantic Ocean stretched from Finisterre to China, and everyone else that it ended in some horrible gulf where its stormy waters poured over the edge of the world into Hell.

In 1492 an Italian Admiral in the service of Spain, sailing westwards in the belief that Cathay lay beyond sunset as well as sunrise, stumbled unawares not on Hell, but on America. The gradual realisation of this was as revolutionary to human thought as would be the discovery to-day of a new planet habitable by man. It was the more so because it coincided with the end of the static European civilisation of the Middle Ages, and the decay of the beliefs on which it was based. At the moment when every ancient door was closing on man's spiritual aspirations, a new one opened into the sunset. Beyond the ocean was a world of boundless opportunity where tired humanity could make a fresh start.

On this bewildering hope the divine discontent of the Christian peoples of Europe engendered the American Dream. At first sight the history of America appears to have been more a chronicle of hard-boiled realities and of mankind in its most materialistic aspects than the story of an ideal. Yet by a curious paradox the material realities of American history have perpetually changed and the dream has remained constant. Thus the nations, which were geographically nearest to those parts of the New World where wealth in a transportable form was most easily obtained, ultimately found their Midas heritage a barren one. For then as later the rainbow of the western world was found to vanish in the crock of gold at the rainbow's end. The treasures which flowed from the mines of the Incas into the coffers of Castile proved less durable than the insubstantial dreams of the visionaries. For more than half a century while Spain and Portugal monopolised the wealth of the western hemisphere and English adventurers struggled to find a route to the East round the frozen coasts of Muscovy or down that steely corridor of dreams, the North-West Passage, English philosophers and poets were toying with the idea of a regeneration of mankind in the transatlantic wilderness. Here the Age of Gold and Innocence, if it had ever existed, might return and society be rebuilt on a basis of humanity and pure reason. Of such stuff as dreams are made on was More's Utopia and Bacon's New Atlantis. And when in the early seventeenth century the greatest of English poets, in the most serene expression of his universal genius, depicted an aged statesman shipwrecked on an enchanted island, it was to make him rub his old, world-blinded eyes at the fresh lush grass around him and fall to babbling of the ideal state he would found there:

Had I plantation of this isle, my lord,—

.   .   .   .   .

I' the commonwealth I would by contraries
Execute all things; for no kind of traffic
Would I admit; no name of magistrate;
Letters should not be known; riches, poverty,
And use of service, none; contract, succession,
Bourn, bound of land, tilth, vineyard, none;

No use of metal, corn, or wine, or oil;
No occupation; all men idle, all;
And women too, but innocent and pure:
No sovereignty;

   .   .   .   .   .

All things in common nature should produce
Without sweat or endeavour: treason, felony,
Sword, pike, knife, gun, or need of any engine,
Would I not have; but nature should bring forth,
Of its own kind, all foison, all abundance,
To feed my innocent people.

   .   .   .   .

I would with such perfection govern, sir,
To excel the golden age.

But the English were not content only to dream of the
New World. Cabot had coasted along the barren shores
of Labrador in a Bristol ship five years after Columbus's
discovery, and as early as 1515 a popular interlude proclaimed to the rough commonalty of England :

O what a great thing had been then
If that they that be Englishmen
   Might have been the first of all
That there should have taken possession
And made first building and habitation
   A memory perpetual.

Shut out from their traditional commercial outlet by the
economic changes in Europe, the merchants of England
sent out expedition after expedition across the ocean for
destinations unknown, and Richard Hakluyt left his quiet
Suffolk rectory of Witheringsett-cum-Brockford and with
' many watchings, toils and wearing out of his weak body '
travelled about the country seeking out record of them.

But it was not in the heroic exploits of Elizabethan
buccaneers in the Spanish Main that the key to the American
future lay, though for a time the majority of English settlers
who crossed the Atlantic—mostly under the pressure of the
economic and political storms that troubled their native

land after the death of Elizabeth—made for the unoccupied West Indian sugar islands. It was Barbados, it will be remembered, that so roused the sanguine hopes of impecunious Tom Verney. But even before the end of the sixteenth century Humphrey Gilbert and Walter Raleigh had experimented with the idea of a settlement of English colonists on the wild mainland of the northern half of the continent, a stretch of whose coast they had tried to colonise and christened after their Queen, Virginia. It was Raleigh's repeated prayer that he might live to see it a new English nation. By 1607 a permanent foothold was established. And though three years later, when the next ship arrived from England, there were only one hundred and fifty survivors, famished, diseased and dispirited—it is said that one man ate part of his wife and salted down the rest—by the middle of the century there were over 60,000 English settlers living in the New World and a third of them on the mainland.

Theirs was no easy struggle. Here was no tropic vegetation nor perpetual sunshine. In the harsh North, christened New England, the first winters brought literal starvation, and even in Virginia the soil and climate were so inhospitable that the Spanish Ambassador in London told his government that the young colony was not worth attacking, since it must inevitably perish of its own. Untamed, encroaching forest, feverish swamp and unfordable river, wild beast and wilder red man, cold, famine and disease stood between the colonists and their dreams. Yet these trials only made their dreams the more precious.

It was natural that those who came should be poor. There was nothing in the primeval condition of North America to tempt the rich and powerful: they were better off in their own country. The early settlers were mostly plain and oppressed men, who braved the horrors of the North Atlantic passage in order to make homes where they might be a little freer than in their native land. The Puritan artisans and husbandmen went to New England and the portionless younger sons of the gentry to the Cavalier settlements of the South. They came with no particular desire of conquest or empire, but for their own personal liberties and to find some sort of a livelihood, however meagre, since hunger with hope in the wilderness was better than hunger without hope at home.

They left government—the ceaseless interference of King, Lord, Bishop, Priest and Squire—behind them. The inequalities of the Old World seemed unbelievably far away on the iron shores of the New World. At their back was the ocean, which few wished to cross again, and in front of them the forest. Every man had to ' root, hog or die.' The few who had influence or wealth in the land from which they had come found that these were almost as hard to carry across the Atlantic as they are said to be across the river of death : the wilderness made everyone the same. Those who came as subordinates found that there was no need to work for others where a whole continent was to be had by anyone who would clear and cultivate it.

The need for labour made men value themselves. The only things that distinguished a settler from his fellows were his own qualities—his strength, courage and resource.

> When Adam delved and Eve span,
> Who was then a gentleman ?

Success could only be measured by what a man achieved for himself : the badges of Europe availed nothing where every man stood on his own rude and hairy legs.

Yet out of this harsh struggle a plain man's dream was born, descended from that older Utopian vision of the Elizabethans. It was a prosaic dream in the English fashion, springing out of the fundamental equality of the plain man in the wilderness :

> We implore
> Free air, free ocean and a harmless shore.

These may not have seemed much, but they were enough, and no man could say that he was being exploited. ' I live a simple life,' wrote one of the settlers, ' and hath builded a shop, and doth follow the weaving of linen cloth, and I have bought 450 acres of land in the woods.' That man should be at liberty to create as he saw good, that work, courage and initiative should not be cheated of their reward, and that every worker should enjoy the fruits of his own labour, such was the American dream. It thrived. By the end of the first century of colonisation there were over a quarter of a million English living along the eastern shores of North America.

To such men freedom and authority seemed at first diametrically opposed. Most of them had left the old world to escape its forms of government. King, Lord of the Council, Priest, Bishop, were words that had no appeal for the American mind.

Yet the very freedom the settlers sought could only be maintained by some system of authority and, with French, Spaniards and red men waging almost perpetual war against them, through some understanding with the mother country. In some places they came to a mutual agreement to ' submit to such government and governors as they should by common consent agree to make and choose '; in others they procured royal charters through the mediation of some great man at home. By the end of the seventeenth century the eastern coast of the continent from Spanish Florida in the south to French Canada in the north was mapped out in states, each managing its own affairs after the English model by representative assemblies, each with a residential Governor appointed by the Crown and each independent of its fellow colonies. But in all the tie between the imperial government and the individual pioneer remained of the lightest : the distance in space and time between them and the absence of bureaucratic machinery ensured that.

In England the imperial connection with these remote colonies, so far as it was not merely regarded as a nuisance, was viewed chiefly in the light of the trading privileges to be obtained from it. The average American, absorbed in making a home for himself in forest and wilderness, had little time for constitutional abstractions, and was ready to let the government make what trading and manufacturing regulations it chose provided that it did not interfere with his hard-earned right to manage his own affairs in his own way. Local government was the only kind of government that as yet affected him, and he had no reason to concern himself with remote checks and controls so long as they remained loose enough for him not to feel them. All he demanded was a law to protect him from unruly neighbours, a local assembly in which to discuss local needs and an assurance that he should not be badgered out of the home he had made for himself by any man.

The dream of the plain man seeking bread in the wilderness thrived ; that is the history of North America. As the sweat poured from his brows, the desert flowered. The primitive society of the seventeenth century was succeeded by something far more complicated. Wealth, with its diversified forms of life, appeared, and in the coast towns a growing merchant community found oppressive the restrictions on trade imposed by the English legislators at Westminster. The rough homespun suit that had once allowed room for every movement became cramping. Freedom was still the first desire of the Englishman in America. But it had to be a larger scale of freedom if it was to continue to suffice.

The Englishman in America ? Yet by the eighteenth century the description was ceasing to be true. A few generations of life in the new country had already made a change in the English stock. The high cheek-bones, the keen look, the fierce tangy speech of modern America were beginning to be noticed as transatlantic phenomena : the sleepy, good-humoured lion of the old world seemed to be taking on talons and wings. Western air in Saxon lungs, the blood of western animals in the veins, the habits of mind and body formed by the battle for life in the western world were making a new race of men. The old English love of law and home was still there, but something fierce and primitive was being added. Soon an eagle would take the air.

Before a new race can grow into a nation, it must breed leaders. An aristocracy does not develop readily in the wilderness; where all have to toil together in the dust, the rare and sensitive are easily crushed. What a modern historian has called the ' down-drag of the frontier ' was a serious factor in the early history of America. There was little time for thought and study, and the instinctive powers, which are born of meditation and the wise use of leisure, were lacking.

Yet leadership came, and from the old Dominion of Virginia. So strangely are good and evil intermixed, that it grew in the rank soil of negro slavery. The use of transported African labour for the cultivation of tobacco on a large scale made the white colonists of Virginia rich without the necessity of working. Estates which had been almost worthless when granted to seventeenth-century pioneers provided their descendants with princely incomes. By the middle of the eighteenth century an American aristocracy had come into being in the tobacco-growing South. Its culture resembled that of the English squirearchy, and was based on classical studies, equestrian exercise and the patriarchal life of the country house. The boarded manorial homes of Virginia boasted libraries, fine furniture, silver and ancestral portraits after the English fashion. They were supported by tobacco and slaves.

Yet at heart the aristocracy that grew up in the American wilderness differed from the comfortable squirearchy of the English shires which it superficially resembled. Beneath the surface of the gay, dancing, fiddling, coach-driving, hard-drinking gentleman of the plantations and the Williamsburg Assembly Rooms were depths unknown in England. At bottom he was *homo Americanus*. Some time or other, like his father before him, he had worn a coonskin cap and tracked the Indians at their own game in the woods. Something of the red man's grim dignity, and of his hatred of compromise and half-measures, had gone to his making.

From such a school of patricians, accustomed from birth to rule, trained by youthful adventure in the primeval forest in the hatchet logic and lonely dignity of the American aboriginal, and maintained by slaves and tobacco, sprang the great Virginians who changed the history of the world. In silk stockings and powdered wigs, they conducted their political and social round according to the decorous conventions of their English motherland, and maintained in more ways than one the English tie. Yet in their innermost hearts England was no longer their country. The stately and slow-witted nobles whom the Court of St. James's sent to govern them, the stupid military officers whose pretences to precedence so maddened their provincial pride, the unimaginative officials who tried to organise their lives, appeared to them increasingly as strangers. The real England of hallowed field and parish lore, which had bred their forefathers, they had never known. Instead they turned in deep, if unexpressed, love to the beautiful and spacious land which gave them and their children so rich and friendly a life. From its forests and rivers and ever-beckoning distances, as much as from the stubborn legal formulas of the unknown island from which their stock had come, their passionate love of individual liberty was derived.

CHAPTER I

THOMAS JEFFERSON

THOMAS JEFFERSON was born on April 13, 1743, in a farm-house on the Virginian frontier. His father was a hard-working, self-made, thriving land surveyor, who had drawn the first map of Virginia, and, having patented a thousand or so acres on the frontier, had built there ' a plain weather-boarded ' house. He was a man of herculean strength, who loved to see his own horizon around him. This rough pioneer married an aristocrat, Jane Randolph, the daughter of an old colonial family. She was of the same stock as the English poet, Thomas Randolph, and the blood of the Princess Pocahontas flowed in her veins.

Their son's youth was passed in the heart of the beautiful district where the farms of Virginia still bordered the great woods of the interior and the habitations of the red men. Coming years were to see the frontier receding ever farther into the west, but wherever it went, in forest, prairie or mountain, it was to remain the home of the American dream, the constant point at which the old world was challenged by the rough promise and hope of the new. Of the great American statesmen of the frontier Thomas Jefferson was the first. He grew up a child of the wilderness, red-headed, strong in body and free in mind, a mighty swimmer and horseman, a lover of the country in all its moods, knowing intimately its birds and beasts and flowers.

To the boy everything American was native. Even the red men were his friends. In after years he loved to recall their visits to his father's home and the impressions of

1

attachment and commiseration he had then first conceived for them. ' I knew much of the great Ontassetè, the warrior and orator of the Cherokees. He was always the guest of my father on his journeys to and from Williamsburg. I was in his camp when he made his great farewell oration to his people the evening before his departure for England. The moon was in full splendour, and to her he seemed to address himself in his prayers for his own safety on the voyage and that of his people during his absence. His sounding voice, distinct articulation, animated action, and the solemn silence of his people at their several fires, filled me with awe and veneration, although I did not understand a word he uttered.' The listening boy was something of a poet, as were so many of these early Virginians.

He was a scholar too. The library at Shadwell was not large, but it contained Shakespeare, Swift and Addison. They made him an enthusiastic learner. Mathematics, music and architecture, mechanics and language, law and folklore, in turn delighted him. And his self-taught father taught him something not to be found in books—never to ask another to do what he could do for himself.

After his father's early death the boy continued his classical education at the famous William and Mary College at Williamsburg—the *alma mater* of the American Revolution where the high Roman republicanism of the great Virginians was nurtured on the writings of Locke and Algernon Sidney. Here he grew to manhood, outwardly a handsome young patrician in the Virginian manner, six foot two in height, a bold rider, taking vigorous part, as befitted his mother's son, in the ' junketing, dancing and high jinks ' of his kind, and absorbing in the society of Governor Fauquier's house the best products of eighteenth-century English culture. Even in such a society he was already distinguished by his accomplishments, which included a mastery of Greek, Latin and French, a knowledge of Spanish and Italian, and a very real love of books, music, philosophy, mathematics and architecture. Yet at heart he remained what his father had been before him, a man of the frontier.

At twenty-one Jefferson entered the chambers of George Wythe, the ' beloved mentor ' of John Marshall and Henry Clay. Aided by Wythe, who always looked on him as his favourite pupil and left him his library when he died, he learnt to understand the old common law of England and added something of its jealous lore of civil liberty to his native passion for freedom. His industry and method quickly made him one of the first lawyers in the State.

He did not neglect other studies. In a course of reading which he drew up at this time for a young friend, he prescribed as the necessary groundwork for a legal education a knowledge of French, Latin, Mathematics and Natural Philosophy. To these were to be added later Physics, Ethics, Religion, Natural Law, Belles Lettres, Criticism, Rhetoric and Oratory. From eight in the morning till bedtime every hour of the day was mapped out. And for each branch of learning Jefferson laid down the detailed rules for its mastery. ' In reading the reporters enter in a common-place book every case of value, condensed into the narrowest compass possible, which will admit of presenting distinctly the principles of the case. This operation is doubly useful, insomuch as it obliges the student to seek out the pith of the case, and habituates him to a condensation of thought, and to an acquisition of the most valuable of all talents, that of never using two words where one will do.'

When he was twenty-eight Jefferson married a rich widow, beautiful and of gentle birth, named Martha Skelton. She gave him children, an addition to his modest independent fortune and ten years of almost unbroken happiness. Through her, from his thirtieth to his fortieth year, that decade in which men of powerful body and strong imagination are most liable to find tempest and frustration, he was freed from all sickness of soul and heart. For her, when his house was burnt to the ground, he built a new home on a beautiful hill named Monticello. He designed it himself, in the Grecian mode that best suited his even

3

temper and mind. It is still one of the finest specimens of domestic architecture in America.

Before he married Jefferson had received his baptism in politics. During his boyhood the Seven Years' War had freed the thirteen English colonies on the American coast from the danger of being cut off from the interior by a chain of French forts from Canada to New Orleans. With the cession of Canada to Britain in 1763 the English in America ceased to be dependent on the armed forces of the Crown for their protection from foreign aggression. At the same time the imperial genius of Chatham and his victories awoke the ruling classes in England to the realisation that they possessed an empire. Unfortunately they therefore assumed that they ought to try to govern it better. Encouraged by a young and energetic sovereign with a high sense of his duty, high-minded legislators at Westminster set themselves to systematise the colonial administration.

The Englishman is a stubborn creature, and the ownership of land renders him more so. Whether he is on the east or west of the Atlantic, he is possessed of an invincible belief that he can manage his own affairs a great deal better than anyone else can manage them for him. In the seventeenth century the benevolent attempts of an officious king and an over-zealous priest to improve their political and ecclesiastical government had driven the people of England into a stubborn rebellion which cost both king and priest their heads. Now a hundred and twenty years later history repeated itself on the other side of the Atlantic.

Well-meant as was the attempt to enforce good government in America, the revolt against it was even better justified. For just as the centralising policy of the Stuart Kings had been frustrated by the hoary corruption and inefficiency of the minor bureaucracy and its utter inadequacy to overcome the strength of English provincialism, so the imperial experiment of the eighteenth century was shipwrecked at the start by the impossibility of arriving at any just and practical measures where rulers and ruled were divided by three thousand miles from one another. To administer a community of Englishmen on the far side of the Atlantic without respect to public opinion was like trying to navigate a ship without regard to the direction of the wind.

Yet the people of England viewed the efforts of their rulers to regulate the affairs of the people of North America with sympathy. There was a good reason for this. The Seven Years' War, like other wars, had cost a great deal of money, and the British taxpayer who had paid for it regarded the American colonist as its principal beneficiary. He was therefore delighted when Parliament, in pursuance of the government's new imperial policy, resolved to shift some part of his burden to the broad backs of the colonists. Unhappily the manner in which she did so was ill suited to the end. By the Stamp Act of 1765 the colonists were not so much asked to contribute to the imperial exchequer as commanded.

In theory the British Government was within its rights. By the legal formulas of the Constitution the Crown in Parliament had sovereign powers over colonial legislatures. Nor was the imposition levied by the Stamp Act onerous or unreasonable in amount. But the principle behind it struck at the hitherto tacitly accepted claim of the colonial assemblies to levy their own internal taxes for revenue, and, what was more dangerous, implied that Englishmen who had crossed the Atlantic were not possessed of the same rights as those who had remained at home. The first of these rights—the sacred charter of the gentlemen of England—was that there should be no taxation without representation.

The independent gentry of Virginia were quick to perceive this. In April 1765 Patrick Henry—

> the forest-born Demosthenes
> Whose thunder shook the Philip of the Seas—

rose in the Virginian House of Burgesses to support a resolution that the colonists were entitled to the full rights of Englishmen. ' Cæsar had his Brutus—Charles the first his Cromwell, and George the third——' here he paused for a moment amid shouts of ' Treason '—' *may profit by their example.* If *this* be treason make the most of it.' Jefferson, born of the same free, forest breed, was listening to Henry at the lobby door. ' He appeared to me,' he said, ' to speak as Homer wrote.' His countrymen thought the same and boycotted the stamps. Impressed by the bold front of the Virginian gentry and the protests of alarmed British merchants, the Government withdrew the Act.

Yet two years later Britain returned to the charge with the Townshend duties on tea, glass and paper. Again Virginia led the American resistance. By this time Jefferson was a member of the House of Burgesses. His first legislative experience was brief, for the assembly was dissolved after five days by the Governor. But it lasted long enough for him to introduce a bill to enable owners to manumit their slaves—characteristically his first political act. It was followed by a more momentous one. On the day after the dissolution he took his part with George Washington and Patrick Henry in the Association at the Raleigh Tavern, Williamsburg, which instituted a boycott of articles of English merchandise till the duties were repealed.

For the second time the colonists gained their point. Yet four years later King George and his chief minister, Lord North, resolved to ' try the question ' once more by the grant of what was for all practical purposes a monopoly to sell tea in America to the East India Company, then in difficulties. It proved the most expensive monopoly ever granted. None of the tea reached the American consumer. At New York it was not admitted to the port and at Charleston it was left to moulder in a vault. At Boston it was thrown into the harbour by the hotheads of the town disguised as Red Indians.

When the news reached England the anger of earth's proudest and most obstinate race broke into flame. The Boston Port Bill of 1774, passed by an assembly of English country gentlemen and place-holders, closed the port, suppressed all town meetings in Massachusetts, and ordered the rioters to be brought to trial in England. In a few minutes an Act passed at Westminster had deprived a part of the English race beyond the Atlantic of the rights of self-government and trial by jury. This time the revolt against the authority of the old world had come from the stark North. But Virginia, New York and Pennsylvania were instant in support. If the mother country were to punish one of her children, she should find the whole nursery in rebellion ! Jefferson himself joined with his Virginian neighbours in drawing public attention to the wrongs of his fellow Americans. ' With the help of Rushworth, whom we rummaged over for revolutionary precedents and forms . . . ' he wrote afterwards, ' we cooked up a resolution . . . for appointing the first day of June, on which the port bill was to commence, for a day of fasting, humiliation, and prayer, to implore Heaven to avert from us the evils of civil war, to inspire us with firmness in support of our rights, and to turn the hearts of the King and Parliament to moderation and justice.' Nothing could have been more English and conservative than this searching for precedents to raise rebellion. It was in the authentic manner of Hampden and Eliot.

The next step of the Virginian gentry was still more significant. Their assembly having been dissolved by the Governor, they set up Committees of Correspondence and appointed deputies to meet the deputies of the other American colonies in a Continental Congress. It was Jefferson, marked out for the task by his political studies, who was set to draft instructions for the Virginian delegates. In doing so he went far beyond the conventional view, held at this time by most of his fellow ' patriots,' that England still had a prescriptive right to regulate colonial commerce and lay duties on it so long as she did not infringe the colonies' privilege of raising their own revenue. Instead he denied that a Parliament elected in Great Britain had any power to tax dwellers in America at all, for by the principles of English freedom a man could only be taxed by his own consent.

The question which Jefferson raised in this revolutionary

document was not what were the legal rights and wrongs of the issue, as interpreted by constitutional pedants, but what were the moral ones dictated by man's reason and nature. He claimed that the first inhabitants of British North America by crossing the Atlantic had exercised the universal right of departing from the country in which chance, not choice, had placed them, in search of a new form of society. In exactly the same way their Anglo-Saxon ancestors had left their native wilds and woods to possess themselves of England, and had established the system of laws which had so long been its glory and protection. America had been conquered, and the settlements established, by the emigrants themselves at the expense of their own blood and fortunes. What they had won, they alone had a right to hold.

From this bold start, Jefferson proceeded to show how the adoption by the settlers of English laws, and their submission to the throne, had in no way altered their fundamental right to govern, tax and judge themselves. Of their own choice they had assumed the laws under which they had lived in England, and continued an association with her by voluntarily acknowledging a common sovereign who thus became the sole link between the component parts of the Empire. The British Parliament, which since the domestic Revolution of 1688 had passed laws regulating American commerce, had usurped functions which had never belonged to it. Thus by an Act of George the Second's reign American subjects were forbidden to manufacture hats out of American fur, and by another to manufacture machinery out of American iron. ' We do point out to his Majesty the injustice of these acts, with intent to rest on that principle the cause of their nullity, but to show that experience confirms the propriety of those political principles, which exempt us from the jurisdiction of the British Parliament. The true ground on which we declare these acts void, is that the British Parliament has no right to exercise authority over us.'

As for such a measure as the Boston Port Bill it was as arbitrary as it would be for legislators in Virginia to deprive the freeholders of Middlesex of their franchise. 'One free and independent legislature hereby takes upon itself to suspend the powers of another, free and independent as itself. . . . Not only the principles of common sense, but the common feelings of human nature must be surrendered up, before His Majesty's subjects here can be persuaded to believe that they hold their political existence at the will of a British Parliament. . . . Can any one reason be assigned why one hundred and sixty thousand electors in the island of Great Britain should give law to four millions in the States of America, every individual of whom is equal to every individual of them in virtue, in understanding, and in bodily strength? Were this to be admitted, instead of being a free people, as we have hitherto supposed and mean to continue ourselves, we should suddenly be found the slaves, not of one, but of one hundred and sixty thousand tyrants.'

From the usurped authority of the British Parliament, Jefferson appealed to the common sense and justice of the British Crown. 'These,' he wrote, 'are our grievances, which we have thus laid before his Majesty, with that freedom of language and sentiment which becomes a free people, claiming their rights as derived from the laws of nature, and not as the gift of their chief magistrate. Let those flatter who fear—it is not an American art. To give praise where it is not due . . . would ill beseem those who are asserting the rights of human nature. They know, and will, therefore, say that kings are the servants, not the proprietors of the people. Open your breast, Sire, to liberal and expanded thought. Let not the name of George the Third be a blot on the page of history. You are surrounded by British counsellors, but remember that they are parties. . . . It behoves you, therefore, to think and to act for yourself and your people. . . . No longer persevere in sacrificing the rights of one part of the empire, to the inordinate desires of another; but deal out to all equal and impartial right. . . . This is the important post in which fortune has placed you, holding the balance of a great, if a well-poised empire. This,

Sire, is the advice of your great American council, on the observance of which may perhaps depend your felicity and future fame, and the preservation of that harmony which alone can continue, both to Great Britain and America, the reciprocal advantages of their connection.

' It is neither our wish nor our interest to separate from her. We are willing, on our part, to sacrifice everything which reason can ask, to the restoration of that tranquillity for which all must wish. On their part, let them be ready to establish union on a generous plan. Let them name their terms, but let them be just. Accept of every commercial preference it is in our power to give, for such things as we can raise for their use, or they make for ours. But let them not think to exclude us from going to other markets, to dispose of those commodities which they cannot use, nor to supply those wants which they cannot supply. Still less let it be proposed that our properties, within our own territories, shall be taxed or regulated by any power on earth, but our own. *The God who gave us life, gave us liberty* at the same time : the hand of force may destroy, but cannot disjoin them. This, Sire, is our last, our determined resolution. And that you will be pleased to interpose . . . to procure redress of these our great grievances, to quiet the minds of your subjects in British America, against any apprehensions of future encroachment, to establish fraternal love and harmony through the whole empire, and that that may continue to the latest ages of time, is the fervent prayer of all British America.'

Such was the remarkable document in which Jefferson outlined those liberal principles of empire which a century and a half later were to animate the British Commonwealth of Nations under the sovereignty of King George V. Unfortunately they were addressed to the chief representative of a people who, however jealous of their own liberties, had yet to learn that these can only be preserved by an equal regard for those of others. As much as any other man Jefferson was responsible for teaching the Anglo-Saxon race that hard lesson.

10

Published in pamphlet form Jefferson's views penetrated to England, where they are believed to have won him the honour of having his name enrolled in a proposed Bill of Attainder and the prouder distinction of being approved by Edmund Burke. The great Irishman wove the raw material of the young Virginian's dream into his own splendid pattern and enunciated, in words that will be remembered so long as men live together in organised societies, the principles that can alone govern the association of free peoples.

My hold of the Colonies is in the close affection which grows from common names, from kindred blood, from similar privileges, and equal protection. These are ties which, though light as air, are as strong as links of iron. Let the Colonists always keep the idea of their civil rights associated with your Government ; they will cling and grapple to you ; and no force under heaven will be of power to tear them from their allegiance. . . . As long as you have the wisdom to keep the sovereign authority of this country as the sanctuary of liberty, the sacred temple consecrated to our common faith, wherever the chosen race and sons of England worship freedom, they will turn their faces towards you. The more they multiply, the more friends you will have ; the more ardently they love liberty, the more perfect will be their obedience. Slavery they can have anywhere. It is a weed that grows in every soil. They may have it from Spain, they may have it from Prussia. But until you become lost to all feeling of your true interest and your natural dignity, freedom they can have from none but you. This is the commodity of price of which you have the monopoly. . . . It is the spirit of the English Constitution, which, infused through the mighty mass, pervades, feeds, unites, invigorates, vivifies every part of the empire, even down to the minutest member. . . .

All this, I know well enough, will sound wild and chimerical to the profane herd of those vulgar and mechanical politicians, who have no place among us ; a sort of people who think that nothing exists but what is gross and material ; and who therefore, far from being qualified to be directors of the great movement of empire, are not fit to turn a wheel in the machine. But to men truly initiated and rightly taught, these ruling and master principles, which in the opinion of such men as I have mentioned, have no substantial existence, are in truth everything, and all in all. Magnanimity in politics is not seldom the truest wisdom ; and a great empire and little minds go ill together.

The profane herd of vulgar and mechanical politicians prevailed, and the world empire of the Anglo-Saxon towards which the compass point of history had been turning for a century was never attained. But out of the disaster that ensued two new conceptions took shape—those of the United States of America and the British Commonwealth of Nations.

At the moment few could discern what was happening. When the first Continental Congress met at Philadelphia in the autumn of 1774, George Washington was so far from foreseeing the issue of the great work to which he was about to put his hand that he declared himself satisfied that no thinking American desired independence. But the terrible obstinacy of the English race was aroused, and for once it had met its match.

' The colonies,' George III wrote to Lord North, ' must either triumph or submit.' When the ' peaceful ' sanctions of ' non-intercourse ' were met by the despatch of British soldiers to Massachusetts, Patrick Henry, standing in the tiny wooden church of Richmond, appealed to the Second Virginian Convention and through it to all America to take arms to protect the country. ' Our brethren are already in the field. Why stand we here idle ? Is life so dear, or peace so sweet, as to be purchased at the price of chains and slavery ? Forbid it, Almighty God ! I know not what course others may take; but as for me give me liberty or give me death ! '

At those arming Resolutions carried in the Virginia Convention by 65 votes to 60, Jefferson and Washington were both present, ' prominent though silent.' A few weeks later, in April 1775, General Gage, on his way to seize the war stores at Concord, was attacked at Lexington. The siege of Boston and the battle of Bunker's Hill followed. After that, great as was the burden to be borne by Washington, the rest was inevitable. King George had lost his Americans.

THOMAS JEFFERSON

But if ultimate independence was assured, nothing else was. What future lay before the thirteen insurgent states? Isolated and divided by provincial jealousies, they might easily have perished or grown into mutually jealous and warring states after the old model of Europe. Inhabited mainly by poor, primitive folk absorbed in the harsh struggle for existence, they might still more easily have become the preserve of a close aristocracy of rich planters and land-owners, applying the principles of Venetian oligarchy to the virgin Western Hemisphere without the old world restraints of king or priest. That America, through the virtues of George Washington or the limitations of George Guelph, became independent, was comparatively unimportant. The revolt of Brazil and the Argentine in the next age neither shook the world nor changed the course of history. But the union of the United States of America on the foundation of the idealistic proposition that all men are created free and equal was the most important social event since the Crucifixion of Christ. At that moment a new hope was born in the tired heart of mankind.

It was due to Jefferson more than to any other man that it was so born. If Washington was the heart and hand of the American Revolution, Jefferson was its spirit. Unlike Washington he was neither an administrator nor a man of the sword. He left to his countrymen only one legacy the ideal of social freedom. Yet that legacy was so finely fashioned out of his vast stores of learning that it has become the talisman, often neglected and sometimes lost, to which America has turned in every crisis of her history. Nor was it exclusive to America. Its virtue lay in its promise, as expressed by Lincoln, that the burden might one day be lifted from the shoulders of all men.

Jefferson's greatness was that he stated that promise and thereafter devoted his life to seeing, so far as lay within his means, that it was not broken. The other leaders of the American revolt against the British connection were no more democratic in their sympathies than the great English parliamentarians and republicans of the seventeenth century. A short while back several of them had taken a prominent part in employing royal troops to suppress a rising of poor agrarians, and had subsequently by skilful pamphleteering turned the unpopularity of this act against the crown for their own ends. This was in the authentic English Whig tradition. Left to themselves they would have freed America from the rule of St. James's only to establish a close transatlantic oligarchy. They were not left to themselves. For twice this tall red-headed man of the frontier, who could never be persuaded to distrust his poorer neighbours, struck at the aristocratic ideal in America —once when he drew up the Declaration of Independence and again when a generation later he flung down the gauntlet to Hamilton and the Federalists. Most revolutionary leaders incite gullible humanity to overthrow the barricades only to re-erect them in a more convenient place further down the street. Jefferson made it his life's work to see that they remained down.

On June 11, 1775, he left his home on a long journey by phæton to the Second Continental Congress at Philadelphia. Here at the age of thirty-two he took a chief part in one of the most momentous gatherings in history. He was no orator, leaving long speeches to the lawyers, whose trade it was ' to contest everything, concede nothing and talk by the hour.' But ' prompt, frank, explicit and decisive,' as John Adams described him, his personality impressed itself on the whole assembly, his very silence pleasing by its absence of self-assertion, while in committee, his keen mind and charm of manner gave him an immediate ascendancy. There was no fuss, no clumsy and unfinished thinking aloud, no irresponsible blustering for the sake of impressing such as mar the work of most men in council. Industrious and resourceful, tactful yet firm, no better chairman of political committees ever existed.

Nor, aristocrat though he was in his intellectual tastes, was there ever a better democrat. Government by the people has usually failed because its advocates have lacked the qualities that Jefferson possessed—disinterestedness, modesty and a generous toleration for the opinions of others. He was the ideal man to state the democratic creed and frame the forms within which it was to work, because it was natural for him to conform to them himself. He was always ready to do the dog's work and ask little or nothing in return. Men of this sort are not common and make themselves indispensable to the assemblies they serve.

At the Second Continental Congress in 1775, Jefferson prepared the rejected draft of the 'Address to the Crown on the Causes of Taking up Arms.' Later he drafted the reply to Lord North's Conciliatory Propositions. The following year brought him greater work. On January 1, 1776, the town of Norfolk was bombarded and burnt by British troops. In May the Virginian Convention unanimously instructed its delegates to Congress ' to propose to that respectable body to declare the United Colonies free and independent States, absolved from all allegiance to, or dependence upon, the Crown or Parliament of Great Britain.' The only question left to be settled was what was to be the nature of the new American nation.

To that question Jefferson provided the answer. His first task was to draft the ' Plan of Government ' for a free Virginia—the famous ' New Model ' which was the first attempt at a written American constitution. Devised for a community of only a few hundred thousand souls, its author, believing that presently the vast virgin continent of North America would be inhabited by millions, felt that what he wrote might decide whether the New World was to repeat the follies of the Old or give mankind a fresh start. ' In truth,' he told a friend, ' it is the whole object of the present controversy ; for should a bad government be instituted for us in future, it had been as well to have accepted at first the bad one offered to us from beyond the water without the risk and expense of contest.'

This was the key to Jefferson's life. In his ' Plan of Government ' for Virginia he set down the fundamental principles and laws which he conceived would best defend the liberty of man. The Legislative, Executive and Judiciary

15

were to be kept separate, power was to be balanced against power, and standing armies in peacetime were to be declared illegal. The House of Representatives was to be elected by all male citizens of adult age who had paid taxes for five years or owned twenty-five acres in the country or a quarter of an acre in the town. This property qualification was added as an additional safeguard for liberty, for a free and incorrupt government could only be maintained where all its members had some degree of personal independence. Otherwise democracy would become a mere form behind which employers and political organisers would tyrannise over the millions by the manipulation of figures and the spread of lies.

Jefferson's 'Plan of Government' for Virginia was not adopted, but his 'Declaration of Independence' is one of the decisive documents of human history. In June 1776, with John Adams, Benjamin Franklin, Roger Sherman and Robert Livingstone, he was appointed by the Continental Congress to prepare a public declaration that the united colonies were free and independent states and absolved of all allegiance to the British Crown. The actual drafting was left to Jefferson. He wrote it in three weeks at the age of thirty-three, in furnished rooms on the second story of a house on the south side of Market Street, Philadelphia. On July 4, 1776, after it had been debated in Congress while its author sat listening in an agony of apprehension, the Declaration was reported, ratified and signed.

This great Charter of human life and happiness began with a general preamble setting out the fundamental principles by which the colonists were guided in their momentous step. 'When, in the course of human events,' it began, ' it becomes necessary for one people to dissolve the political bands which have connected them with another, and to assume among the powers of the earth the separate and equal station to which the laws of nature and of nature's God entitle them, a decent respect to the opinions of mankind requires that they should declare the causes which impel them to the separation.

' We hold these truths to be self evident: that all men are created equal; that they are endowed by their creator with certain inalienable rights; that among these are life, liberty, and the pursuit of happiness; that to secure these rights, governments are instituted among men, deriving their just powers from the consent of the governed; that whenever any form of government becomes destructive of these ends, it is the right of the people to alter or to abolish it, and to institute new government, laying its foundation on such principles, and organizing its powers in such form, as to them shall seem most likely to effect their safety and happiness.' Such a state of affairs had now arisen and, though prudence dictated that governments long established should not be lightly discarded, a long train of abuses and usurpations had made it the right and even the duty of the colonists to make a change.

From man's perverted law, Jefferson appealed to natural and divine law. ' We, therefore, the representatives of the United States of America, in General Congress assembled, appealing to the Supreme Judge of the world for the rectitude of our intentions, do, in the name, and by the authority of the good people of these colonies, solemnly publish and declare, that these united colonies are, and of right ought to be, free and independent states; that they are absolved from all allegiance to the British crown, and that all political connection between them and the state of Great Britain is, and ought to be, totally dissolved; and that as free and independent states, they have full power to levy war, conclude peace, contract alliances, establish commerce, and to do all other acts and things which independent states may of right do.

' And for the support of this declaration, we mutually pledge to each other our lives, our fortunes and our sacred honour.' Jefferson had written the end of one long chapter in mankind's history and the beginning of another.

A nation had been made: it had still to be fought for. While the stately Washington rode through the forest at the head of his ragged colonials to drive back the Redcoats into the sea, Jefferson withdrew to his native state and took his seat in the Virginian House of Representatives at Williamsburg. Here, amid the alarums and excursions of war, he devoted himself, a local man in a local theme, to the remodelling of Virginia's laws and institutions. In this act of provincialism he was true to his English ancestry; in his curious aloofness from the turmoil of the hour to some transatlantic strain in his make-up, which has constantly recurred in *homo Americanus*, from Whitman standing cold and remote from the opening struggles of Civil War to the Middle West's long indifference to the agonies of European democracy in 1914.

Jefferson's work for the future administration of Virginia was conceived on broad and humanistic lines. He took the principal part in reorganising the Courts of Justice and in ending the established system of primogeniture by freeing landowners to dispose of their estates as they pleased among their younger children. By this measure he dealt a fatal blow at the patrician order and stopped the development in the South of an hereditary caste. Aristocrats there have been in America, and always will be in any community, but since Jefferson's time, with the possible exception of the Adams family, they have been of mushroom growth.

Two of his favourite plans for the betterment of his native state Jefferson was not yet able to carry to fulfilment. With great care he had worked out a scheme of general education, including a state university and a public library. But his countrymen, poverty-stricken and engaged in a life-and-death struggle with England, were scarcely in a position to pursue such philosophical perfection, and it was not till he was an old man that his proposal was adopted even in part. Nor did his plea for the abolition of negro slavery commend itself to his fellow slave-owners. For that consummation of his creed he had to wait his whole life in vain. ' The public mind would not bear the proposition.'

Freedom of the press and religion he did establish, though

THOMAS JEFFERSON

it was not till 1786 that his ' Bill for Establishing Religious Freedom ' finally became law in Virginia. Based on the proposition that ' Almighty God hath created the mind free . . . ,' it advanced the revolutionary claim that ' all attempts to influence it by temporal punishments or burdens, or by civil incapacitations, tend only to beget habits of hypocrisy and meanness, and are a departure from the plan of the Holy Author of our religion, who being Lord both of body and mind, yet chose not to propagate it by coercions on either, as was in his Almighty power to do, but to extend its influence on reason alone.' Hence, Jefferson argued, it was ' time enough for the rightful purposes of civil government for its officers to interfere when principles break out into overt acts against peace and good order; . . . that truth is great and will prevail if left to herself; that she is the proper and sufficient antagonist to error, and has nothing to fear from the conflict unless by human inter-position disarmed of her natural weapons, free argument and debate; errors ceasing to be dangerous when it is permitted freely to contradict them.'

Jefferson's name is usually associated with the inde-pendence of the United States of America. Yet his chief work was not so much that he freed a nation—for this was Washington's achievement—as that he freed the individual mind. Against persecution and compulsion of every sort he set his face. ' Is uniformity attainable ? ' he asked. ' Millions of innocent men, women, and children, since the introduction of Christianity, have been burnt, tortured, fined, imprisoned; yet we have not advanced one inch towards uniformity. What has been the effect of coercion ? To make one half of the world fools, and the other half hypocrites. To support roguery and error all over the earth. Let us reflect that it is inhabited by a thousand million of people; that these profess probably a thousand different systems of religion; that ours is but one of that thousand; that if there be but one right, and ours that one, we should wish to see the nine hundred and ninety-nine wandering sects gathered into the fold of truth. But against such a

19

majority we cannot effect this by force.' Reason and free enquiry and persuasion were the only effectual instruments against error.

Three years after the Declaration of Independence, in the midst of the War of Independence Jefferson was elected Governor of Virginia. He was not a particularly good one. But for two years, a philosopher in action, he bore the brunt of a grievous and distasteful office with a sweet patience that touched even his enemies. He found the Treasury empty, trade and agriculture half ruined, and the currency so depreciated that his Governor's salary of £4500 a year did not even suffice to buy bread for his household. Throughout his term of office the infant state was constantly threatened by the enemy. All the while Jefferson had to meet out of depleted and diminishing resources Washington's requests for men and money. In 1780 Virginia was invaded, its capital taken and its farms devastated. Jefferson himself was almost captured in his own house. But amidst the bitter criticism which these calamities aroused against his government, he made no attempt to cast the blame on his subordinates and advisers.

After his withdrawal into private life the tide turned and the principal English army laid down its arms at Yorktown. For Jefferson, personally, the next year was a tragic one. Yet, calumniated and misunderstood, struggling with the embarrassments consequent on the collapse of the currency and public credit, and deprived by death of the wife whose companionship had meant so much to him, he still retained his serenity of spirit. In the quiet of Monticello he found escape from the present by contemplating the future of his country. A learned correspondence with a French *savant* supplied him with the necessary incentive.

In his ' Notes on Virginia ' Jefferson enshrined his love for his native land—a patriotism based on an intimate knowledge of its ways of life. No man knew more of Virginia than he—its geography, climate, scenery, plants and animals. So he wrote of the great Mississippi river that bordered its farthest confines, that it ' yields turtle of a peculiar kind, perch, trout, gar, pike, mullets, herrings, carp, spatula-fish of fifty pounds weight, cat-fish of an hundred pounds weight, buffalo-fish and sturgeon. Alligators or crocodiles have been seen as high up as the Acansas. It also abounds in herons, cranes, ducks, brant, geese, and swans.' And he prophesied the day when it would come to be one of the chief channels of American commerce.

In his answers to his correspondent's queries, Jefferson touched also on his country's laws and institutions. He was not blind to certain faults inherent in them. The greatest of these was slavery—' a circumstance,' he wrote sadly, ' of great tenderness, where our conclusion would degrade a whole race of men from the rank in the scale of beings which their Creator may perhaps have given them.'

Jefferson was under no illusion about the blacks, such as weakened the efficacy of the abolitionist arguments of a later generation. He believed the negro to be the inferior, intellectually and morally, of the white man. Familiar with the habits and capacities of his own slaves, he wrote of them sympathetically but without sentimentality. ' Their griefs are transient. Those numberless afflictions which render it doubtful whether heaven has given life to us in mercy or in wrath, are less felt, and sooner forgotten with them. In general, their existence appears to participate more of sensation than reflection. To this must be ascribed their disposition to sleep when abstracted from their diversions, and unemployed in labour. An animal whose body is at rest, and who does not reflect, must be disposed to sleep of course.'

Yet, though he knew that the majority of the slaves in his native state were well treated and not unhappy, his ultimate judgment on the institution of slavery was damning. Its existence threatened the political and moral character of every citizen, and undermined the foundations of freedom. ' The whole commerce between master and slave is a perpetual exercise of the most boisterous passions, the most unremitting despotism on the one part, and degrading submissions on the other. Our children see this, and learn to imitate it; for man is an imitative animal. . . . The parent storms, the child looks on, catches the lineaments of wrath, puts on the same airs in the circle of smaller slaves, gives a loose to the worst of passions, and thus nursed, educated, and daily exercised in tyranny, cannot but be stamped by it with odious peculiarities. The man must be a prodigy who can retain his manners and morals undepraved by such circumstances.' The future was to prove how right this prediction was.

Another peril that Jefferson foresaw for his country was the manufacturing ideal, then first taking root in northern England. He had no wish to see urban industry protected at the expense of the farming population. Democracy to be effective required that every citizen should play an intelligent and independent part in its maintenance. A community of small farmers owning their own land and understanding their interests offered the only durable basis for such a system of government. The 'mobs of great cities' were incompatible with real freedom because, having no independence, they had no means of resisting corruption and intimidation, and could always be cheated of their liberty by those who knew how to use these weapons.

If it guarded against such dangers, Jefferson held, democracy would succeed, and Virginia and its fellow American states would present the spectacle of the least corrupt and most benevolent polity yet seen on earth. But he added one final word of caution. They must be careful to keep clear of European entanglements and above all of war. For them the future offered something better than the barren prizes of military glory and power. A whole continent of boundless possibility was awaiting their peaceful development. 'Young as we are, and with such a country before us to fill with people and with happiness, we should point in that direction the whole generative force of nature, wasting none of it in efforts of mutual destruction. It should be our endeavour to cultivate the peace and friendship of every nation, even of that which has injured us the most, when we shall have carried our point against her. Our interest will be to throw open the doors of commerce, and to knock off all its shackles, giving perfect freedom to all persons for the vent of whatever they may choose to bring into our ports, and asking the same in theirs. Never was so much false arithmetic employed on any subject, as that which has been employed to persuade nations that it is their interest to go to war. Were the money which it has cost to gain, at the close of a long war, a little town, or a little territory, the right to cut wood here, or to catch fish there, expended in improving what they already possess, in making roads, opening rivers, building ports, improving the arts, and finding employment for their idle poor, it would render them much stronger, much wealthier and happier. This I hope will be our wisdom.'

In the winter of 1782, after his wife's death, Jefferson was recalled to the service of his country. He was about to sail on a mission of peace to Europe when Britain, exhausted at last, gave up the struggle and for the first time in two centuries admitted her inability to accomplish her purpose. In the following autumn he was re-elected to Congress. Here, as Chairman of the Currency Commission, he was responsible for selecting the Spanish dollar as the monetary unit of the new nation.

While the American Constitution was being framed Jefferson was no longer in the country, and the credit or discredit of its details belongs to others. In the summer of 1784 he sailed for Europe with his eldest daughter, Martha, to assist Benjamin Franklin and John Adams in the task of negotiating treaties of commerce with the states of the Old World. Nine months later he succeeded Franklin as American Minister Plenipotentiary at the Court of France. For the next five years, an exile from the soil of his country, he served her by labouring to secure for her recognition and concessions from the indifferent rulers of Europe.

It was no easy task. 'They seemed,' he wrote, ' to know little about us, but as rebels who had been success-ful in throwing off the yoke of the Mother country. They

23

were ignorant of our commerce, which had always been monopolised by England.' But more than any other man Jefferson with his wide and cultured tastes was fitted to give a favourable impression of *homo Americanus* to the statesmen of the *ancien régime*. To some it seemed as if the dreams of the Utopian philosophers of the past had come back in the shape of this open-hearted, intelligent, red-headed son of the West.

Jefferson's residence in France coincided with the death throes of the old monarchical system and the outbreak of the Revolution. As the representative of America and her free principles, he was much consulted by the French 'patriots,' on whom he consistently urged moderation. His own revolutionary methods had been very different from theirs, for he had based them on observations of man's needs and environment. In the advice which he gave to a noble young reformer about to set out on a journey, he indicated the practical bent of his politics: 'You must be absolutely incognito; you must ferret the people out of their hovels as I have done, look into their kettles, eat their bread, loll on their beds on pretence of resting yourself, but in fact to find if they are soft. You will feel a sublime pleasure in the course of this investigation, and a sublimer one hereafter, when you shall be able to apply your knowledge to the softening of their beds or the throwing a morsel of meat into their kettle of vegetables.'

In November 1789 Jefferson returned to America on leave. He was overjoyed to do so. 'I am savage enough,' he had written from Paris, 'to prefer the woods, the wilds and the independence of Monticello to all the brilliant pleasures of this gay capital.'

But he was not permitted to enjoy that which he loved for long. Early in 1790 he was invited by President Washington, who had undertaken to save the country from the anarchy into which it was fast sinking, to serve as Secretary of State. Reluctantly he accepted and in February left Monticello for New York to take up the task of making the democratic institutions in which he believed work in practice.

For all his nostalgia for country life and the cultured labours of his library and garden, Jefferson did so with hope. The air at that time was full of gloomy prophecies for the future of democracy, and most thinking men believed that the fond dream of popular government would soon pass; even Washington confessed that the Republic was on probation and might easily fail. But Jefferson remained confident. 'We have been fellow-labourers and fellow-sufferers,' he wrote to a friend, 'and Heaven has rewarded us with a happy issue from our struggles. It rests now with ourselves alone to enjoy in peace and concord the blessings of self-government, so long denied to mankind; to show by example the sufficiency of human reason for the care of human affairs; and that the will of the majority—the natural law of every society—is the only sure guardian of the rights of man. Perhaps even this may sometimes err; but its errors are honest, solitary, and short-lived. Let us then, my dear friends, forever bow down to the general reason of the society. We are safe with that, even in its deviations, for it soon returns again to the right way.'

Jefferson's tenure of the Secretaryship of State is largely remembered for his great duel with Alexander Hamilton. This brilliant young man, proud, high-spirited, with talents for war and administration which might have made him another Napoleon, was born to champion the aristocratic idea at its highest. Washington, whose secretary he had been during the war and who knew his genius, had appointed him Secretary of the Treasury, a post for which he was fitted by financial talents of the first order. But of Jefferson's faith in the ordinary man and love of social equality, born of his home on the frontier, Hamilton had no share. Democracy he distrusted, and his ideal of government was a strong, rich and aristocratic system based on English lines. To establish this, he worked constantly to strengthen the powers of the federal government over the states and to build up a permanent monied interest which should 'keep in check demagogues and knaves in the disguise of patriots' and so exert a sobering influence on the heady politics of the young Republic.

But wise and realist as this policy seemed, and still seems to many, it was anathema to Jefferson. Where Hamilton with his keen nose for a scoundrel wished to place strong controlling powers in the hands of organised authority, Jefferson, with his belief in the integrity of the plain man and of his right to be trusted with his own government, was all for keeping society untrammelled. He set his face against every extension of the authority of the Federal government; ' the powers not delegated to the United States by the Constitution, nor prohibited by it to the States, are reserved to the States or to the people.' Low taxes, an absence of all restrictive duties on commerce, and an army and navy on the lowest possible scale, were his objects. To Jefferson government was a mere negative safeguard and nothing more, and the individual citizen's happiness and free development all and everything. To Hamilton government was a religion: the positive and almost sacred act from which all progress and virtue flowed.

Between such opposing principles there could be no compromise. An almost open state of warfare between the Secretary of State and the Secretary of the Treasury divided Washington's cabinet. Only their common devotion to the great President and the absence of meanness and littleness in their own characters enabled the two men to work together at all. Their principal battleground was the cost of administration. Hamilton consistently sought to build up a large civil service and a powerful class of fund-holders who could be trusted to make the government strong in order to secure the money they had lent it. Jefferson, who hated public debt and was all for paying it off at once, pronounced it a crime for one generation to entail its extravagance on posterity. His own Secretary of State's office he ran with almost ostentatious frugality, on four grossly underpaid clerks and a messenger.

When his term of office ended, he asked to be excused further service, and in January 1794 set out joyfully for his beloved Monticello. Here he spent three peaceful and happy years, devoting himself to plantations, books and

26

scientific pursuits. 'I return to farming,' he wrote in the spring of his release, 'with an ardour which I scarcely knew in my youth, and which has got the better entirely of my love of study. Instead of writing ten or twelve letters a day, which I have been in the habit of doing as a thing in course, I put off answering my letters now, farmer-like, till a rainy day.' 'I would not give up my own retirement for the empire of the universe.' Now, a free man in a free country, he planned, created and planted to his heart's content, making experiments in new manures, patent ploughs and rotating crops, rebuilding Monticello and filling it with every species of ingenious and labour-saving device—a new kind of desk, a mechanical dumb-waiter, a table that turned into something else—collecting maps, books and plants and pursuing every study that could enlarge his knowledge of the land of which he had been born a citizen. It was all part of his political system: the consequence of ensuring to man 'life, liberty and the pursuit of happiness.' As the late Mr. Vachel Lindsay pointed out, one side of Jefferson's doctrines might be stated: 'All men are ingenious when they have a chance, because I am,' and the other : 'All men are magnificently versatile when they have a chance, because I am.' [1] It still remains an American ideal.

In such felicity, even the misdoings of politicians at Washington and warring kings in Europe almost ceased to trouble him. 'I am still warm,' he wrote to a friend, 'whenever I think of these scoundrels, though I do it as seldom as I can, preferring infinitely to contemplate the tranquil growth of my lucerne and potatoes. I have so completely withdrawn myself from these spectacles of usurpation and misrule that I do not take a single newspaper nor read one a month; and I feel myself infinitely the happier for it.'

Yet the very freedom from turmoil and political restraint which he loved was dependent on active participation by such men as himself in the unpleasing business of politics.

[1] Vachel Lindsay, *The Litany of Washington Street*, 1929, p. 112.

That was the inescapable price for the privilege of citizenship of a free community. When the time came Jefferson was again ready to pay it. In 1796 the increasing cost of government and the subservience of Congress to the Treasury recalled him to public affairs.

The situation was alarming. In place of the simple democracy he had hoped to found, there appeared to be growing up a complicated system of loans, taxes and paid public offices, the whole enveloped in an atmosphere of high financial mystification, which no ordinary man could hope to penetrate. Jefferson protested vigorously: ' The accounts of the United States ought to be, and may be made, as simple as those of a common farmer, and capable of being understood by common farmers. I wish it were possible to obtain a single amendment to our Constitution. I would be willing to depend on that alone for the reduction of the administration of our government to the genuine principles of its Constitution; I mean an additional article, taking from the federal government the power of borrowing.' For such power, in his view, ended inevitably in the rule of bankers. And though in the case of war the necessity of meeting expenditure out of revenue would be hard, it would not be so hard as having ten wars instead of one, the usual fate of loan-mongering states. Besides, he could see no necessity for America entering a war at all.

Yet this was what the Federalist Party, led by Hamilton, was trying to bring about. The excesses of the French Revolution had led to a reaction against liberal and equalitarian sentiments, and the well-to-do classes of the eastern ports were now demanding intervention against France abroad and vigorous repression of disorder and licence at home. ' The aspect of our politics has wonderfully changed since you left us,' Jefferson wrote to a friend. ' In place of that noble love of liberty and republican government which carried us triumphantly through the war, an Anglican, monarchical, aristocratical party has sprung up, whose avowed object is to draw over us the substance, as they have already done the forms, of the British Government. The main body of our citizens however remain true to their republican principles; the whole landed interest is republican and so is a great mass of talents. Against us are the Executive, the Judiciary, two out of three branches of the legislature, all the officers of the government, all who want to be officers, all timid men who prefer the calm of despotism to the boisterous sea of liberty, British merchants and Americans trading on British capital, speculators and holders in the banks and public funds. . . . In short we are likely to preserve the liberty we have obtained only by unremitting labours and perils.'

None the less Jefferson felt little doubt that it could be preserved. ' We have only,' he wrote, ' to awake and snap the Lilliputian cords with which they have been entangling us during the first sleep which succeeded our labours.' With such feelings he put himself forward, on Washington's retirement in 1796, as presidential candidate.

For the moment the influence of the Treasury was too strong, and Jefferson was beaten by a narrow margin by the great Bostonian, John Adams. He accordingly became Vice-President and Chairman of the Senate. But his real part during the four years of Adams's presidency was as unofficial leader of the democratic opposition. During the last three years of the century the depredations of French privateers brought the United States within an inch of war with France and of that closer union and more authoritarian form of government which was Hamilton's dream. Even reunion with Great Britain was not unthinkable and would probably have been welcomed by many in the harassed young Republic.

The course of the future was resolved by Jefferson. So long as his dream was threatened, this friendly, red-headed man was ready to go to any lengths to preserve it. For three years he opposed Hamilton, and where necessary his own President, Adams, on every issue that touched the freedom of the individual. When the excesses of a few American Jacobins led to the passage through Congress of the Alien

Law and the Sedition Act, Jefferson calmly declared them unconstitutional and advised his fellow citizens to treat them as a nullity. In the same way he secretly advised dissentient states that the Federal government had no power to coerce them into measures which were uncovered by the Constitution, and that the residuary mass of rights not given to Congress remained inalienably with them. As resolutely he opposed the attempts of the shipowners and the Federalists to involve the nation in war with France, and Hamilton's plan of a military alliance with Great Britain to conquer Spanish South America.

Jefferson triumphed. Though the last four years of the century saw the expenditure of the Federal government doubled, no war took place, and in 1799 a mission was despatched to reopen negotiations with the French government. The panic subsided, and young America turned her eyes westwards again towards her true destiny. Jefferson's eyes had never been anywhere else: in the very worst moment of anti-revolutionary and bellicose fever he had been quietly corresponding, as President of the American Philosophical Society, with the naturalists of the border state of Kentucky about the herds of wild horses in the unknown country beyond the Mississippi. Against that vast promise of hope and untrammelled life for unborn generations, all the fears and desires of New York bankers and Boston merchants weighed with him as nothing.

In the last month of the old century both Washington and Patrick Henry died, leaving Jefferson the chief repository of the American dream. A year later, after one of the vital presidential elections of American history, he became President. In his first Inaugural Address he laid down the principles that were to govern the future of his country. 'We are all Republicans: we are all Federalists. If there be any among us who would wish to dissolve this Union, or to change its republican form, let them stand undisturbed as monuments of the safety with which error of opinion may be tolerated where reason is left free to combat it.'

At the time Jefferson's victory passed almost unnoticed

in a world absorbed by the great struggle between France and Great Britain. Yet it was as decisive in its result as any of Creasy's fifteen battles. It decided, once and for all, that America should follow the republican course with its full democratic implications. Hitherto republics had only survived in small states like Holland and Venice, and where they had done so had taken on an aristocratic form. It was now to be shown that in a country of almost boundless extent, neither monarchy, aristocracy nor privilege were necessary to maintain order and secure wealth. 'The storm through which we have passed has been tremendous indeed,' Jefferson wrote. 'The tough sides of our Argosy have been thoroughly tried. . . . We shall put her on her republican tack, and she will now show by the beauty of her motion the skill of her builders. . . . A just and solid republican government maintained here will be a standing monument and example of the aim and imitation of the people of other countries; and I join with you in the hope and belief that they will see from our example that a free government is of all others the most energetic.'

Jefferson's ideal was 'a frugal government, which shall restrain men from injuring one another, shall leave them otherwise free to regulate their own pursuits of industry and improvement, and shall not take from the mouth of labour the bread it has earned.' To put it into practice he endeavoured to make his eight years of presidency a period of peace abroad and retrenchment at home. Quiet and immunity from the turmoils of the outer world was all that the country needed to develop as no nation had ever done before. At present it was in its infancy—a rural and agricultural community of a few millions, scattered along a 1300 mile coast, with as yet no more than 50,000 settlers moving out beyond the Alleghanies into the interior wilderness. The capital, Washington, was still only a primitive settlement, with its Congressmen living crowded together in half a dozen boarding-houses and the White House standing in a naked field above the Potomac marshes—a ' metropolis where fancy sees squares in morasses, obelisks in trees.' At this stage of the nation's development time was everything. 'Peace is our most important interest and a recovery from debt,' Jefferson declared. 'We feel ourselves strong and daily growing stronger. The census just now concluded shows we have added to our population a third of what it was ten years ago. This will be a duplication in twenty-three or twenty-four years. If we can delay but for a few years the necessity of vindicating the laws of nature on the ocean we shall be the more sure of doing it with effect. The day is within my time as well as yours when we may say by what laws other nations shall treat us on the sea. And we will say it.'

So he resisted the importunities of American traders and bankers whose ships were suffering from privateers and blockade, and kept his country out of a war from which she had little to gain and everything to lose. When, during his second period of office, the gravest tension was produced by the lengths to which the British government enforced its claim to search and impressment on the high seas, he braved public opinion by laying an embargo on American ships trading with Europe and averted hostilities at the expense of the mercantile class. Whatever suffering it might entail, it seemed to him a lesser evil than war. For though the traders of the eastern ports, whom it hurt, were the wealthiest section of the nation, they were not the most important. Jefferson's eye was forever on the frontier and on the lonely farms and the westward-moving wagons with whom the promise of the future lay. Compared with their peace and well-being the glamour of national glory was only a little thing. 'Were I in Europe,' he wrote to a friend in the troubled year 1807, 'pax et panis would certainly be my motto. Wars and contentions indeed fill the page of history with more matter; but more blest is that nation whose silent course of happiness furnishes nothing for history to say. This is what I ambition for my own country, and what it has fortunately enjoyed for now upwards of twenty years, while Europe has been in constant volcanic eruption.'

Yet Jefferson, the pacifist, added to the possessions of the United States the greatest single imperial conquest ever made by a nation, and without the cost of a single life. To the west of the infant republic was the vast territory of Louisiana, over which Spain had long exercised a vague and insubstantial suzerainty, and through which the produce of three-eighths of the soil of the United States passed down the Mississippi to market. In 1801 the port of New Orleans was suddenly closed to American commerce and Jefferson learnt that France had acquired Louisiana by a secret purchase from Spain.

That the mouth of the Mississippi should be held and the path to the interior closed by the bayonets of a militant European power was intolerable to Jefferson. As the trustee of the American future he felt bound to act. Pacifist though he was, he therefore intimated to France that on the day on which French troops occupied New Orleans the American nation would marry itself to the British fleet. At the same time he despatched his fellow-Virginian, Monroe, to Paris, with an appropriation of two million dollars secured from Congress, to try the effect of bargaining. ' On the event of this mission,' he told Monroe, ' depends the future destinies of this republic.'

Monroe succeeded beyond expectation. Napoleon, absorbed in the affairs of Europe, offered to sell, not New Orleans alone, but the whole of Louisiana. Jefferson accepted the offer on his own responsibility and sealed his triumph by finding the fifteen million dollars for the purchase without increasing the public debt. In one stroke he doubled the size of his country, and added a million square miles, representing ultimately fourteen new states, to the territories of the Union. The Mississippi was freed, the long trail to the Pacific opened, and ' the realms of liberty ' widened by an area two thousand by four thousand miles—' a great achievement to the mass of happiness which is to ensue.' What was even more important was that for nearly a century to come America was assured of a perpetual frontier, where the young hope and idealism of the western democracy could grow up in each generation untrammelled by the established wealth of the urban East. The balance of

33   D

American power shifted to the farms and the pioneers, where Jefferson had always wished it to rest.

It was given to Jefferson to see his dreams realised as it is to few statesmen. The Federal Party, whose designs had seemed so threatening a few years before, declined as rapidly as it had arisen, and the President's refusal to victimise his defeated opponents disarmed opposition. Taxes were drastically reduced, though at the expense of half the government's patronage, and a sinking fund established for the purpose of paying off the public debt in a generation. Peace was preserved, faction exorcised and the liabilities of the growing republic met without mortgaging the future, and all this under a system of freedom of speech, press and opinion. Whatever the administrative limitations of Jefferson's presidency—and there were many—this must be regarded as his achievement. His mistakes and executive deficiencies belong to the transient *minutiae* of contemporary chronology: his free and triumphant trial of democracy to the enduring history of human progress. ' Nor was it uninteresting to the world,' he said, ' that an experiment should be fairly and fully made, whether freedom of discussion, unaided by power, is not sufficient for the propagation and protection of truth—whether a government, conducting itself in the true spirit of its Constitution, with zeal and purity, and doing no act which it would be unwilling the whole world should witness, can be written down by falsehood and defamation.'

In one important respect Jefferson failed. He always believed that pure democracy could only survive in a community of small farmers. ' Generally speaking, the proportion which the aggregate of the other classes of citizens bears in any state to that of its husbandmen, is the proportion of its unsound to its healthy parts, and is a good enough barometer whereby to measure its degree of corruption.' He, therefore, wished to keep America mainly rural, limit manufactures and avoid the growth of large urban populations, which, he wrote, ' add just as much to the support of pure government as sores do to the strength of the human

34

body.' But before he became President the seeds of commercial and banking supremacy had already been sown in the North and the industrial revolution was fast spreading to America. But even here Jefferson was not entirely unsuccessful, in so far as he impressed on his countrymen an ideal which, for all the vast urban development of the last hundred years, they still retain: that a small farmer on his own land is the freest and happiest man in the world.

In 1804, at the age of sixty-one, Jefferson was re-elected President by fifteen out of the seventeen states and by a hundred and sixty-two votes against fourteen in the electoral college. His second term of office was clouded by the British blockade of Napoleonic Europe and by the bitterness engendered by his pacific system of embargo. Yet even the embargo, though unsuccessful, helped to point a way for the future guidance of American statesmen, providing them with a touchstone to test, as Jefferson put it, ' whether war is the most efficacious mode of redress in our case, or whether, having taught so many other useful lessons to Europe we may not add that of showing them that there are peaceable means of repressing injustice by making it the interest of the aggressor to do what is just and abstain from future wrong.' And though, in accordance with his principles he yielded to public opinion and withdrew the embargo, in another great question even dearer to his heart he was able to carry the people with him. In 1807 the Act which forbade the future importation of negro slaves to America was passed.

Then, in 1809, having completed forty years of public service, Jefferson withdrew into private life, ' with hands as clean as they were empty,' leaving his country peaceful, prosperous and expanding. He was as happy as a boy at his release. ' Within a few days,' he wrote, ' I retire to my family, my books, and farms; and having gained the harbour myself I shall look on my friends still buffeting the storm, with anxiety indeed, but not with envy. Never did a prisoner released from his chains feel such relief as I shall on shaking off the shackles of power.' He settled down to a happy, patriarchal life at his Grecian paradise, Monticello, farming, raising tobacco and manufacturing agricultural tools and showing all the world how an independent American citizen might live in usefulness and happiness. Here he collected and arranged the finest library in America, which in the hour of his country's need he made a virtual present of to Congress, studied philology, astronomy, botany and meteorology, presided over the Philosophical Society, corresponding with every part of the world, and made experiments with pendulums and mathematical instruments. 'No person,' he explained cheerfully, 'will have occasion to complain of the want of time who never loses any. It is wonderful how much may be done if we are always doing.'

To the student of political institutions it is pleasant to picture the republican father enjoying in his old age the peaceful and useful existence which he had helped to ensure for millions of his future countrymen, while his pupils, Madison and Monroe, took the supreme watches on the bridge he had vacated. In his correspondence he sketched the outline of these calm and happy days. 'I am retired to Monticello, where in the bosom of my family and surrounded by my books I enjoy repose to which I have been long a stranger. My mornings are devoted to correspondence, from breakfast to dinner I am in my shops, my garden, or on horseback among my farms; from dinner to dark I give to society and recreation with my neighbours and friends; and from candle light to early bedtime I read. My health is perfect; and my strength considerably reinforced by the activity of the course I pursue; perhaps it is as great as usually falls to the lot of near sixty-seven years of age. I talk of ploughs and harrows, of seeding and harvesting, with my neighbours; and of politics too, if they choose, with as little reserve as the rest of my fellow citizens, and feel at length the blessing of being free to say and do what I please, without being responsible for it to any mortal.' It was the domestic life of Anglo-Saxon America to perfection.

One who was often a childish visitor at Monticello

completed the portrait in after years: 'On winter evenings, when it grew too dark to read, in the half hour which passed before candles came in, as we all sat round the fire, he taught us several childish games, and would play them with us. I remember that "Cross-questions," and "I love my love with an A," were two I learned from him; and we would teach some of ours to him. When the candles were brought, all was quiet immediately, for he took up his book to read; and we would not speak out of a whisper, lest we should disturb him; and generally we followed his example and took a book; and I have seen him raise his eyes from his own book, and look round on the little circle of readers and smile, and make some remark to mamma about it. When the snow fell, we would go out, as soon as it stopped, to clear it off the terraces with shovels, that he might have his usual walk on them without treading in snow.'

In the closing years of his life Jefferson made two further contributions to the future of his country. In 1819 he laid the foundations of the University of Virginia. He himself collected the money for it and secured the Legislature's approval, chose the site—a few miles from his home—designed the building in the Grecian mode which he loved, and gathered professors from all over the learned world to model its future studies. He became its first Rector and in 1825, at the age of eighty-two, had the satisfaction of seeing it opened to students.

In a more indirect way Jefferson helped to influence his pupil, President Monroe, in one of the most momentous decisions in American foreign policy. For a long while the nations of the world had watched with varying feelings the struggle between the South American colonies and their mother country, Spain. To Jefferson the rebellion seemed to herald a day of which he had long dreamed, 'when we may formally require a meridian of partition through the ocean which separates the two hemispheres, on the hither side of which no European gun shall ever be heard, nor an American on the other.' Of these hopes he now wrote to Monroe.

' I have ever deemed it fundamental for the United States never to take active part in the quarrels of Europe. Their political interests are entirely distinct from ours. Their mutual jealousies, their balance of power, their complicated alliances, their forms and principles of government, are all foreign to us. They are nations of eternal war. All their energies are expended in the destruction of the labour, property, and lives of their people. On our part, never had a people so favourable a chance of trying the opposite system, of peace and fraternity with mankind, and the direction of all our means and faculties to the purposes of improvement instead of destruction. With Europe we have few occasions of collision, and these, with a little prudence and forbearance, may be generally accommodated. Of the brethren of our own hemisphere, none are yet, or for an age to come will be, in a shape, condition, or disposition to war against us. And the foothold which the nations of Europe had in either America, is slipping from under them, so that we shall soon be rid of their neighbourhood.'

There were naturally many in Europe who did not share Jefferson's hopes. The Conference Statesmen of that time, like their Geneva successors of a hundred years later, chiefly wanted to preserve the *status quo*, for which such vast sacrifices of treasure and blood had been made in the Revolutionary and Napoleonic wars, and were inclined to view the disturbances in South America only as another symptom of that unrest which it was always their object to smother. There was consequently talk among the old monarchies of Europe of sending troops and ships to aid Spain in the suppression of her rebellious subjects.

It was this threat that led to the enunciation of the famous Monroe Doctrine, in its details the handiwork of John Quincy Adams, Secretary of State to the President who gave it its name. It was facilitated by the enlightened attitude of an English Minister who, weaning his country from the fussy directorate of continental powers which had governed the affairs of Europe since 1815, invited Monroe to join with him in a bold declaration of opposition to European intervention.

THOMAS JEFFERSON

Confronted with Canning's invitation, President Monroe took counsel of his political mentor, the aged sage of Monticello. As in the drafting of the Declaration of Independence and the Louisiana purchase, Jefferson at once saw the magnitude of the opportunity. 'The question presented by the letters you have sent me,' he replied, ' is the most momentous which has ever been offered to my contemplation since that of Independence. That made us a nation, this sets our compass, and points the course which we are to steer through the ocean of time opening on us. And never could we embark on it under circumstances more auspicious.

'Our first and fundamental maxim should be, never to entangle ourselves in the broils of Europe. Our second, never to suffer Europe to intermeddle with cis-Atlantic affairs. America, North and South, has a set of interests distinct from those of Europe, and peculiarly her own. She should therefore have a system of her own, separate and apart from that of Europe. While the last is labouring to become the domicile of despotism, our endeavour should surely be, to make our hemisphere that of freedom. One nation, most of all, could disturb us in this pursuit; she now offers to lead, aid, and accompany us in it. By acceding to her proposition, we detach her from the band of despots, bring her mighty weight into the scale of free government, and emancipate a continent at one stroke, which might otherwise linger long in doubt and difficulty. Great Britain is the nation which can do us the most harm of any one, or all on earth; and with her on our side we need not fear the whole world.

'With her, then, we should most sedulously cherish a cordial friendship; and nothing would tend more to knit our affections than to be fighting once more side by side, in the same cause. Not that I would purchase even her amity at the price of taking part in her wars. But the war in which the present proposition might engage us, should that be its consequence, is not her war, but ours. Its object is to introduce and establish the American system of keeping out

39

of our land all foreign powers, of never permitting those of Europe to intermeddle with the affairs of our nations. It is to maintain our own principle, not to depart from it. And if, to facilitate this, we can effect a division in the body of the European powers, and draw over to our side its most powerful member, surely we should do it. But I am clearly of Mr. Canning's opinion, that it will prevent instead of provoking war. With Great Britain withdrawn from their scale, and shifted into that of our two continents, all Europe combined would not undertake such a war. For how would they propose to get at either enemy without superior fleets ? '

Jefferson therefore advised Monroe to join cordially with Canning and so bring nearer one of the great and historic objects of American policy, the isolation and permanent peace of the western hemisphere. ' I could honestly, there-fore, join in the declaration proposed, that we aim not at the acquisition of any of those possessions, that we will not stand in the way of any amicable arrangement between them and the mother country; but that we will oppose, with all our means, the forcible interposition of any other power, as auxiliary, stipendiary, or under any other form or pretext, and most especially, their transfer to any power by conquest, cession, or acquisition in any other way. I should think it, therefore, advisable, that the Executive should encourage the British government to a continuance in the dispositions expressed in these letters, by an assurance of his concurrence with them as far as his authority goes; and that as it may lead to war, the declaration of which requires an act of Congress, the case shall be laid before them for consideration at their first meeting, and under the reasonable aspect in which it is seen by himself.

' I have been so long weaned from political subjects, and have so long ceased to take any interest in them, that I am sensible I am not qualified to offer opinions on them worthy of any attention. But the question now proposed involves consequences so lasting, and effects so decisive of our future destinies, as to rekindle all the interest I have heretofore felt on such occasions, and to induce me to the hazard of opinions, which will prove only my wish to contribute still my mite towards anything which may be useful to our country.' A few weeks later, on December 2, 1823, Monroe issued his famous message to Congress that the United States would view, as dangerous to their peace and safety, any attempt by European states to extend their system in any portion of the New World.

The end had now almost come. Professor Ticknor, who visited Jefferson in December 1824, described him as a vivid old man, ' now eighty-two years of age, very little altered from what he was ten years ago, very active, lively, and happy, riding from ten to fifteen miles every day, and talking without the least restraint very pleasantly upon all subjects.' Neither the financial troubles which came to him in his old age and threatened to deprive him of his home, nor the approach of death, disturbed his serene temper. Orthodox Christians who regarded him as an atheist had expected his end to be clouded, but he told a friend that he did not feel the smallest solicitude for the result. ' To the corruptions of Christianity I am, indeed, opposed; but not to the genuine precepts of Jesus himself. I am a Christian, in the only sense in which he wished any one to be; sincerely attached to his doctrines, in preference to all others; ascribing to him every *human* excellence; and believing he never claimed any other.'

An unbeliever in the strict sense of the word, no man ever believed more ardently in the future of humanity and the essential goodness of his fellow men. Nor had forty years of political life soured his creed. ' I do not believe with the Rochefoucaulds and Montaignes,' he said, ' that fourteen men out of fifteen are rogues. I believe a great abatement from that proportion may be made in favour of general honesty.' That rogues usually contrived to ' nestle them-selves into places of power and profit ' and monopolise offices of authority did not detract from the essential decency of mankind. The moral was to keep society as simple and unrestricted as possible and to confine the actions of governments to an indispensable minimum.

Such was Jefferson's unshakable creed. ' I am for a

government rigorously frugal and simple, applying all the possible savings of the public revenue to the discharge of the national debt; and not for a multiplication of officers and salaries merely to make partisans. . . . I am for free commerce with all nations; political connection with none; and little or no diplomatic establishment. And I am not for linking ourselves by new treaties with the quarrels of Europe; entering that field of slaughter to preserve their balance, or joining in the confederacy of kings to war against the principles of liberty.' Nor did any mathematical machinery for ensuring the sovereignty of the people's representatives over the people appeal to his clear and far-seeing mind : ' an elective despotism was not the government we fought for.' The liberties of the future he bequeathed to the independent freeholders and farmers of his vast country, ' the true representatives of the great American interest, and . . . alone to be relied upon for expressing the proper American sentiments.'

In the summer of 1826 he began to fail. His last wish was to live till July 4, the fiftieth anniversary of the Declaration of Independence. Like so many of his wishes it was granted. He died on that famous day leaving to his country the principles of individual freedom to which she has recurred at every crisis of her history. His trust in her future he had expressed in a letter a little before his death. ' We are destined to be a barrier against the returns of ignorance and barbarism. Old Europe will have to lean on our shoulders, and to hobble along by our side, under the monkish trammels of priests and kings as she can. What a Colossus shall we be when the Southern continent comes up to our mark. . . . I like the dreams of the future better than the history of the past— so good night ! '

CHAPTER II

ABRAHAM LINCOLN

THE American dream had begun as an ideal in the minds of the Elizabethans. It first took on actuality on the barren shores of North America, where the plain and oppressed made their appeal to the wilderness for the freedom and well-being which the old and established world, with its dead hand of custom and privilege, had denied them. It continued, as the land was settled, wherever the poorer and less influential colonists, turning their faces westwards, moved farther into the forest to make new homes. Every increase of wealth and civilisation saw a fresh trek of ' poor whites ' westwards, till the tide of them flowed over the Alleghanies and into the great Mississippi valley.

The ' buckskins,' as such poor and ignorant frontiersmen were called, were looked down on by the established and well-to-do who stayed on their inherited acres or in counting-houses in the settled lands near the coast. But their numbers were reinforced by new tides of European emigration— Germans after the Thirty Years War, Catholic Irish and Highlanders after the English Revolution and poor English colonials at all times. Whenever a few thousand of them were gathered together they were free, by the terms of the Constitution, to form a new state which, however rude and uncultured, was entitled to enter the Union on terms of absolute equality with the older states of the East. One such, Kentucky, was founded in 1792, and another, Tennessee, in 1796. And after Jefferson's purchase of Louisiana, at the beginning of the nineteenth century, the scope for new states became almost illimitable. Thus the frontier was constantly being called in to counterbalance the inevitable

43

tendency of the rich and powerful to weigh down the scales of the Union in favour of the established order.

In this way the ideal of democracy was ever renewed. Life on the frontier was almost unbelievably harsh and primitive, and there was no leisure for culture or any but the most elementary virtues. Yet it was lit by hope, the perpetual religion of the western world. It was a hope expressed by the words of a simple ballad of the time:

> To the west, to the west, to the land of the Free
> Where the mighty Missouri rolls down to the sea,
> Where a man is a man if he's willing to toil,
> And the poorest may gather the fruits of the soil.

Into this world Abraham Lincoln was born on February 12, 1809, in a log cabin in the backwoods of Kentucky. His grandfather, who had English Quaker blood, had trekked westwards in the eighteenth century from the Shenandoah valley and had been shot by an Indian while working on a claim located in Kentucky. His father, Thomas Lincoln, was an unprospering but hopeful farmer, ever moving west as tales of new and better land reached him from the farthest foam of the flowing tide of settlement. His mother, Nancy Hanks, was the illegitimate daughter of a Virginian gentleman and a poor serving girl, who had travelled the wilderness road into Kentucky with her unwanted babe in her arms.

Lincoln's boyhood was one of incessant hardship. In after years he spoke of it but little, once saying sadly to a questioner: 'Why: it is a great folly to attempt to make anything out of me or my early life. It can all be condensed into a single sentence; and that sentence you will find in Gray's Elegy:

> The short and simple annals of the poor.

That's my life, and that's all you or anyone else can make out of it.' The chief factors in it were poverty, the crude vitality and downward drag of the frontier, and his father's repeated moves into the wilderness.

When he was eight he lost his mother. The fever that

carried her off spared him, but he mourned her all his life and idealised her memory. He used to say that he owed everything he was to her. About this time his father had settled on the Indiana shore in the new state of Ohio. ' It was a wild region,' Lincoln wrote, ' with many bears and other wild animals still in the woods. There I grew up. There were some schools, so called, but no qualification was ever required of a teacher beyond "readin', writin', and cipherin'," to the rule of three.'

His father married again, and his stepmother, Sarah Johnston, a kindly, sensible woman with a family of her own, did her best to assist Abe's passionate attempts at learning. With no other encouragement, in the midst of the ceaseless manual labour by which the family gained a livelihood in that wild place, he contrived to master a few books—the Bible, ' Æsop's Fables,' ' Robinson Crusoe,' the ' Pilgrim's Progress,' a ' History of the United States,' and a copy of the ' Laws of Indiana.' These he gradually acquired and constantly re-read. His absorption in such pursuits, which seemed incongruous to his neighbours, was afterwards remembered by one of his early employers :

I found him cocked up on a haystack with a book.
' What are you reading ? ' I said.
' I'm not reading, I'm studying,' says he.
' What are you studying ? ' says I.
' Law,' says he, as proud as Cicero.
' Good God Almighty,' says I.

Lincoln grew to a giant's size. At nineteen he was six feet four inches high, with long ungainly arms and legs, and with deep lines already scored across his face, the result of deep, unaided thought and early under-feeding. He looked, a friend said, as if he had been rough-hewn with an axe and needed smoothing with a jackplane. His strength was such that he was in great demand for felling trees and splitting timber rails for fences. He also became a notable wrestler.

But his chief fame in that primitive countryside was as a story-teller. For this he had a natural if not very decorous genius, and he could make almost anybody laugh. The crudity of his tales was not founded on any debauchery of life— where women were concerned he was shy and awkward— but from the rough human environment from which he sprang.

> Abraham Lincoln, his hand and pen,
> He will be good but God knows when,

was scrawled across the title page of one of his early books. He intended to be.

Before he was in his teens Abe was earning his own keep, shucking corn, skinning and curing hides, and later splitting rails, digging wells and butchering for his father's neighbours. No man who achieved his distinction ever received so broad a basis to his education. When he was nineteen he took a flat-boat with farm produce a thousand miles down the Mississippi to New Orleans, holding his own with the tough kings of western democracy, 'half-men, half-alligator,' who made 'ole man river' their own. Theirs was a rough and picturesque equality: one of them kicked a Frenchman, who was boasting of royal blood, out of a tavern parlour into the middle of the street with a 'What if you are a king. Ain't we all kings over here?' 'I'm little Billy,' the leader of a rival gang used to cry, 'all the way from North Fork of Muddy Run, and I can whip any man in this section of the country. Maybe you never heard of the time the horse kicked me an' put both his hips out o' j'int—if it ain't true, cut me up for catfish bait. I'm one o' the toughest—live forever and then turn to a white-oak post. I can outrun, outjump, outswim, chaw more tobacco and spit less, drink more whisky and keep soberer, than any man in these parts.' In this society the young husky from Indiana moved as to the manner born. Yet he also held a little aloof from it, almost as if he had one of his long legs in another world.

For Lincoln combined with his rude social sense queer, wistful longings of which he seldom spoke. It was his custom, in the silent hours of his employment, to weave

stories to himself very different from the purely masculine
kind he told to his fellows. It was a habit begun in boyhood, when a passing family moving west stayed for a
few days in the neighbourhood of his father's cabin; there
were daughters, and one of the girls, shyly admired at a
distance while her mother read stories aloud to him and
the other children, set his imagination working. 'When
they had gone I thought of her a great deal, and one day
when I was sitting out in the sun by the house I wrote
out a story in my mind. I thought I took my father's
horse and followed the waggon, and finally I found it,
and they were surprised to see me. I talked with the girl
and persuaded her to elope with me; and that night I put
her on my horse, and we started off across the prairie.
After several hours we came to a camp; and when we rode
up we found it was the one we had left a few hours before,
and we went in The next night we tried again, and the
same thing happened—the horse came back to the same
place; and then we concluded we ought not to elope.
I stayed until I had persuaded her father to give her to
me. I always meant to write that story out and publish it;
but I concluded that it was not much of a story.'

Early in 1830 the Lincoln family again moved west,
naked as they had come, into the Sangamon country of the
new state of Illinois. Soon afterwards Abe said good-bye
to his father and set up on his own, going down the
Sangamon River by canoe to New Salem, a log township
of a dozen families, where he took a job as salesman in a
local store. He had taught himself to do figures and write—
'Oh I guess I can make a few rabbit tracks '—and so felt
himself well qualified for the learned labours of clerkship
and accountancy.

Somehow, in that little whisky-drinking, cock-fighting
community, the store never thrived. His partner drank, and
bills and bad debts accumulated, and in the end Lincoln was
left to shoulder the debts, which he did most manfully,
ultimately paying them off after fifteen years of pinching.
Meanwhile he earned his livelihood as a land surveyor and

for a time as local postmaster. He used to say that he carried the office round in his hat. Except for the Presidency of the United States it was the only one he ever held.

He also had a brief experience of campaigning against the Indians, joining up as a volunteer and being elected by his comrades to the command of a company. It was a campaign more humorous than heroic, as afterwards, during his brief middle period in Congress, he related to his amused fellow legislators. ' Yes, sir ; in the days of the Black Hawk War, I fought, bled, and came away. Speaking of General Cass's career reminds me of my own. I was not at Stillman's defeat, but I was about as near it as Cass was to Hull's surrender ; and, like him, I saw the place very soon afterwards. It is quite certain I did not break my sword, for I had none to break ; but I bent a musket pretty badly on one occasion. If Cass broke his sword, the idea is he broke it in desperation ; I bent the musket by accident. If General Cass went in advance of me in picking huckle-berries, I guess I surpassed him in charges upon the wild onions. If he saw any live, fighting Indians, it was more than I did ; but I had a good many bloody struggles with the mosquitoes, and although I never fainted from the loss of blood, I can truly say I was often very hungry.'

All the while he was quietly making himself a better man. Kirkham's ' Grammar,' Gibbon, Rollin's ' History of the World,' the ' Statutes of Illinois,' and an old volume of Blackstone bought from an emigrant's sack, contributed in turn to his process of self-education. Encouraged by a neighbouring Justice, who was kind to him, he abandoned the idea of being a blacksmith and resolved to become a lawyer. In a state where the population was doubling every few years, and everyone had some claim to land, it did not seem a bad choice.

It was well attuned to another of Abe's interests. Like everyone in the West who had brains to spare, he was absorbed in politics. Outside farming and the natural philosophy of the bar-room it was almost the only thing a man could talk about. It interested Lincoln so much that at twenty-three he decided to stand for the infant State legislature. He was an uncouth-looking customer for such aspirations, even in so primitive a place as Illinois, and knew it. But, being a born raconteur, he was used to holding forth to his neighbours and so boldly put himself forward.

His election address was a mixture of parish-pump politics and that curious idealism which he always contrived to blend with a shrewd knowledge of the world he lived in. Thus he added to his practical project of improving the navigation of the Sangamon River certain views on the question of education. ' I can only say that I view it as the most important subject which we as a people can be engaged in. That every man may receive at least a moderate education, and thereby be enabled to read the histories of his own and other countries, by which he may duly appreciate the value of our free institutions, appears to be an object of vital importance, even on this account alone, to say nothing of the advantages and satisfaction to be derived from all being able to read the Scriptures, and other works both of a religious and moral nature, for themselves. . . . For my part, I desire to see the time when education—and by its means, morality, sobriety, enterprise, and industry—shall become much more general than at present.'

There was a personal touch, too, at the end of the address. ' I was born, and have ever remained, in the most humble walks of life. I have no wealth or popular relations or friends to recommend me. My case is thrown exclusively upon the independent voters of the country; and, if elected, they will have conferred a favour upon me for which I shall be unremitting in my labours to compensate. But if the good people in their wisdom shall see fit to keep me in the background, I have been too familiar with disappointments to be very much chagrined.'

In August 1832, Lincoln, who had just returned from campaigning against the Indians, began his electoral campaign by stepping on to a wooden box in the street of Pappville to address his fellow citizens. After telling them a few stories and temporarily leaving his box to pick up a rowdy opponent by the seat of his breeches and throw him out, he came speedily to the point. ' Gentlemen and fellow citizens: I presume you all know who I am. I am humble Abraham Lincoln. I have been solicited by many friends to become a candidate for the legislature. My politics are short and sweet, like the old woman's dance. I am in favour of a national bank. I am in favour of the internal-improvements system and a high protective tariff. These are my sentiments and political principles. If elected, I shall be thankful; if not, it will be all the same.' He was not elected.

Comic backwoodsman as he was, he stood again. He attached himself to the unpopular ' Whig ' or conservative party, then much discredited in the western states. ' Can't the party raise any better material than that? ' someone asked. But he got in, and from his twenty-sixth to his thirty-fourth year served his neighbours in the State legislature of Illinois at a fee of three dollars a sitting.

He proved a quaintly honest politician, and in the end became the more popular because of it. ' I am too poor to own a carriage,' he told an audience of farmers, ' but my friend '—pointing to the Democratic candidate—' has generously invited me to ride with him. I want you to vote for me if you will; but, if not, then vote for my opponent, for he is a fine man.' He helped the Whigs to win the state from the Democrats and took a leading share in the legislation for developing the public resources of the young community. In this there was much scope for peculation in the American political mode,[1] but Lincoln, to the great annoyance of some of his colleagues, would have none of it. Once he kept the Assembly sitting all night through his refusal to purchase an important block of votes by

---

[1] ' Mr. Chairman, this work is exclusively the work of politicians; a set of men who have interests aside from the interests of the people, and who, to say the most of them, are, taken as a mass, at least one long step removed from honest men. I say this with the greater freedom because, being a politician myself, none can regard it as personal.'

lending his support to a corrupt measure. For there was no moving this big, gaunt fellow. ' You may burn my body to ashes,' he said, ' and scatter them to the winds of heaven; you may drag my soul down to the regions of darkness and despair to be tormented for ever; but you will never get me to support a measure which I believe to be wrong, although by doing so I may accomplish that which I believe to be right.'

But if he was unbending where his conscience was aroused, he was supple in things immaterial. He loved to sit amidst his fellow politicians, with his knees drawn up to his chin, drinking and telling tall stories, especially when a friend had brought a fiddle. For all the lines on his face, he was a companionable soul and, as such, a born politician. He had a genius for drawing the best out of his fellow men in the most informal kind of way, and he never stopped learning from them. His knowledge of human nature therefore was perpetually expanding. And he became a master at pulling wires.

Yet the Lincoln who kept every company in a roar with his droll stories and ways of speech had melancholy moods. When he was alone he was haunted by dreams of something tenderer and lovelier than life had offered him, and he found the contrast of the harsh reality about him almost more than he could bear. He once told a friend that he never dared carry a pocket-knife for fear lest in one of his fits of gloom he might kill himself. Altogether he was an enigma, now uproariously funny in company, now sad and alone, rough and awkward in appearance with a terrible strength, yet tender as a girl towards anyone helpless or in trouble. As for his appearance, a friend wrote that he was the most uncouth-looking young man he had ever seen. ' He seemed to have but little to say, seemed to feel timid, with a tinge of sadness visible in the countenance, but when he did talk all this disappeared for the time, and he demonstrated that he was both strong and acute. He surprised us more and more at every visit.'

One of the measures which Lincoln helped to coax through

the Illinois legislature was the removal of the state capital to Springfield. Here Lincoln moved also and set up as a lawyer. As usual at this period of his life, though the soul of independence, he seemed to have no money. On this occasion he walked into a local store to buy himself some bedding and explained to the storekeeper that, having only seventeen dollars in the world, he would like to purchase it on a system of deferred payment. The storekeeper, whose name was Joshua Speed, looked up at the young giant and decided that he had never seen so melancholy a face in all his life or one so honest. He offered him a share of his own bed and became his lifelong friend.

Springfield at this time was a fast-growing little town with a population of 1500 or more, quite a number of shops, two churches and the kind of society which comes into being whenever women, raised above the line of bare subsistence, are gathered together. To Lincoln they were a little-known quantity and a rather terrifying one. For the next seven years they became a disturbing and revolutionary factor in his life.

For, fearless of everyone else, he was afraid of women, and the more he admired them the more he feared them. His ignorance of them was the result of shyness, caused by acute consciousness of his own uncouth figure, and by a certain fastidiousness which was part of his idealism and prevented him from ever acquiring the sort of experience which men of coarser grain so easily obtain. Yet, though he kept his thoughts to himself, he thought about women a great deal, and wove them into his dreams. In one of his rare, half-humorous, half-tragic passages of self-revelation, he replied in the form of a parable to an acquaintance who had asked why he seemed to take so little pleasure in feminine society. 'When we lived in Indiana, once in a while my mother used to . . . make some gingerbread. . . . One day I smelled the gingerbread, and came into the house to get my share while it was still hot. My mother had baked me three gingerbread men. I took them out under a hickory-tree to eat them. There was a family near us poorer than we were, and their boy came along as I sat

down. . . . " Abe," he said, " gimme a man ! " I gave
him one. He crammed it into his mouth in two bites, and
looked at me while I was biting the legs off my first one.
" Abe," he said, " gimme that other'n." I wanted it myself,
but I gave it to him, and it followed the first. I said to him,
" You seem to like gingerbread." " Abe," he said, " I don't
s'pose anybody on earth likes gingerbread better'n I do—and
gets less'n I do." '

The love affairs that ensued in his life were not happy :
those of men who, growing up in ignorance of women,
idealise them, seldom are. The first was tragic enough.
With many misgivings he courted the daughter of a storekeeper with whom he had boarded in Kentucky. For a
time she favoured a rival, and Lincoln, who saw himself
as an unattractive fellow with no chance, withdrew. But
the successful suitor proved false, and the girl turned to
Lincoln. For three months they were engaged—months of
exquisite happiness in his starved life. Then suddenly she
sickened of a fever and died in his arms.

The tragedy made a deep impression on his melancholy
nature. For a time his reason seemed to be shaken : then
the hard core of manhood inside saved him. Yet once
he told a friend that the thought that the snows and rains
fell on her grave filled him with indescribable grief. The
memory of that brief fulfilment brought out all the latent
poetry in Lincoln and left behind a dream that he nursed
to his dying day. It made him a much bigger man but it
made him a sadder one.

His next love affair, though it was also unhappy, had a
humorous aspect. After mourning Ann Rutledge for three
years he gradually found himself associating with a certain
Mary Owens. She was a woman of commanding and comfortable aspect, and was no longer young. But she needed
a husband, and her friends decided that Lincoln, who was a
good-natured sort of fellow, would do very well, for he was
so uncouth that he could not afford to be particular. Lincoln
did not love her, but, as he said, he had ' no good objection,'
and it was generally understood that sooner or later, since

their doing so could deprive no one but themselves of anything, they would marry.

To Lincoln the situation grew increasingly distasteful. Poor Mary Owens' prosaic womanly mind and still more prosaic figure only heightened the saddening contrast between dreams and reality that drove him into woman's society. On the other hand he was a kind-hearted, scrupulous man and easily frightened of any woman. 'I spent my time,' he told a friend, 'planning how I might get along through life after my contemplated change of circumstances should have taken place, and how I might procrastinate the evil day for a time, which I really dreaded as much, perhaps more, than an Irishman does the halter.'

In the end he decided that it was his duty to make a formal proposal to her. He braced himself for the ordeal, and to his astonishment, she refused him. Like Mr. Collins, he put the refusal down to feminine modesty and repeated his offer. But she still declined, and as often as he returned to the subject, refused again. 'I finally was forced to give it up,' he confided afterwards to the wife of a fellow legislator, ' at which I very unexpectedly found myself mortified almost beyond endurance. I was mortified, it seemed to me, in a hundred different ways. My vanity was deeply wounded by the reflection that I had been too stupid to discover her intentions, and at the same time never doubting that I understood them perfectly ; and also that she, whom I had taught myself to believe nobody else would have, had actually rejected me with all my fancied greatness. And, to cap the whole, I then for the first time began to suspect that I was really a little in love with her. But let it all go. I'll try and outlive it. Others have been made fools of by the girls; but this can never with truth be said of me. I most emphatically, in this instance, made a fool of myself. I have now come to the conclusion never again to think of marrying, and for this reason: I can never be satisfied with anyone who would be blockhead enough to have me.'

It was a melancholy confession and a comic sort of affair. Fat, comfortable Mary Owens came out of it rather well, for she refused to put a noose round the neck of an honest man who did not love her. She always spoke of him afterwards with affection as ' a man with a heart full of human kindness and a head full of common sense.' At the time it must sometimes have seemed to her that the former was more developed than the latter.

At the third encounter Lincoln met his match. In 1839 there came to Springfield, on a visit to her married sister, a young woman of good birth named Mary Todd. She was a vivacious, lively creature, with a spark of fire in her, more ambitious than tender and with an intense will of her own. Socially she was far superior to any of the Springfield girls, the daughter of a Kentucky Bank President, with a host of elegant accomplishments, fine clothes and an armful of winning feminine graces. Lincoln, who had never seen anything like her before, was quite awe-stricken in her presence. And she, with a sure eye for power, saw just what she needed to further her ambition in the gawky young legislator with the enormous arms and legs and the great brow. After a brief period of flirting with the idea of marrying the rising star of Illinois, the politician Stephen Douglas, she plumped for Lincoln as the one man she had met who she believed, in her innermost heart, might take her to the White House. She set her cap at him and in 1840 they became formally engaged. Nor could the arguments of all her friends persuade her that she was throwing herself away.

But once he had got her for himself Lincoln found that Mary Todd was not an ideal in petticoats, but a human being like himself, and a very imperious and exacting one at that. He began to see that marriage with her would not resolve his dreams after all. Though even more frightened of her than her predecessor, he tried to break it off, but failed miserably. ' When I told Mary I did not love her, she burst into tears, and, almost springing from her chair and wringing her hands as if in agony, said something about the deceiver being herself deceived. It was too much for me. I found the tears trickling down my own cheeks. I caught her in my arms and kissed her.' His friend Speed, to whom this confession was made, told him he had made a fool of himself. But poor Lincoln replied, ' Well, if I'm in again, so be it. It's done, and I shall abide by it.'

After that he was at the mercy of his nerves. He became ill, depressed and lifeless. He did not know what he should do and walked about the streets of Springfield like a man awaiting imprisonment. There was no possible escape. When the day fixed for the wedding came, he went down to the Legislature and sat there all day, listening to the debate. The bride waited in the church but no bridegroom came. Afterwards Lincoln was distraught at what he had done: he had shamed himself in the eyes of his neighbours and friends, thrown away his only chance of happiness and humiliated the woman he had once loved. He thought again of taking his life, and told his partner that he was the most miserable man living and that if what he was feeling was distributed over the whole human family there would not be a cheerful face left on earth. For a time he put himself in the hands of a mental doctor and sounded the lowest depth of shame and agony.

His friend Joshua Speed made his trouble his own, took him to his home in the warm South, nursed and tended him like a child. It was part of Lincoln's greatness that he could inspire such affection. Gradually his balance and his sense of humour returned. When he went back to Springfield he was able to take up his old pursuits of law and politics; even to advise Speed himself, who had just become engaged to a southern girl and now found himself the victim of the same sort of nerves as Lincoln himself. ' The first special cause,' he wrote, ' is your exposure to bad weather on your journey, which my experience clearly proves to be very severe on defective nerves. The second is the absence of all business and conversation of friends, which might divert your mind, give it occasional rest from the intensity of thought which will sometimes wear the sweetest idea threadbare and turn it to the bitterness of death. The third is the rapid and near approach of that crisis on which all your thoughts and feelings concentrate.'

Then with a rare intermixture of insight and common sense he advised Speed how to cure himself. ' Let me, who have reason to speak with judgment on such a subject, beseech you to ascribe it to the causes I have mentioned, and not to some false and ruinous suggestion of the Devil. The general cause—nervous debility, which is the key and conductor of all the particular ones, and without which they would be utterly harmless—though it does pertain to you, does not pertain to one in a thousand. It is out of this that the painful difference between you and the mass of the world springs.' And he told him that like himself it was his misfortune to dream dreams beyond the capacity of attainment. But that was no reason why Speed should throw away the substance of a real happiness.

' I know what the painful point with you is at all times when you are unhappy; it is an apprehension that you do not love her as you should. What nonsense! How came you to court her? Was it because you thought she deserved it, and that you had given her reason to expect it? If it was for that, why did not the same reason make you court at least twenty others of whom you can think, and to whom it would apply with greater force than to her? Did you court her for her wealth? Why, you know she had none. But you say you reasoned yourself into it. What do you mean by that? Was it not that you found yourself unable to reason yourself out of it? Did you not think and partly form the purpose of courting her the first time you ever saw her or heard of her? . . . There was nothing at that time for reason to work upon. Whether she was moral, amiable, sensible, or even of good character, you did not, nor could then know, except, perhaps, you might infer the last from the company you found her in. All you then did or could know of her was her personal appearance and deportment; and these, if they impress at all, impress the heart, and not the head.

' Say, candidly, were not those heavenly black eyes the whole basis of all your early reasoning on the subject? Did you not go and take me all the way to Lexington and back, for no other purpose but to get to see her again? What earthly consideration would you take to find her scouting and despising you, and giving herself up to another? But of this you have no apprehension; and therefore you cannot bring it home to your feelings. I shall be so anxious about you that I shall want you to write by every mail.'

Speed took his advice and married his black-eyed Fanny and was happy. When the chance came again, Lincoln applied the same lesson to his own case. After two years a meeting with Mary Todd was effected by mutual friends. Feeling that he had cruelly wronged her, he did her every service within his power and, when they were fully reconciled, laid his heart at her feet. They became engaged again.

In October 1842 he wrote to Speed to ask his counsel. 'You have now been the husband of a lovely woman nearly eight months. You are happier now than the day you married her. Returning elasticity of spirits is manifested in your letters. But I want to ask you a close question, " Are you in feeling as well as judgment glad that you are married as you are? " From anybody but me this would be an impudent question, not to be tolerated; but I know you will pardon it in me. Please answer it quickly as I am impatient to know.' But it was more a reassurance than advice that he required. For he had resolved to cross his Rubicon, and this time there was no turning back. On November 4 he and Mary were married according to the rites of the Episcopal Church, a preference of Mary's, who, true to her southern breeding, liked to have the best of everything. When the bridegroom placed the ring on her finger and repeated the form ' With this ring I thee endow with all my goods, chattels, lands, and tenements,' his friend and neighbour Judge Brown, unaccustomed to such ceremony, burst out in blunt amazement, ' God Almighty, Lincoln, the statute fixes all that.'

Lincoln made a brave show of it, but, as those who knew him best were sadly aware, he was not happy. Nor was he afterwards. For all her prettiness and cleverness, deep in his inner consciousness he knew that she was second best to him. Her impetuous will and acrimonious temper soon made his home a far from easy place. And for a man of catholic and democratic tastes her social pretences were a considerable trial. Once, when asked by a friend why his wife's relations spelt their name with two *d*'s, he replied, ' For God one *d* is enough, but the Todds need two.'

Nor, to a woman of elegant accomplishments and social aspirations, was Lincoln the most satisfactory of husbands. In refined society, neither his appearance nor his over-droll conversation was any asset. Though in most things he let her have her own way, he was unaccountable in his hours, slovenly in dress and little of a lady's companion. In a moment of bitterness she confided to a friend : ' He is of no account when he is at home. He never does anything except to warm himself and read. He never went to market in his life. He is the most useless, good-for-nothing man on earth.' Yet she believed in him, and fostered his secret ambitions. For, though others might laugh, she meant to make a statesman of him.

In another way, too, all unconsciously she helped him to become one. Though after his children were born he loved to be with them and play with them, his fellow lawyers and politicians noticed that he did not hurry home after business was over. To him home was rather a restless, nagging sort of place, and though his wife gave him a spur to his ambition, she give him little of what he had craved so much, tenderness and companionship. So he put aside all hope of fulfilling his inner dreams—renounced them—and turned elsewhere for something on which to lavish his idealism. He found it in the service of his fellow men. Henceforward he devoted ever more of his time to public affairs, seeking in the pursuit of law and politics the means of releasing all the love that was imprisoned in his lonely heart.

His marriage, mistaken as in certain lights it must appear, had done something else for Lincoln. It had restored his confidence in his own ability to keep his resolves, which he had once taken pride in as the chief gem of his character and which he felt he had lost when he failed to turn up on his first wedding day. Now he knew that he could overcome his own temperament and go through with whatever life set him. He returned to politics with a graver manner and a more resolved purpose, and deliberately laid aside the clownishness which till now had prevented men from taking him seriously. The old flashes of humour still recurred—the use of homely agricultural illustrations, which his rustic listeners could understand, and his quizzing grasp of life's contradictions and absurdities. But there was also in his speeches a growing note of conviction and even intensity.

In 1846, urged by his wife, he stood and was elected to Congress by the Illinois Whigs. There followed an interlude of two years at Washington. Here he lived in a boarding house and was only conspicuous as one who could always make the House rock with laughter. An amusing example was his attack on General Cass, whom the Democrats were trying to popularise as a military hero against the next Presidential election.

Mr. Speaker, I adopt the suggestion of a friend that General Cass is a general of splendidly successful charges—charges, to be sure, not upon the public enemy, but upon the public treasury. He was governor of Michigan Territory and ex-officio superintendent of Indian affairs, from the 9th of October, 1813, to the 31st of July, 1831—a period of seventeen years, nine months, and twenty-two days. During this period he received from the United States treasury, for personal services and personal expenses, the aggregate sum of ninety-six thousand and twenty-eight dollars, being an average of fourteen dollars and seventy-nine cents per day for every day of the time. This large sum was reached by assuming that he was doing service at several different places, and in several different capacities in the same place, all at the same time. . . . But I have introduced General Cass's accounts here chiefly to show the wonderful physical capacities of the man. They show that he not only did the labour of several men at the same time, but that he often did it at several places, many hundreds of miles apart, at the same time. And at eating, too, his capacities are shown to be quite as wonderful. From October, 1821, to May, 1822, he ate ten rations a day in Michigan, ten rations a day here in Washington, and near five dollars' worth a day on the road between the two places ! And then there is an important discovery in his example—the art of being paid for what one eats, instead of having to pay for it ! Hereafter, if any nice young man should owe a bill which he cannot pay in any other way, he can just board it out.

Mr. Speaker, we have all heard of the animal standing in doubt between two stacks of hay and starving to death. The like of that would never happen to General Cass. Place the stacks a thousand miles apart, he would stand stock-still midway between them, and eat them both at once, and the green grass along the line would be apt to suffer some too, at the same time. By all means make him President, gentlemen. He will feed you bounteously—if—if there is any left after he shall have helped himself.

But though Lincoln's power of ridicule and mimicry was almost as potent in Congress as in his native state, he was too much of a backwoodsman to be taken seriously by people who pretended to culture and refinement. Besides he supported the unpopular pacifist side over the Mexican war then waging. After his two years he did not seek re-election, and withdrew, a tired and disappointed man at the age of forty, to Springfield. As some reward for his services to the Party, which in matters of lobbying and wire-pulling were considerable, he was offered the governorship of Oregon Territory in the Far West. The post, which meant virtual retirement from active politics, was the most he could reasonably expect. But his wife, who still believed in his star, persuaded him not to take it. In her bones she knew what no one else knew, that the future would bring something greater.

After his retirement from Congress, Lincoln, with a growing family to feed, returned to his profession. For the next five or six years he was the prairie lawyer, gradually winning the confidence of all Illinois. His was a queer practice, and critics sometimes said that Lincoln carried it round with him in his hat—a tall, battered object which, with his brolly and his satchel, became inseparably associated with him. In the ramshackle, untidy office at Springfield, which he shared with his young partner, Herndon, he was generally to be found with his long shanks spread across the table or stretched against the mantelpiece. More often he was away on circuit, jolting in a buggy across the prairie, telling droll tales to all the neighbourhood in country inns or pleading in rough, outlandish little courthouses.

For all his untidiness and his quaint ways of conducting business he was a good lawyer. For one thing he was absolutely straight, so that everybody trusted him, including the judges. The whole western world knew that ' honest Abe ' would not charge an excessive fee or accept a doubtful brief. ' I can win your case,' he once told a client, ' I can get you 600 dollars. I can also make an honest family miserable. But I shall not take your case, and I shall not take your fee. One piece of advice I will give you gratis. Go home and think seriously whether you cannot make 600 dollars in some honest way.' Nor did he ever resort to those little arts of chicanery by which bad lawyers make fortunes at the expense of public stability. Litigiousness he loathed. ' Persuade your neighbours to compromise whenever you can,' he said to a young lawyer. ' Point out to them how the nominal winner is often a real loser—in fees, expenses, and waste of time. As a peacemaker, the lawyer has a superior opportunity of being a good man. There will still be business enough.'

But if Lincoln was honest he was not simple. There was no shrewder advocate in Illinois. A fellow lawyer testified that anyone who took him to be an artless, harmless fellow would soon find himself undeceived—in the ditch. Some of his cases became famous for their wit, such as his advocacy for a poor old farmer who had sold a waggon and team to two young men who subsequently pleaded ' infancy ' to avoid the debt. Instead of attempting to defeat the letter of the law by a sentimental appeal on behalf of his client, who stood to be ruined by the cheat, he lay back during the case for the defence with his hands in his pockets, capping each point of opposing counsel with a bland, drawling, ' I reckon that's so.' But when it came to his turn to rise, he gazed at the defendants with an air of extraordinary benevolence and turned to the jury with a ' Gentlemen of the Jury: are you prepared that these two young men shall enter upon life and go through life with the stain of a dishonourable transaction for over affixed to them ? ' The jury thought not and found against them.

There was a homely directness and originality about his advocacy which was exquisitely attuned to the rough western mind he knew so well. ' My client,' he explained in one case, ' was in the position of a man who was walking along the road with a pitchfork on his shoulder when suddenly a savage dog ran out of a farmhouse he was passing and attacked him. To save himself, the man killed the dog with the pitchfork. " Why did you kill my dog ? " said the angry farmer. " Why did the dog try to bite me ? " " Why didn't you fend him off with the blunt end ? " " Why didn't your dog go for me with his blunt end ? " '

It was this kind of crazy humour that made Lincoln so difficult to resist. Once, when he was challenged to a duel and offered the choice of weapons, he replied gravely, ' How about cow-dung at five paces ? '

But there was another side to Lincoln. At one moment he would be the life and soul of a party of lawyers and local politicians in some little western inn, telling mocking story after story over the pipes and glasses : the next he would be lost and far away in some unfathomable world of his own. One who was with him on circuit described him as sitting alone in a corner of the bar, remote from everyone, wrapped in abstraction and gloom. ' I watched him for some time. He seemed to be pursuing in his mind some specific painful subject, regularly and systematically through various sinuosities, and his sad face would assume, at times, deeper phases of grief. No relief came till he was roused by the adjournment of court, when he emerged from his cave of gloom, like one awakened from sleep.' His neighbours naturally could not make it out.

For Lincoln was doing what men, and politicians least of all, seldom do—thinking. His mind did not move quickly, but it never ceased to move. All the while he was making himself a bigger man: reading and musing over what he read and doing what he called figure things out. At this time the Bible, Shakespeare and Burns were his inseparable companions; on his lonely journeys across the prairie he used to turn them over in his mind and reach out to his own hard-wrought conclusions. ' My mind is like a piece of steel,' he told a friend, ' very hard to scratch anything on it, and almost impossible after you get it there to rub it out.' Sometimes it seemed as though the strong thought within him must break out: in a sudden burst of confidence he once turned to Herndon with a ' How hard it is to die and leave one's country no better than if one had never lived for it ! The world is dead to hope, deaf to its own death struggle. One made known by a universal cry, What is to be done ? Is anything to be done ? Do you ever think of these things ? ' Lincoln did.

And when his hour came he was ready. For in the late forties of his life a great question arose which threatened the very existence of the American ideal and in doing so tested Lincoln's character to the core. Upon the back of this lonely man, with nothing to love but his dreams and his rough fellow men, a tremendous burden was placed.

The question was the position of slavery in the United States, and another, even more momentous, depended upon it. When the Union was first made, negro slavery on the tobacco plantations was already firmly established in the Southern states from which the chief wealth and talent of the country was then drawn. The Fathers, basing their independence and nationhood on the dictum that all men are created equal and with the right to freedom, would have liked to have abolished it there and then. But the institution was an essential part of the economic structure of Southern society, and immediate abolition would have meant widespread ruin. It was therefore left to time to eliminate, with the clear understanding that it was an evil that was to be regarded unequivocally as such and on no account to be allowed to spread. ' The whole commerce

64

between master and slave,' wrote Jefferson, who, though a slave-owner himself, always hoped to achieve abolition, ' is a perpetual exercise of the most boisterous passions, the most unremitting despotism on the one part and degrading submissions on the other. . . . I tremble for my country when I think of the negro and remember that God is just.'

There probably, but for the intervention of an economic revolution, the matter would have rested until in the course of time slavery had been superseded and eliminated. But the invention of the cotton gin and the vast extension of cotton growing, for which the Mississippi states of the far South were peculiarly suited, altered the whole position. The value of slaves became greater than it had ever been before, and their breeding a lucrative industry.

All this happened in Jefferson's own lifetime, and his later thoughts were much clouded by the difficulty of reconciling his beloved democracy to the institution of slavery. Unlike most of his Southern neighbours he knew that they could not be reconciled. His Louisiana purchase complicated the matter still further, for it was followed by a new tide of emigration westwards into country much of which was suitable to cotton growing and therefore to slavery. The evil, instead of being kept within a ring fence as the Fathers had intended, spread. The six original slave states became fifteen. ' This momentous question,' he wrote in his old age, ' like a fire-ball in the night, awakened and filled me with terror.'

Six years before Jefferson's death a settlement of a sort was found in the famous Missouri Compromise. Slavery, it was agreed, was to be tacitly permitted south of latitude 36° 30', on condition that it was never allowed to spread north of that line. But the Missouri Compromise was only a stop-gap and not a solution. Before long the perilous question arose again in a new and more alarming form.

For the very dispute that the existence of slavery involved between the Northern and Southern states called the whole foundation of the Union and of the democratic ideal into

F

question. The North did not want slavery, for on its harsher soil unintelligent slave labour was useless. On the other hand it resented the presence within the nation of a species of human relationship which made the Declaration of Independence in the hands of the irreverent seem a cynical mockery. And with the itch of human nature to condemn unrighteousness in others, the average Northerner was apt to say very hard things about slavery.

This was unfortunate, because in some respects the Southerner was a finer citizen than the Northerner. He was more cultured, better educated and lived an agrarian life far more suited to the free American ideal of Jefferson and the ' Fathers ' than the urban industrial existence which was growing up in the big towns of the North. There was a humanitarianism about Southern society which recalled the Utopias of the Elizabethan philosophers who had first conceived the American dream. The graceful Southern gentlemen whom the plantations sent to Washington compared well with the ill-educated, vulgar, cocksure, get-rich-quick ' Yankee ' manufacturer.

For the moment the South still controlled the weak central government of the Union. Its politicians were by far the most able and their alliance with the untutored Democrats of the West had given them a long ascendancy over the ' Whigs ' of the North who carried on the traditions of big business and federal power of the defeated Hamiltonians. The Southern gentlemen provided the leadership and the Western states the votes that kept the Democratic Party in power.

But during the second quarter of the nineteenth century developments occurred that threatened to destroy this balance. The industrial revolution spread to America, bringing new forms of life and wealth to the North. A great tide of emigration from the poorest parts of Europe flowed into the Northern states, enormously increasing their population and voting power. These newcomers, being uneducated, unpropertied and unused to liberty, could easily be induced to vote as their employers dictated. Soon they

ABRAHAM LINCOLN

might be used to destroy the political predominance of the South. And that might well mean the ultimate destruction of the South, for the North stood not only for the abolition of slavery but for a high protective tariff on manufactured goods which would bring ruin to the free-trading, cotton-growing, agrarian South.

It was this fear to the very basis of their life, in many respects a fine and gracious one, that made the Southern politicians of the third, fourth and fifth decades of the nineteenth century meet the challenge of the North to the moral basis of slavery with an arrogant counter-cry that slavery was good in itself. A conviction ripened in Southern minds that domestic slavery—' our Institution at the South '—was not only an economic necessity but a wise and even noble relationship. The negroes, it was pointed out, were contented, well treated, and employed in the only way of which their primitive intellects admitted. In fact it was plain that God meant them to be so employed.

This doctrine, which was broadcast from every Southern platform, was accompanied by a vigorous campaign to strengthen the electoral power of the South by extending the institution of slavery to new Western states north of the Missouri Compromise line. The Mexican war which Lincoln had opposed had brought fresh accessions of territory, which at once became a bone of contention between North and South. After a bitter struggle between contending politicians a further compromise was effected in 1850, by which the South was compensated for its failure to legalise slavery in California by the passage through Congress of a new and strict fugitive slave law, by which slaves who escaped into free states were to be returned, regardless of public opinion, to their masters. But in the course of the controversy Southern politicians had begun to speak openly of their right to secede and to form a new Union of States, dedicated to the proposition that slavery was in accordance with divine law.

Meanwhile the bitterness between North and South grew worse. It was all very well for Southern politicians to

67

point out that slave-owners were more humane than the Northern manufacturers and that most slaves were happy. All along the boundary that divided the slave from the free states there was a constant succession of escaping fugitives, who were pursued and taken back to servitude by professional slave-chasers. Nor could the ordinary Northerner, unaccustomed to such a society, witness with composure during his visits to the South the sight of the slave auction or of gangs of blacks chained together on their way from one part of the country to another. Such had been Lincoln's own experience on his early trips down the Mississippi, and he had not forgotten it. ' Lincoln saw it,' a companion afterwards testified, ' said nothing much, was silent. I can say, knowing it, that it was on this trip that he formed his opinion of slavery. It ran its iron into him, then and there, May, 1831. I have heard him say so often.'

Angry and irresponsible denunciations by Northern abolitionists, and duckings and horsewhippings inflicted by angry Southerners on such as dared to speak against slavery within their domains, were driving events to a crisis. Some of the Southern states made it a criminal offence, punishable by death, to incite the slaves to mutiny, and, the widest construction being put on the word incitement, freedom of speech and press virtually ceased to exist. For Southerners, growing frantic with fear and anger, felt they would sooner die in the last ditch than let the damned Yankees insult them or threaten the cherished ways of life.

To this inflammatory stuff the match was now applied by an opportunist politician furthering his career. In 1854 Lincoln's countryman and erstwhile rival for the hand of Mary Todd, Stephen Douglas, made a bold bid for Southern support for his leadership of the Democratic Party by championing a Bill to permit the new state of Kansas, which was north of the Missouri Compromise line, to vote itself a slave state. By astute political management and the application of a doctrine which he called popular ' sovereignty,' affirming the right of the people of every state, if they so wished, to establish slavery without restriction, Douglas carried the Bill and at one blow destroyed the compromises of 1820 and 1850.

But Douglas had been too clever. There was, of course, a howl of indignation from the North, which was only to be expected, for the South had gained the senatorial votes of a new state. What Douglas had not counted on was that in his own stronghold, the West, which hitherto had supported the Democratic Party and so kept the minority South in power, public opinion was outraged. When he visited Chicago and other Western towns he was howled down. As Lincoln put it, 'You can fool all the people some of the time, and some of the people all the time, but you cannot fool all the people all the time.'

Lincoln's own view of the slavery question, based on his experience and his reading of American history, was that of the original founders of the Republic. Slavery was deeply rooted in the South and could not be abolished, as the irresponsible philanthropists of the North demanded, without grave injustice to innocent individuals and an equally grave infringement of state rights. But that did not justify its extension to areas where it had never existed, however much Southern statesmen, for political and voting purposes, might desire it. 'As the Fathers of the country did not abolish slavery,' he wrote, ' we must not do so either; but we must make laws for the new States, which the Fathers could not foresee.' His desire was to put back slavery where they had left it.

In short, slavery, though rendered temporarily necessary by the inevitable limitations placed on the present by the past, was an evil, and it was wrong to regard it as anything else. ' I must hold it to be the paramount duty of us in the free States, due to the Union of the States, and perhaps to liberty itself (paradox though it may seem), to let the slavery of the other States alone; while, on the other hand, I hold it to be equally clear that we should never knowingly lend ourselves, directly or indirectly, to prevent that slavery from dying a natural death—to find new places for it to live in, when it can no longer exist in the old.' If this principle

was universally realised, Lincoln believed, what the Fathers
had hoped for would ultimately come to pass, and slavery
would gradually disappear.

This was not the view either of Northern abolitionists or
Southern politicians. The former, swept forward on the
wave of a great popular religious emotion aroused by the
publication of Mrs. Beecher Stowe's ' Uncle Tom's Cabin '—
a sensational novel which depicted a negro slave as a kind
of second Christ—talked and behaved as if the whole South
was a sink of moral iniquity that needed violent cleansing
by the righteous Northerners. And the Southerners, instead
of resting calmly on their unchallengeable state rights to the
maintenance of their ancient institutions, talked wildly about
seceding if they were not permitted to introduce slavery into
the new states of the West. ' I see how it is,' said one of
them. ' You may force freedom as much as you like, but we
are to beware how we force slavery.'

In a letter to his old friend Joshua Speed, who was a
Kentucky man and a slave-owner, Lincoln crystallised the
real issues. ' You know,' he said, ' I dislike slavery, and
you fully admit the abstract wrong of it. So far, there is
no cause of difference. But you say that sooner than yield
your legal rights to the slaves, especially at the bidding of
those who are not themselves interested, you would see the
Union dissolved. I am not aware that anyone is bidding
you yield that right; very certainly I am not. I confess
I hate to see the poor creatures hunted down and caught and
carried back to their stripes and unrequited toil; but I bite
my lips and keep quiet. In 1841, you and I had together a
tedious low-water trip on a steamboat from Louisville to
St. Louis. You may remember, as well as I do, that from
Louisville to the mouth of the Ohio there were on board
ten or a dozen slaves shackled together with irons. That
sight was a continued torment to me; and I see something
like it every time I touch the Ohio or any other slave border.
It is not fair for you to assume that I have no interest in a
thing which has, and continually exercises, the power of
making me miserable. . . .

ABRAHAM LINCOLN

' I do oppose the extension of slavery because my judgment and feelings so prompt me, and I am under no obligations to the contrary. If for this you and I must differ, differ we must. You say, if you were President, you would send an army and hang the leaders of the Missouri outrages upon the Kansas election; still, if Kansas fairly votes herself a slave State, she must be admitted or the Union must be dissolved. You say that if Kansas fairly votes herself a free State, as a Christian you will rejoice at it. All decent slaveholders talk that way, and I do not doubt their candour. But they never vote that way. . . .

' Our progress in degeneracy appears to me to be pretty rapid. As a nation we began by declaring that " all men are created equal." We now practically read on " all men are created equal except negroes." When the Know-Nothings get control, it will read " all men are created equal, except negroes and foreigners and Catholics." When it comes to this, I shall prefer emigration to some country where they make no pretence of loving liberty—to Russia, for instance, where despotism can be taken pure, without the base alloy of hypocrisy.'

For to Lincoln this was the biggest question of all. The manner in which the disputants, and especially the Southerners, were conducting their quarrel, was threatening to break up the Union and so to terminate the dream of a united and peaceful continent which had been the motive inspiration of Washington and Jefferson. Slavery was an issue which time and patience would probably solve. ' All such questions must find lodgment with the most enlightened souls who stamp them with their approval. In God's own time they will be organised into law, and thus woven into the fabric of our institutions.' But the Union, once gone, was gone for ever, and North America would turn into another Europe, for ever torn by wasteful rivalries and wars. And on its preservation, he believed, the whole future of democracy depended.

In 1854, when this great problem first began to dominate all others, Lincoln seemed to have abandoned any hope of

71

a political career. He was merely a hard-working prairie lawyer with a reputation for astuteness as a party manager and wire-puller, and regarded by few as fitted for anything but the back-stairs of politics. His chief asset was his knowledge of his Western neighbours and their manifest trust of him.

But here at last was an issue which demanded precisely the qualities and the experience he possessed. The crucial point in the controversy was the attitude of the West, since that of the South and North was already determined. And probably no one in all America knew the West as well as Lincoln. What was as important was that by the accident of early choice he belonged to the Whig Party, which had hitherto had little hold in the West but was not committed to the Southern politicians like the popular and predominant Democratic Party. He thus became a natural leader in the new Republican Party, which after the passage of the Kansas-Nebraska Bill was formed by an alliance between the Whigs and those Northern democrats who repudiated their old allegiance in order to combat the extension of slavery.

In the fight for the West which now began and culminated six years later in his election as President, Lincoln played the chief part. His protagonist was his old rival and the villain of the Kansas-Nebraska Bill, Stephen Douglas. The 'little giant,' as he was called, was one of the first orators of the day and already spoken of as the next presidential candidate of the Democratic Party. Lincoln was unknown to all but his neighbours, and even by them thought of as a very homely fellow. Douglas was rich, and a favourite of the new capitalists who with the help of railways and banks were developing the virgin resources of the country: Lincoln was poor as a church mouse. Douglas took himself very seriously and was so taken by others: Lincoln was still something of a joke.

The first round between them was fought over the election of 1856 when Lincoln, chosen by the Republican Party in Illinois as its Senatorial candidate, tried to oust Douglas, the sitting Senator and choice of the Democrats. In this duel, waged in every town throughout the state, Lincoln, though he did not win, caused a tremendous sensation. For it was suddenly realised that this obscure, shabby lawyer, who toured the country in public conveyances and stopped at ramshackle inns, was a fair match for the redoubtable Douglas with his shouting crowds and bands and special trains. In accepting his nomination Lincoln made a speech that, by showing how clearly he saw the issue, brought him at once before a far wider public than that of his own state. ' " A house divided against itself," ' he declared, ' " cannot stand." I believe this Government cannot endure permanently half slave and half free. I do not expect the Union to be dissolved—I do not expect the house to fall—but I do expect that it will cease to be divided. It will become all one thing or all the other. Either the opponents of slavery will arrest the further spread of it, and place it where the public mind shall rest in the belief that it is in course of ultimate extinction; or its advocates will push it forward till it shall become lawful alike in all the States, old as well as new—North as well as South.'

Lincoln as a public figure was something new. Till now everyone from his wife downwards had thought of him as one of the most ungainly-looking men alive. But about this time people began to notice certain other things about his appearance—the great forehead, the earnestness of the deep-set eyes, the finely chiselled chin and lines of his face, and a certain brooding nobility about his expression that made those who saw him while speaking forget the clumsiness of his gaunt body. At such moments he seemed to be lit by hidden fires; the eyes kindled and the long arms were raised as he spoke of the lot of the slave: ' reaching his hands towards the stars of that still night he proclaimed " In some things she is certainly not my equal, but in her natural right to eat the bread that she has earned with the sweat of her brow, she is my equal, and the equal of Judge Douglas, and the equal of any man." '

The intensity of such moments was enhanced by the crazy

humour of others. Lincoln knew just how to appeal to his Western audiences, to make them laugh at his mimicry and droll jokes. When a Southern lady angrily dangled a nigger doll in front of him as he spoke, he enquired, with exaggerated deference, ' Ma'am, is that your baby ? ' And his speeches were always rich in homely metaphors of a bucolic kind that Western farmers could grasp in a moment. ' The whole thing is as simple as figuring out the weight of three small hogs,' he explained. To pioneers accustomed to the life of the wilderness he illustrated the importance of keeping new territories free of slavery by saying that they must be given a clean bed with no snakes in it.

But the real force of Lincoln's speeches was that he was speaking about fundamentals, of which he had thought deeply and of whose importance he was wholly convinced. His neighbours and countrymen, who had not thought of them as he had done, did not as yet understand them. Lincoln's claim to greatness as a statesman rests on the fact that he made them understand. In explaining, he used simple socratic arguments which led by simple steps to an irresistible conclusion : it was not for nothing that he had recently been studying logic. As he spoke he seemed to be thinking aloud and so made his audience think with him. Witness his destruction of his opponents' contention that, because things apparently good in themselves depended on it, there was some moral basis for slavery.

If A can prove, however conclusively, that he may, of right enslave B, why may not B snatch the same argument, even prove equally, that he may enslave A ?

You say A is white and B is black.—It is *colour*, then ; the lighter having the right to enslave the darker ? Take care.—By this rule, you are to be slave to the first man you meet, with a fairer skin than your own.

You do not mean *colour* exactly ? You mean the whites are *intellectually* the superior of the blacks, and, therefore, have the right to enslave them ? Take care again.—By this rule, you are to be slave to the first man you meet with an intellect superior to your own.

But, say you, it is a question of *interest*; and, if you can make it your *interest*, you have the right to enslave another.—Very well—and if he can make it his interest he has the right to enslave you.

For there, as Lincoln pointed out, was the real objection to slavery. It was double-edged and could not exist in a country dedicated to the proposition that men were free and equal without ultimately endangering the freedom and equality of everyone. ' This,' he said, ' is a world of compensation; and he who would be not slave, must consent to have no slave. Those who deny freedom to others deserve it not for themselves.' ' When we freed ourselves from political slavery to King George, we said the principle " all men were created equal " was an immanent truth. Now, when we are full fed, and have no fear of being made slaves again ourselves, we have become so greedy to be masters that we declare the very reverse of this maxim to be an immanent truth.'

For Lincoln was conscious that what was at stake was more than the well-being of the negro slave. It was the freedom of his own countrymen that was endangered by the new attitude which had grown up towards slavery. And, as he was well aware, there were already a great many citizens of white blood in the United States whose hold on liberty was, to say the least of it, precarious. Mr. Agar, in his brilliant book ' The American Presidents,' suggests that, in his anxiety to prevent the extension of negro slavery and preserve the Union, Lincoln, living in a rural Western community, overlooked the helot system which was already established in the Northern factories and was growing every year with the increasing tide of cheap emigrant labour. But in fact Lincoln was painfully aware of it, and fought the contention that slavery was justifiable because he realised that there was only a step to its virtual application to whites as well as blacks. ' If we once abandon the principle of our fathers that all men are born free and equal, and if we declare that negroes are not the equals of whites, the next step will be to declare that not all the whites are equal. . . . What will then become of the fundamental idea of our Constitution, that no one is entitled to issue orders to another, unless that other be a consenting party ? ' ' God be thanked,' he said on another occasion, ' that we have a labour system in which people can go on strike ! '

In 1856 Lincoln was defeated because public opinion was still not fully aroused as to the issues at stake. But he did not cease his campaign and, as he had foreseen, the course of events made the truth of his contention increasingly clear. Shortly after the return of the new Democratic President, Buchanan, to Washington, the Supreme Court pronounced its famous decision in the Dred Scott case that a slave could not sue for his freedom in a United States court, so that even if long settled in a free state, he could always be taken back to captivity. The judicial *obiter dicta* which accompanied this decision, by appearing to legalise the utmost claims of the Southern states to independence from Federal control, aroused the deepest feelings throughout the North. Three years later a fanatic abolitionist, John Brown, who had made a spectacular but hair-brained raid into a slave state to free the negroes, was solemnly executed by the government of Virginia. ' Even as I write,' wrote Longfellow, ' they are leading old John Brown to execution in Virginia for attempting to rescue slaves. This is sowing the wind to reap the whirlwind, which will soon come.'

One result of the Dred Scott case and the raid at Harper's Ferry was to split the Democratic Party from top to bottom. Henceforward the South would have to stand alone. This meant that for the first time in American history the issue at the next Presidential Election would be North *versus* South, with the inevitable result that the South would be outvoted. The Southern politicians thereupon declared that if defeated and deprived of their power, they would lead those they represented out of the Union. The right of secession and not that of slavery became the issue.

In this crisis the attitude of the West was all-important. The logic of events showed that the Republican Party would oust the Democrats from power by the adoption of a Western presidential candidate. The leading Western Republican was Lincoln. Among the Northern politicians there were many men with far more refinement, far more political experience and far better claims to the leadership of the party. But they were none of them Westerners and Lincoln was and could bring his own people with him. Moreover, incongruously enough, he commended himself to the big financial interests of the North, who had not definitely thrown in their lot with the Republicans and approved of his lawyer's sense and his rigidly honest views about the sanctity of private property. They did not want an abolitionist crank who, in his blind enthusiasm for the slaves, would undermine the sacred foundations of private ownership. 'The Republican standard is too high,' said one of them, 'we want something practical.'

And on the question of Union, a deeper issue to the ordinary American than slavery, Lincoln was absolutely sound. In his view no Southern politician had any right, because he could not get his own way at the polls, to wreck the great American experiment for which the Fathers of the Republic had risked their lives and fortunes. To do so was the very antithesis of democracy. In a free state there could be no appeal from ballots to bullets.

Gravely Lincoln warned the South of the folly and peril of the course its leaders were pursuing. 'You will not abide the election of a Republican President! In that supposed event, you say, you will destroy the Union; and then, you say, the great crime of having destroyed it will be upon us! That is cool. A highwayman holds a pistol to my ear, and mutters through his teeth, "Stand and deliver, or I shall kill you, and then you will be a murderer!"'

Will you make war upon us, and kill us all? Why, gentlemen, I think you are as gallant and as brave men as live; that you can fight as bravely in a good cause, man for man, as any other people living; that you have shown yourselves capable of this upon various occasions; but, man for man, you are not better than we are, and there are not so many of you as there are of us. You will never make much of a hand at whipping us. If we were fewer

77

in number than you, I think that you could whip us; if we were equal, it would likely be a drawn battle; but, being inferior in numbers, you will make nothing by attempting to master us.

So it came about that this queer, rough diamond of a Western lawyer, who a short while before had seemed doomed to a round of prairie court-houses for the rest of his days, found himself, at the age of fifty-one, in the running for the presidential nomination of what was now the predominant Party in the Union. Yet it was not such an incongruous choice as it might have seemed a year or two back, for beneath the surface Lincoln's mental and spiritual capacity had been growing with amazing rapidity.

In the opening months of 1860 he made his first appearance before Eastern audiences. Those who saw and heard him were shocked by his awkwardness and ungainly figure and the ill-cut clothes of which he was so painfully conscious, but they were impressed by what he had to say. One who was present at a speech which he gave in February at the Cooper Institute at New York recorded his impressions: ' He appeared in every sense of the word like one of the plain people among whom he loved to be counted. At first sight there was nothing impressive or imposing about him; his clothes hung awkwardly on his giant frame; his face was of a dark pallor without the slightest tinge of colour; his seamed and rugged features bore the furrows of hardship and struggle; his deep set eyes looked sad and anxious; his countenance in repose gave little evidence of the brilliant power which raised him from the lowest to the highest station among his countrymen; as he talked to me before the meeting he seemed ill at ease. . . . When he spoke he was transformed; his eye kindled, his voice rang, his face shone and seemed to light up the whole assembly. For an hour and a half he held his audience in the hollow of his hand. His style of speech and manner of delivery were severely simple. What Lowell called " the grand simplicities of the Bible," with which he was so familiar, were reflected in his discourse. . . . It was marvellous to see how this untutored man, by mere self-discipline and the chastening of his own

78

ABRAHAM LINCOLN

spirit, had outgrown all meretricious arts, and found his way to the grandeur and strength of absolute simplicity.'

In May, at the Convention of the Republican Party at Chicago, Lincoln was put forward by his friends for the White House nomination. 'Just think of such a sucker as me being President,' he observed. It was morally certain that if chosen he would become so, for with the Democratic Party split from top to bottom the Republicans were almost bound to carry their candidate. After the usual huckstering and bargaining, Lincoln was nominated, not unaided by the adroit production by his supporters of two rails made ' by Abraham Lincoln and John Hanks in the Sangamon Bottom in the year 1830.' Abe the rail-splitter became the political fancy of the hour. 'A poor flatboatman!' wrote the poet William Cullen Bryant, 'such are the true leaders of the nation.'

Lincoln received the news at Springfield. 'I reckon there's a little short woman down at our house that would like to hear that,' he remarked and went home to tell Mary. When the Republican Convention waited on him they thought they might have picked a handsomer article, yet doubted if they could have chosen a better.

On November 6, 1860, waiting with the operator in a telegraph box at Springfield, Lincoln learnt that he had been chosen President of the United States, nearly 1,900,000 votes going to him, 1,400,000 to Douglas, and rather over 1,000,000 to the other two candidates. The news was greeted by a howl of derision from the South. The North had used its numerical strength to put a clodhopper in the chair of Washington and to debase the whole level of public life. 'Free society?' wrote a Southern newspaper. 'We sicken of the name. What is it but a conglomeration of greasy mechanics, filthy operatives, small-fisted farmers, and moon-struck theorists! All the Northern and especially the New England States are devoid of society fitted for well-bred gentlemen. The prevailing class one meets with is that of mechanics struggling to be genteel, and small farmers who do their own drudgery, and

79

yet who are hardly fit for association with a Southern gentleman's body-servant.'

Sooner than accept a ' Black Republican President ' the South prepared to secede. Before the end of the year South Carolina had led the way by declaring for secession. In place of the old Union of the Fathers, the Southern states would form a new Confederation dedicated to the ' inequality of man.' Alexander Stephens, the Vice-President of the ' Confederate States of America,' which was formed with Jefferson Davis as its President in February 1861, put the matter clearly. ' The new constitution makes an end, once for all, of the disturbing problems that have arisen out of our institution, slavery. This was the immediate cause of the rupture and of the revolution. The prevailing ideas entertained by Jefferson and most of the leading statesmen at the time of the formation of the old Constitution, were that the enslavement of the Africans was in violation of the law of nature; that it was wrong in *principle*, socially, morally, and politically. . . . Our new government is founded upon exactly the opposite idea. Its foundations are laid, its corner-stone rests upon the great truth, that the negro is not equal to the white man; that slavery—subordination to the superior race—is his natural and normal condition. This, our new government, is the first, in the history of the world, to be based upon this great physical, philosophical, and moral truth. Secession became necessary when the North refused to recognize the great moral, political, and religious truth that there can be no other solid foundation than the slavery of the negro. . . . It is, indeed, in conformity with the ordinance of the Creator. . . . The great objects of humanity are best attained when there is conformity to His laws and decrees, in the formation of Governments as well as in all things else.'

To Lincoln, waiting at Springfield for the end of the six months which according to the Constitution divided his election from his inauguration, all this was bitter agony. He was no abolitionist and, for all his rough, hard schooling, he sympathised much with what the proud, cultured South stood for. In private correspondence with Stephens, who was an old acquaintance, he tried to allay Southern fears that a Republican administration would interfere with the established rights of slave-owners. ' I wish to assure you, as once a friend, and still, I hope, not an enemy, that there is no cause for such fears. The South would be in no more danger in this respect than it was in the days of Washington.' The only difference between them in this respect was that the Southern politicians thought that slavery was right and ought to be extended, while Lincoln, like the founders of the Republic, thought that it was wrong and ought to be restricted.

But the maintenance of the Union was another matter. An English statesman contemplating its disintegration prophesied that the America of the future would be one ' of armies, of diplomacy, of rival states and manœuvring cabinets, of frequent turbulence and probably of frequent wars.' This vision of Disraeli's was precisely that which haunted the imagination of an American patriot like Lincoln. So, in an earlier age, the pacifist Jefferson had been ready to follow the New Englanders into a commercial foreign war which he hated sooner than break the ultimate unity of the North American continent. ' Whatever follies we may be led into as to foreign nations,' he had written, ' we shall never give up our Union, the last anchor of our hope, and that alone which is to prevent this heavenly country from becoming an arena of gladiators. Much as I abhor war, and view it as the greatest scourge of mankind, and anxiously as I wish to keep out of the broils of Europe, I would yet go with my brethren into these rather than separate from them.' In the same way Lincoln felt it better to face civil war than allow the South to secede.

For the issue, he knew, admitted of no compromise. Others in the North, brought face to face with the actual threat of secession, were seeking frantically for expedients to give the South what it wanted in the matter of extension of slavery and so save their own faces. But Lincoln knew that compromise in essentials never settles anything, but only postpones the evil day and makes it more tragic when it comes. ' There is no possible compromise upon it but which puts us under again, and leaves all our work to do over again.' A decision had been taken at the polls which showed that the nation was opposed to the extension of slavery, and if that decision was now to be reversed by the threat of the dissatisfied minority to break up the state, democratic government by popular majority would have failed. The future of American Union and of democracy as a means of human government were equally at stake.

In the meantime Lincoln could do nothing, for until his inauguration he was powerless. Meanwhile the outgoing Democratic administration at Washington hastily sold the pass. President Buchanan told Congress that, though a state had no constitutional power to secede, the Federal government had equally none to prevent secession. In other words, the Union could not be maintained. And he allowed his Secretary of War, a Southerner, to remove arms and munitions from Northern arsenals to the South and the Secretary of the Treasury to do the same with Union funds. ' Never before,' wrote an onlooker, ' did I hear of any instance of a ruler sending a member of his own Cabinet to organize a revolution against his own Government.' Secession was being encouraged rather than repressed.

Poor Lincoln, waiting at Springfield, knew that every day that the process of delay and condonation continued the seceding South was growing stronger and more irretrievably committed to a position that must bring either the horror of civil war or the end of the American dream. For this choice he would have to bear the responsibility, and yet now, while there was still time, he could do nothing. ' I know it is an awful thing for me to say,' he told a friend, ' but I already wish someone else was here in my place. . . . I have read, upon my knees, the story of Gethsemane, where the Son of God prayed in vain that the cup of bitterness might pass from him. I am in the Garden of Gethsemane now, and my cup of bitterness is full and overflowing.'

At last his hour came, and, when almost all hope of bringing the South to reason by peaceful means had gone, he was permitted to take up his barren heritage. In the manner of the West, he roped his own trunks and wrote his labels, and then stood, in stovepipe hat, on the platform of the railway car that was to take him to Washington, and bade farewell to his Springfield neighbours. He told them, as they stood listening in the rain, that no one not in his situation could appreciate his feeling of sadness at such a parting. ' To this place, and the kindness of these people, I owe everything. Here I have lived a quarter of a century and have passed from a youth to an old man. Here my children have been born and one is buried. I now leave, not knowing when or whether I may ever return, with a task before me greater than that which rested upon Washington.' He never saw Springfield again.' On his way to Washington he broke his journey to speak to the peoples of the cities of the North and East. At Indianopolis he told them to remember that the events now in progress were their concern and not his, and that if the Union of the States was lost it could mean but little to a man like himself of fifty-two years of age, but a great deal to the thirty million inhabitants of the States and to their posterity. ' Constantly bear in mind that not with politicians, not with Presidents, not with office-seekers, but with you, is the question. Shall the Union and shall the liberties of this country be preserved to the latest genera- tion?' In the Hall of Independence at Philadelphia he explained why. ' I have never had a feeling politically,' he said, ' that did not spring from the sentiments embodied in the Declaration of Independence. I have often pondered over the dangers which were incurred by the men who assembled here and framed and adopted that Declaration of Independence. I have pondered over the toils that were endured by the officers and soldiers of the army who achieved that independence. I have often inquired of myself what great principle or idea it was that kept the Confederacy so long together. It was not the mere matter of separation of the colonies from the motherland, it was the sentiment in the Declaration of Independence which gave liberty, not alone to the people of this country, but I hope to the world, for all future time. It was that which gave promise that in due time the weight would be lifted from the shoulders of all men.' He must have made a strange figure standing there in the unwonted clothes that hung from his vast, gaunt frame, speaking words which not his listeners but posterity were to treasure. All the while the Southern Congress was sitting in Alabama.

At Washington Lincoln was received coldly by his Cabinet, who despised him as an upstart, and still more coldly by the people, who saw him only as a barbarian who had come to smash the civilisation of the South. He tried to set them at their ease and break the chill with which they surrounded him by his words. 'I think much of the ill-feeling that has existed and still exists between the people in the section from which I came and the people here is dependent upon a mis-understanding of one another. I therefore avail myself of this opportunity to assure you, and all the gentlemen present, that I have not now, and never have had, any other than as kindly feelings toward you as to the people of my own section. I have not now, and never have had, any disposition to treat you in any respect otherwise than as my own neighbours . . . in a word, that when we shall become better acquainted—and I say it with great confidence—we shall like each other better. I thank you for the kindness of this reception.' The town was full of spies and traitors, the treasury was empty and the South was in arms beyond the Potomac.

Under such circumstances Lincoln was inaugurated President of the United States on March 4, 1861. Before he began to speak it was noticed that he was extremely embarrassed, for he did not know what to do with his hat and his stick, both brand new and very large and produced by his wife to lend distinction to the occasion. Everyone was aware that he appeared out of place, and he more than any: ' he looked so uncomfortable,' said an onlooker, ' that it was quite pathetic ! '

Yet when he began to speak he forgot himself and became

bigger than himself or than anyone there present. He made it clear that he regarded the Union as indissoluble and that, at whatever cost, he would take the necessary steps to preserve it. Beyond the bare essentials he would not press his power an inch or interfere with any state right. 'The power confided to me will be used to hold, occupy, and possess the property and places belonging to the Government, and to collect the duties on imports; but beyond what may be necessary for these objects there will be no invasion, no using of force against or among the people anywhere.'

Then he appealed to the South to abide by the people's decision and the forms of democracy. 'Is there any better or equal hope in the world? In our present differences, is either party without faith of being in the right? If the Almighty Ruler of Nations, with His eternal truth and justice, be on your side of the North, or on yours of the South, that truth and that justice will surely prevail by the judgment of this great tribunal of the American people.'

Towards the end he became inspired by the intensity of his feeling. The poet in him took control and transformed the prose words which his accomplished Secretary of State, Seward, had tried to impose on him. 'In your hands, my dissatisfied fellow-countrymen, and not in mine, is the momentous issue of civil war. The Government will not assail you. You can have no conflict without being yourselves the aggressors. I am loath to close. We are not enemies but friends. We must not be enemies. Though passion may have strained, it must not break our bonds of affection. The mystic chords of memory, stretching from every battlefield and patriot grave to every living heart and hearthstone all over this broad land, will yet swell the chorus of the Union, when again touched, as surely they will be, by the better angels of our nature.'

During the next month, the plight of a small government post at the mouth of Charleston harbour, from which the South were withholding supplies, brought the issue to a head. For so long as he was able Lincoln delayed the final decision, while all around him urged him to compromise on the main question and yield to the South. At the beginning of April, when Fort Sumter was at its last gasp, and its Governor reported that he had no other resort but to haul down the Stars and Stripes and yield to the Southerners, he ordered the despatch of a ship of provisions for its relief. The South countered by opening fire on the American flag and taking possession of the fort.

Lincoln had refused to be cowed by the Southern display of force, but there had been good grounds for the fears of his colleagues. At that moment there was scarcely a soldier in Washington and the total forces at the disposal of the Federal government did not amount to more than three thousand scattered troops. Until the New York Regiment arrived a few days later the President was actually in danger of being captured by the Southerners who swarmed in the capital or by raiders from across the Potomac. The treasury and most of the military and naval magazines were empty. Most of the best officers in the army, being drawn from the South, were with the Confederate forces.

For the moment the advantage was altogether with the South. Its people were high-spirited, accustomed to field sports and to command, and believed, rightly or wrongly, that they were fighting to preserve everything in life that mattered to them. They knew what they wanted and were prepared to go to any lengths to secure it. The North was divided and uncertain, ill-disciplined and untrained to arms. A few quick blows, it was believed, would soon settle the business.

In the long run, of course, the odds were all in favour of the North, whose population much outnumbered that of the Confederate states, and whose wealth and manufacturing resources were far greater. But it did not seem as though there would be any long run. Few people in England, the one outside country whose intervention could decide the struggle, seemed to think so. Indeed, the natural preference felt by the English ruling class for an aristocratic, free-trading, cotton-growing Confederation for a time overcame even its traditional dislike of slavery. The leading London papers were filled with interesting and not unsympathetic articles about the 'peculiar domestic institution' of the South, and there were pictures by special correspondents of grinning negroes being sold at auctions or conversing affectionately and respectfully with their masters: 'I found them well dressed, well fed and apparently happy and contented.' Yet perhaps the truth of the matter was better expressed by the black barman who, being asked by one of these correspondents if the slaves were contented with their lot, quietly put a tumbler over two or three flies eating crumbs on the counter. Immediately the captive flies ceased to eat and began buzzing about at the walls of their glass prison, though there was food enough within to last them a week.

However well shrewd observers thought of the South's chances of victory, the North meant to fight. Lincoln's stand had made that certain. The star-spangled banner had been fired upon, and thousands of simple Americans, who thought little enough about the slaves and not very much about the future of democracy, were not going to stand for that. Lincoln appealed for 75,000 volunteers for ' the suppression of an unlawful combination ' and the North sprang to arms. By June 300,000 men were in training.

It was now to be tested whether a democracy could maintain itself in an emergency. It was Lincoln's task to lead that democracy which he could not coerce, to keep it true to itself and to persuade it to make the sacrifices and sustained voluntary effort which alone could give it victory. ' It is a struggle,' he said, ' for maintaining in the world that form and substance of Government whose leading object is to elevate the condition of men—to lift artificial weights from all shoulders; to clear the paths of laudable pursuit for all; to afford all an unfettered start, and a fair chance in the race of life. . . . It is now for them to demonstrate to the world that those who can fairly carry an election can also suppress a rebellion; that ballots are the rightful and peaceful successors of bullets; and that when ballots have fairly and constitutionally decided, there can be no successful appeal back to bullets. . . . Such will be a great lesson of peace : teaching men that what they cannot take by an election, neither can they take by a war; teaching all the folly of being the beginners of a war.'

At first all the odds seemed against Lincoln. His Cabinet, who thought his shabby clothes and clumsy manners indicated the man within, lobbied and intrigued against him, while every sectional interest in the North with wild indiscipline pulled in different directions. Meanwhile the South proved to have got yet another asset in two soldiers of the highest genius, the chivalrous Commander-in-Chief, Lee, and his brilliant lieutenant, Jackson. The North, on the other hand, had many extravagant pretenders to military genius but none who seemed able to win a victory. A series of calamitous and ignominious defeats marked the first eighteen months of the war. The Northern generals, whose fault it was, thereupon turned round and publicly abused the President, who they declared had failed to support them though he had poured troops upon them even more quickly than they lost them. It was, as he himself once put it, ' like shifting fleas across a barn floor with a shovel, not half of them ever get there.'

But as the dreary months of war and waiting passed, it began to be seen that the North had one supreme asset, its President. Democracy, whatever its failings, had bred a man. His Ministers and his generals were always thinking about their dignity and their careers : Lincoln did not seem to mind if he was abused by unjust newspapers, patronised by members of his own Cabinet or insulted by his generals so long as the United States was properly served. ' I will hold McClellan's stirrup for him,' he said of one tiresome and disloyal marshal, ' if he will only win us victories.' Lincoln's patience was phenomenal : he was prepared to be the Aunt Sally of the whole nation if he could in the least serve its cause by doing so. ' I do the very best I know how, the very best I can,' he said, ' and I mean to keep doing so until the end. If the end brings me out all right, what is said against me won't amount to anything. If the end brings me out wrong, ten angels swearing I was right would make no difference.'

For it was Lincoln's supreme greatness that he loved the people so much that nothing could kill his love. He had dedicated himself to their service and bowed his patient back to the yoke. The humblest soldier at the hour of attack did not serve his country more devotedly and purely than he. All the shabby awkwardness of his appearance, the uncouth things he said, the painful social *gaucheries*, could not now conceal the dignity and stature of his detachment.

Even the ambitious, scheming Washington politicians were not able to resist the appeal of his simple dignity: he seemed ignorant, but there could be no doubt of his sincerity and honesty. Nor, for that matter, of his strength; one after another of his bustling, omniscient subordinates was courteously but firmly put in his place. He was always ready to take responsibility and, once his mind was made up, was unshakable. He might be mad—the Tycoon, the ancient with his awful old hat and his habit of telling ribald stories at solemn moments of state—but he had to be reckoned with.

Cultured and refined people who did not know him still laughed at him, but the best among them were changing their views. Motley, the historian, who visited him in June 1861, left an interesting impression of his interview. ' I went and had an hour's talk with Mr. Lincoln. I am very glad of it, for, had I not done so, I should have left Washington with a very inaccurate impression of the President. I am now satisfied that he is a man of very considerable native sagacity; and that he has an ingenuous, unsophisticated, frank, and noble character. I believe him to be as true as steel, and as courageous as true. At the same time there is doubtless an ignorance about State matters, and particularly about foreign affairs, which he does not attempt to conceal, but which we must of necessity regret in a man placed in such a position at such a crisis. Nevertheless his very modesty in this respect disarms criticism. We parted very affectionately, and perhaps I shall never set eyes on him again, but I feel that, so far as perfect integrity and directness of purpose go, the country will be safe in his hands.' Another intellectual leader of America who encountered him at this time made a remarkable prediction. ' Free from the aspirations of genius, he will never be a danger to a free community. . . . He is the people personified. . . . His government is the most representative known to history. I will venture a prophecy that may sound strange. Within fifty years, and perhaps sooner, Lincoln's name will be inscribed in the honourable annals of the American Republic beside that of Washington. . . . The children of those who now persecute him will bless him.'

The common people understood him instinctively. To them he was ' old Abe '—one of themselves, with a goodness, a patience and a wisdom which they knew they did not possess. He went out of his way to make himself accessible to them, and stretched even the traditional latitude of the White House to callers in order to ensure that every claimant should be admitted to his presence. Superior persons could not understand this almost reverent attention of the President's to the trivial demands of common people, and saw it with the eyes of the indignant general who found him ' closeted with an old Hoosier from Illinois, telling dirty yarns, while the country was quietly going to hell.' But to Lincoln himself all this was an essential and outward form of the democracy he was fighting to preserve. ' I happen, temporarily, to occupy this big white house,' he told a delegation. ' I am a living witness that any one of your children may look to come here as my father's child has. It is in order that each one of you may have, through this free government which we have enjoyed, an open field and a fair chance for your industry, enterprise, and intelligence— that you may all have equal privileges in the race of life with all its desirable human aspirations—it is for this that the struggle should be maintained, that we may not lose our birthright.'

The burden that this devotion placed on Lincoln was enormous. Old friends were shocked to see how cadaverous he had grown and how sunk his eyes. He was conducting at the same time the ordinary administration of a free country and the conduct of a vast, improvised war, yet added to it the self-imposed task of comforting every widow and taking the rough hand of every country farmer who came up to Washington to see his President. The drain on his nervous resources was dangerous. He knew it. ' I sometimes fancy,' he once confided, ' that every one of the numerous grist ground through here daily, from a senator seeking war with France down to a poor woman after a place in the Treasury Department, darted at me with finger and thumb, picked out their especial piece of my vitality, and carried it off. When I get through with such a hard day's work there is only one word which can express my condition, and that is flabbiness.' But he did not spare himself the less.

One thing sustained him—his all-embracing gift of human sympathy. Unlike other statesmen and administrators, he never saw government as an abstract science, remote and detached from the realities of individual experience. To him it was no office problem. His great heart made him realise what the man in the street and the field, the soldier on the battlefield and the wife waiting in her lonely home were feeling, and, understanding, he could never blame them or be angry with them. It is this which explains the unfailing consideration which, however tired he was, he showed to others and the touching patience and self-effacement of his letters. ' My dear Sir, God help me,' one of them ran. ' It is said that I have offended you. I hope you will tell me how.'

He held the North together, and little by little the tide of war turned in his favour. The disastrous mistakes of early days were not repeated, the volunteer armies learnt to stand to their guns, and the tawdry, showy generals of an undisciplined democracy who were unable to learn were replaced by others who could cross swords even with the giant Lee. Thereafter superior numbers and wealth began to tell. If the vast conglomeration of the Northern states could be kept

THE AMERICAN IDEAL

firm for a little longer, the South must inevitably be defeated and the Union saved.

Yet the turn of the tide brought new problems to the tired leader of American Democracy. There was the question of the slaves. So far as the South was concerned, Lincoln had never been an abolitionist, honouring as he did the rights of the individual and the contractual position of the Southern states. At the beginning of the war he had had to fight against a tremendous outcry from his keenest supporters for negro emancipation, which if acceded to would have alienated the border states and, by causing them to throw in their lot with the South, have made the restoration of the Union impossible. As the war continued the clamour increased. So long as victory was far out of sight Lincoln would do nothing: a Proclamation of Emancipation under such circumstances could do no good and would only acerbate already bitter feelings. The slaves, he pointed out, would not be freed merely by passing a decree to that effect any more than a calf would be given five legs by calling its tail a leg. He therefore begged the irresponsible and self-righteous reformers to be patient.

I am approached with the most opposite opinions and advice, and that by religious men who are equally certain that they represent the divine will. I am sure that either the one or the other class is mistaken in that belief, and perhaps in some respects both. I hope it will not be irreverent for me to say that, if it is probable that God would reveal His will to others, on a point so connected with my duty, it might be supposed He would reveal it directly to me. What good would a proclamation of emancipation from me do especially as we are now situated? I do not want to issue a document that the whole world will see must necessarily be inoperative like the Pope's Bull against the comet. Do not misunderstand me, because I have mentioned these objections. They indicate the difficulties that have thus far prevented my acting in some such way as you desire. I have not decided against a proclamation of liberty to the slaves, but hold the matter under advisement. And I can assure you that the subject is on my mind, by day and night, more than any other. Whatever shall appear to be God's will, I will do.

92

But after the battle of Antietam the situation began to change. If it stuck to its guns the North was going to win. For the first time in the history of the United States there was a chance of ending the evil of slavery without ending the Union also. And if that chance was not taken, the North itself would be split. The President decided to act.

It was his wish to bring about emancipation gradually, both for the sake of the Southern planters and the slaves themselves, for whose interests, unlike the unthinking New England abolitionists, he genuinely cared. It was part of his make-up that to him a negro was neither an economic pawn nor an object for sentimental self-satisfaction, but another man like himself with similar difficulties and temptations. To free the slaves without careful provision for their future employment and moral welfare would be to do them, not a kindness, but a grave injury.

It was part of the tragedy of Lincoln's position that in the end he was forced to do so. The gradual emancipation with compensation for the owners which he required was made impossible by the obstinacy of the South, and neither the occasion nor the North would wait any longer. Before the end of the war freedom for the slaves had come. Lincoln's own last word on the subject was spoken a few days before his death, when he addressed the hysterical cheering negroes who for mile after mile blocked his passage on his visit to Richmond in the spring of 1865.

My poor Friends, you are free—free as air. You can cast off the name of slave and trample upon it; it will come to you no more. Liberty is your birthright. God gave it to you as He gave it to others, and it is a sin that you have been deprived of it for so many years. But you must try to deserve this priceless boon. Let the world see that you merit it, and are able to maintain it by your good works. Don't let your joy carry you into excesses. Learn the laws and obey them; obey God's commandments and thank Him for giving you liberty, for to Him you owe all things. There, now, let me pass on; I have but little time to spare. I want to see the capital, and must return at once to Washington to secure to you that liberty which you seem to prize so highly.

Even when victory in the field seemed assured, it was not certain that the North would hold together. War-weariness, divided aims, the sapping of public morality and honour which every war brings, were all taking their toll of the Republic. Without Lincoln's leadership the appalling effort and waste of those terrible years would have been spent in vain. By his words and his life he kept his countrymen mindful of that for which they were fighting. In the dedication of the National Cemetery for those who fell at Gettysburg he followed the two hours' oration of the cultured Edward Everett with a speech of a few minutes that defined for all time the nature and ideals of Democracy.

Four score and seven years ago our fathers brought forth on this continent a new nation, conceived in liberty and dedicated to the proposition that all men are created equal. Now we are engaged in a great civil war, testing whether that nation, or any nation so conceived and so dedicated, can long endure. We are met on a great battlefield of that war. We have come to dedicate a portion of that field as a final resting place for those who here gave their lives that that nation might live. It is altogether fitting and proper that we should do this. But, in a larger sense, we cannot dedicate—we cannot consecrate—we cannot hallow—this ground. The brave men, living and dead, who struggled here have consecrated it far above our poor power to add or to detract. The world will little note nor long remember what we say here, but it can never forget what they did here. It is for us, the living, rather to be dedicated here to the unfinished work which they who fought here have thus far so nobly advanced. It is rather for us to be here dedicated to the great task remaining before us—that from these honoured dead we take increased devotion to that cause for which they gave the last full measure of devotion; that we here highly resolve that these dead shall not have died in vain; that this nation, under God, shall have a new birth of freedom; and that government of the people, by the people, for the people, shall not perish from the earth.

Such moments do not occur often in the mist and turmoil of everyday politics. As the Presidential Election of 1864 drew near, every species of political self-seeker and intriguer thronged the approaches to Washington. On the surface it seemed improbable that Lincoln would be returned, and he himself, worn out by his ceaseless labours, gravely doubted it. Yet it was morally certain that if he was not returned the South would be saved at the eleventh hour. He expressed his readiness to withdraw in favour of any more acceptable candidate who was ready and capable of holding the weary North together till the struggle was won. But none was forthcoming. ' I have not permitted myself, Gentlemen,' he therefore advised his countrymen, ' to conclude that I am the best man in the country; but I am reminded in this connection of a story of an old Dutch farmer, who remarked to a companion once : " It is not best to swap horses when crossing a stream." '

But whatever the carrion who usually batten on democracy had anticipated, the upshot proved them wrong. The plain people were overwhelmingly on Lincoln's side: ' up here,' said an old farmer in the Northern highlands, ' we believe in God and Father Abraham.' He was returned by a great majority. It was a vindication of democracy and a proof, as Lincoln said, that a government not too strong for the liberties of its people could maintain its existence in a great emergency. Until that day it had not been known that this was a possibility.

In his second Inaugural Address Lincoln spoke of the past and the future. He saw the war as a great tragedy, but one that could only be explained by God's anger for an ancient national crime. ' If we shall suppose that American slavery is one of those offences which, in the providence of God, must needs come, but which, having continued through His appointed time, He now wills to remove, and that He gives to both North and South this terrible war as the woe due to those by whom the offence came, shall we discern therein any departure from those divine attributes which the believers in a living God always ascribe to Him ? Fondly do we hope—fervently do we pray—that this mighty scourge

95

of war may speedily pass away. Yet, if God wills that it continue until all the wealth piled by the bondsman's two hundred and fifty years of unrequited toil shall be sunk, and until every drop of blood drawn with the last shall be paid by another drawn with the sword, as was said three thousand years ago, so still it must be said, " The judgments of the Lord are true and righteous altogether." '

But the ancient crime had been expiated at last, and it was for the nation, and for Lincoln as its chosen leader, to see that it was not repeated in some new form. ' With malice towards none ; with charity for all; with firmness in the right, as God gives us to see the right, let us strive on to finish the work we are in ; to bind up the nation's wounds; to care for him who shall have borne the battle, and for his widow and for his orphan—to do all which may achieve and cherish a just and lasting peace among ourselves and with all nations.'

Yet all the while the victorious North was clamouring for revenge, and its baser elements for plunder. Lincoln, who knew that this would not benefit by one iota the plain man for whom he had fought the war, threw all his great influence into the opposing scale. To the rebellious states who were still fighting gamely he insisted on the unconditional surrender of their claim to secession, but resolutely opposed every suggestion of victimisation. Even their leaders he would not touch. ' No one,' he said, ' need expect me to take any part in hanging or killing these men, even the worst of them. Frighten them out of the country, open the gates, let down the bars, scare them off. Shoo ! ' Unmoved by the clamour of those about him, he kept his unchanging end in view, the union of the nation.

At heart he was sad. He knew how many vile passions had been loosed by the war, and how dangerous to the future of democracy was the force of human greed and self-seeking. He seemed to be quite alone. He was ill and exhausted. The deep lines on his face were like furrows now and his legs were always cold. ' I hardly know how to rest,' he told a friend who begged him to lie down. ' It may be good for the body. But what is tired in me lies within, and can't be got at.'

In the spring of 1865 he took a brief holiday, riding in his top hat among the troops who had been called into being by the magic of his name and staying with the rough General whom his trust had raised from a life of waste and failure to an hour of wonderful achievement. For a few days, mixing with the simple folk he loved, he was happy. But nothing could lift the burden of his weariness, and in after years those who were with him remembered the deep emotion with which he read aloud Shakespeare's lines :

> Duncan is in his grave,
> After life's fitful fever he sleeps well;
> Treason has done his worst; nor steel, nor poison,
> Malice domestic, foreign levy, nothing
> Can touch him further.

On April 11 he returned to Washington amid cheering crowds. The final victory had come. Three days later the Union flag was hoisted at Fort Sumter where it had first been shot down.

That morning before the Cabinet met Lincoln was curiously excited. He told his colleagues of a dream that he had had that night and which always preceded momentous tidings—of being carried in a ship of strange build swiftly towards an unknown shore. At that moment they were awaiting the news of the final surrender of the South.

At the Cabinet meeting the President spoke of the future. Everything must henceforward be done to restore the South to its proper place in the nation and to quiet the passions of hatred and jealousy which the war had raised. ' I think it providential that this great rebellion is crushed just as Congress has adjourned and there are none of the disturbing elements of that body to hinder and embarrass us. If we are wise and discreet we shall reanimate the States and get their governments in successful operation, with order prevailing and the Union re-established before Congress comes

THE AMERICAN IDEAL

together in December. . . . I hope there will be no persecution, no bloody work after the war is over.'

But there was to be bloody work, and it was done that
night. In the hush of the crowded theatre, the assassin
Booth fired the fatal shot. Lincoln, borne unconscious to
a neighbouring house, died before morning.

CHAPTER III

EMERSON AND WHITMAN

In that part of the States that lay to the northward the spiritual character of the original settlers was for long transmitted to their descendants. Here the first fight against the forces of nature had been fiercer than in any other part of the continent, and those who survived carried with them their marks and scars as a proud reminder of their manhood. Their hard-earned arrogance was fortified by their religion—Calvin's stark philosophy of God's elect, brought with them in the *Mayflower* from the Old World. They saw themselves as perpetually setting out from the City of Destruction, leaving behind them, with mingled feelings of pity and contempt, the generality of mankind.

The nature of life in the early days of settlement left its permanent impress on the New England character. Thrift was an everyday and indispensable virtue: in Massachusetts the elect could make a penny go as far as sixpence anywhere else. Poverty was a universal attribute and regarded as a virtue: it was a badge that all God's chosen people wore. It left the soul free and untainted for the higher activities of existence. These were the contemplation of the Divine Being, severe argument concerning the austere operation of His laws, and thanksgiving for His goodness to His saints. This last was a constant source of wonder and comfort. Everything was foreseen and predestined by Providence—the disease that slew the savages, the storm that wrecked the house of the ungodly, the wonderful catch of herrings or African slaves, which in due season rewarded the righteous man. 'We are as a city set upon a hill,' wrote one of them, ' in the open view of all the earth, the eyes of the world are upon us, because we profess ourselves to be a people in Covenant with God.' With such divine and irresistible Intent to advance their cause, forest, famine, disease and winter could not keep God's people from the attainment of their Destiny. Ever best was found at the close.

From such stock came Ralph Waldo Emerson. One of his forbears was the famous Peter Bulkley, rector of Odell, Bedfordshire, who crossed the Atlantic in the sixteen-thirties because Archbishop Laud had dared to try to silence him and became the first of the preaching aristocracy of New England—' the painful preachers ' who civilised the wilderness. His great-great-grandfather, the Rev. Samuel Moody, had been wont to thunder so terribly at his parishioners that they sometimes tried to steal out of church during his sermons to hide their shame, only to be recalled by a terrible shout from the pulpit, ' Come back, you graceless sinners, come back.' Such was the contempt of this good man for worldly treasure that he once gave away his wife's only shoes to a beggar. His son, Emerson's great-grandfather, took after him and used to pray every night that none of his descendants might ever suffer the curse of being rich. The prayer was answered. The next in the line died of fever as a chaplain in the Army of Independence. ' Great, grim, earnest men,' wrote Emerson of them in after years, ' I belong by natural affinity to other thoughts and schools than yours, but my affection hovers respectfully about your retiring footprints, and sad offices; the iron-grey deacon and the wearisome prayer rich with the diction of ages.'

Emerson's father, the cultured and music-loving minister of the First Church at Boston, was a softer fruit of this vigorous tree. He was the centre of the learned and artistic society of the town and a preacher of much charm. His eldest son, Ralph Waldo, was born to him on May 25, 1803, in the old parish house of the First Church. It stood amidst orchards and gardens in a town still famed for its pastoral beauty. Here, and at the village of Concord, Emerson spent almost all his fourscore years, and here, and in the spirit of those hardy and religious forbears from whom he sprang, the spirit of his work must be sought. The lives of literary men are seldom rich in external incident. As Emerson said, theirs are the shortest biographies. ' Their cousins can tell you nothing about them. They lived in their writings, and so their home and street life was trivial and commonplace.' Of his own childhood and youth there is little to relate. An early schoolfellow remembered him as a ' spiritual looking boy in blue nankeen,' a little remote from his fellows. When he was eight his father died, leaving his mother with six children to bring up on a pension of five hundred dollars a year. Together they underwent the discipline of poverty. It was a species of legacy.

It was a kindly one. The children, as their aunt said, were born to be educated, and nothing was allowed to deprive them of this right. Sometimes they were hungry: a friend once found the whole family sitting supperless while Aunt Mary, a fierce Calvinist of remarkable spiritual gifts, sustained them with tales of heroic endurance. But a serene and hereditary trust in Providence defended them. A letter of Ralph's, written at the age of thirteen, reveals the nature of their life :

In the Morning I rose, as I commonly do, about five minutes before six. I then help Wm. in making the fire, after which I set the table for Prayers. I then call mamma about quarter after six. We spell as we did before you went away. I confess I often feel an angry passion start in one corner of my heart when one of my Brothers gets above me, which I think sometimes they do by unfair means, after which we eat our breakfast; then I have from about quarter after seven till eight to play or read, I think I am rather inclined to the former. I then go to school, where I hope I can say I study more than I did a little while ago. I am in another book called Virgil, and our class are even with another which came to the Latin School one year before us. After attending this school I go to Mr. Webb's private school, where I write and cipher. I go to this place at eleven and stay till one o'clock. After this, when I come home I eat my dinner, and at two o'clock I resume my studies at the Latin school, where I do the same except in studying grammar. After I come home I do mamma her little errands if she has any; then I bring in my wood to supply the breakfast room. I then have some time to play and eat my supper. After that we say our hymns or chapters, and then take our turns in reading Rollin, as we did before you went. We retire to bed at different times. I go at a little after eight, and retire to my private devotions, and then close my eyes in sleep, and there ends the toils of the day.

Sharing his overcoat with his brother, learning to look on the world of thought and the spirit as the only source of true happiness, and reading Plato in a fireless garret, muffled up in a woollen cloak for warmth so that the dialogues were ever after associated in his mind with the smell of wool, such were his early memories. He always recalled them gratefully and pictured in his writings the blessed and guarded children of such a home. ' What is the hoop that holds them stanch ? It is the iron band of poverty, of necessity, of austerity, which, excluding them from the sensual enjoyments which make other boys too early old, has directed their activity into safe and right channels, and made them, despite themselves, reverers of the grand, the beautiful, and the good. Ah, short-sighted students of books, of nature, and of man ! too happy could they know their advantages; they pine for freedom from that mild parental yoke; they sigh for fine clothes, for rides, for the theatre, and premature freedom and dissipation which others possess. Woe to them if their wishes were crowned ! The angels that dwell with them, and are weaving laurels of life for their youthful brows, are Toil and Want and Truth and Mutual Faith.'

At the Latin School at Boston Emerson mastered the classics and learnt to love history. Thence he passed in 1817 to Harvard, as President's Freshman and a waiter at Commons. Quiet, unobtrusive and gently aloof, he made little impression on his contemporaries. He was only a fair scholar, developing late like many men of genius as his confidence grew. To earn a livelihood he entered the teaching profession, but found it uncongenial. One of his pupils described him as looking like ' a captive philosopher set to tending flocks; resigned to his destiny but not amused with its incongruities.' He does not seem to have been much of a disciplinarian, for it is recorded that his usual comment after the offences of his charges was ' Oh sad !' For a time he taught in an old-fashioned academy at Chelmsford in Middlesex County, and later helped his brother to teach a girls' school. ' A hopeless schoolmaster,' he wrote of himself, ' just entering upon years of trade, to which no distinct limit is placed; toiling through this miserable employment without even the poor satisfaction of discharging it well; for the good suspect me, and the geese dislike me.'

At twenty-one he drifted into the Ministry, the hereditary calling of his family. After two years at a Divinity school he was approbated to preach and ascended the popular Unitarian pulpit, ' the meek ambassador of the highest.' In 1829 he was ordained and succeeded to the Ministry of the Second Unitarian Church in Boston. In the same year he married the eighteen-year-old daughter of a Boston merchant.

Yet his days in the Ministry were not happy. For one thing his health was a continual anxiety, a family tendency to consumption manifesting itself in a stricture on the right side of the chest. ' The lungs,' he wrote, ' in their spiteful lobes sing sexton and sorrow whenever I only ask them to shout a sermon for me.' He was forced to winter in Florida and South Carolina to escape the terrible northern winds that swept over New England from frozen Canada, and for some years his chances of survival seemed small. ' It is a long battle, this of mine betwixt life and death,' he told a friend, ' and it is wholly uncertain to whom the game belongs.'

In the midst of it he lost his wife, who died of the same disease in 1832. His brother followed her. Emerson was prostrated. For two years he visited his wife's grave at Roxbury every day.

It was not only ill health and the loss of loved ones that vexed his ministry ; his own conscience troubled him. It was his misfortune to see every side of a question, and he found a growing dislike in himself to what he called the flimsy sophistries and unclean dogmas of established creeds. He was unable, like his parishioners, to bring himself to view God as a person: a spirit could not be interpreted in such mundane terms. 'The talk of the kitchen and the cottage is exclusively occupied with persons. And yet, when cultivated men speak of God, they demand a biography of him as steadily as the kitchen and the bar-room demand · personalities of men. . . . Theism must be, and the name of God must be, because it is a necessity of human mind to apprehend the relative as flowing from the absolute, and we shall always give the absolute a name.' Such feelings did not make his task congenial. Nor were those to whom he ministered pleased. One of them complained that he did not seem so much as to understand the business of consolation.

Yet the spirit that was to make Emerson so great a force in his continent and generation was already taking shape: behind the mask of his fragile, anxious face ideas of indestructible strength were forming. 'I preach half of every Sunday,' he wrote to a friend. 'When I attended church on the other half of a Sunday, and the image in the pulpit was all of clay, and not of tunable metal, I said to myself that if men would avoid that general language and general manner in which they strive to hide all that is peculiar, and would say only what was uppermost in their own minds, after their own individual manner, every man would be interesting. Every man is a new creation, can do something best, has some intellectual modes and forms, or a character the general result of all, such as no other agent in the universe has: if he would exhibit that, it must needs be engaging, must be a curious study to every inquisitive mind.' What he found in himself he found also in his fellows.

After three years in the Ministry Emerson resigned his living on the ground that he could not conscientiously administer the Communion service. He saw it, he explained, merely as a spiritual commemoration and held that it confused the idea of God to transfer the worship of Him to Christ: at such moments ' the soul stands alone with God, and Jesus is no more present to your mind than your brother or child.' His parishioners could not follow him in these spiritual flights.

He made his resignation without fuss or argument. Unassertive and tolerant, he was content that others should hold their views as he held his. There was no pretence of martyrdom: he just explained his position with courtesy and went. ' Having said this, I have said all. I have no hostility to this institution; I am only stating my want of sympathy with it. Neither should I ever have obtruded this opinion upon other people, had I not been called by my office to administer it. That is the end of my opposition, that I am not interested in it. I am content that it stand to the end of the world if it please men and please Heaven, and I shall rejoice in all the good it produces.' A fellow clergyman, who regarded his view as blasphemy, found it impossible to be angry with so gentle a heretic: he just could not make him out. ' Mr. Emerson is one of the sweetest creatures God ever made,' he wrote; ' there is a screw loose somewhere in the machinery, yet I cannot tell where it is, for I never heard it jar. He must go to heaven when he dies, for if he went to hell the devil would not know what to do with him.'

Emerson had sacrificed his principal income without a complaint or gesture, and was now his own master. He was unfeignedly glad. ' I hate preaching,' he said, ' whether in pulpits or in teachers' meetings. Preaching is a pledge, and I wish to say what I feel and think to-day, with the proviso that to-morrow perhaps I shall contradict it all. Freedom boundless I wish.' Now he could explore the world and bring his own soul into tune with it.

With this intent he set sail on Christmas Day, 1832, for Europe, in a 236-ton brig bound for Malta. The glorious air of the Atlantic filled his lungs and gave him a truckman's health and stomach, bringing him for the first time in his life the blessing of conscious health. Then he landed in the Old World, a pilgrim in quest of a teacher ' full of truth and of boundless benevolence and heroic sentiments,' who could reveal to him the elixir of life.

With this hope he visited the old poet, Landor, in Italy, Coleridge in London, and Wordsworth among his native hills at Rydal. None of them could give him what he sought. Then with difficulty he tracked down an obscure pamphleteering prophet, named Thomas Carlyle, in whose writings he fancied he discerned the light of genius. He found him at Craigenputtock, a Nithsdale farm, ' amid desolate heathery hills, where the lonely scholar nourished his mighty heart.' Of him he made a lifelong friend though he was one more difficult to make a friend of than almost any man on earth.

His search accomplished, Emerson returned to America with a knowledge of his own powers and mission. He had seen the accumulated art of Europe in its antiquity and beauty: it had inspired him, but it had not overawed him as it had other Americans. For its secret was plain: it sprang from a single and everlasting source, whose springs were ready to gush out in all ages for whoever chose to seek them. There was no need to grovel in the art galleries of Europe or repeat religious formulas by rote like the Calvinists and Unitarians among whom he had been bred. ' I believe,' he wrote, ' that the error of religionists lies in this: that they do not know the extent, or the harmony, or the depth of their moral nature; that they are clinging to little positive verbal formal versions of the moral law,—and very imperfect versions too,—while the infinite laws, the great circling truths whose only adequate symbol is the material laws, . . . are all unobserved, and sneered at, when spoken of, as frigid and insufficient. I call Calvinism such an imperfect version of the moral law. Unitarianism is another, and every form of Christian and of Pagan faith in the hands of incapable teachers. On the contrary, in the hands of a true teacher, the falsehoods, the pitifulnesses, the sectarianisms of each are dropped, and the sublimity and depth of the original penetrated and exhibited to men.'

All that man had to do was to open his eyes to the universe around him and receive its inspiration. He was born for it. 'A man contains all that is needful to his government within himself. He is made a law unto himself. All real good or evil that can befall him must be from himself. He only can do himself any good or any harm. Nothing can be given to him or taken from him, but always there's a compensation. There is a correspondence between the human soul and everything that exists in the world; more properly, everything that is known to man. . . . The purpose of life seems to be to acquaint man with himself. He is not to live to the future as described to him, but to live to the real future by living to the real present. The highest revelation is that God is in every man.'

> The heavens that now draw him
> With sweetness untold,
> Once found,—for new heavens
> He spurneth the old.

Priests, churches, dogmas, these were but isolated facets of the truth. Emerson did not condemn them: they revealed only a fraction of the whole, but it was something that they revealed even that. 'The church aerates my good neighbours, and serves them as a somewhat stricter and finer ablution than a clean shirt, or a bath, or a shampooing. When they have spent all their week in private and selfish action, the Sunday reminds them of a need they have to stand again in social and public and ideal relations, beyond neighbourhood, higher than the town-meeting, to their fellow-men. They marry; and the minister, who represents this high Public, celebrates the fact. Their child is baptized; and again they are published by his intervention. One of the family dies; he comes again, and the family go up to church to be publicized or churched in this official sympathy of mankind. It is all good so far as it goes. It is homage to the ideal

Church, which they have not; which the actual Church so foully misrepresents. But it is better so than nohow. These people have no fine arts, no literature, no great men to Boswellize, no fine speculation to entertain their family board or their solitary toil with. Their talk is of oxen and pigs and hay and corn and apples. Whatsoever liberal aspirations they at any time have, whatsoever spiritual experiences, have looked this way; and the Church is their fact for such things. It is still to them the accredited symbol of the religious idea.'

Yet if man would only use his eyes and open his soul and be himself, such aids to spiritual understanding of God's universe would no longer be necessary. For it was all staring him in the face. ' I think the robin and finch the only philosophers. I listen attentively to all they say, and account the whole spectacle of the day a new speech of God to me; though He speaks not less from the wharf and the market.' Man, the heir to a world of marvels, blindly failed to see his own heritage though it was staring him in the face.

Such was the glad tidings that Emerson felt himself called upon to proclaim : that was an inexhaustible well of inspiration and happiness lodged in the soul of every created creature. ' But now . . . man begins to hear a voice that fills the heavens and the earth, saying that God is within him; that *there* is the celestial host. I find this amazing revelation of my immediate relation to God a solution to all the doubts that oppressed me. I recognize the distinction of the outer and the inner self; the double consciousness that, within this erring, passionate, mortal self sits a supreme, calm, immortal mind, whose powers I do not know, but it is stronger than I; it is wiser than I; it never approved me in any wrong; I seek counsel of it in my doubts; I repair to it in my dangers; I pray to it in my undertakings. It seems to me the face which the Creator uncovers to his child. It is the perception of this depth in human nature, this infinitude belonging to every man that has been born, which has given new value to the habits of reflection and solitude. In this doctrine, as deeply felt by him, is the key by which the words that fell from Christ upon the character of God can alone be well and truly explained. "The Father is in me: I am in the Father, yet the Father is greater than I." ' All this came to Emerson with the conviction and joy of a prophet: he had discovered a most wonderful truth and wanted mankind to share it.

He took no credit for his discovery, nor sought any reward. It was so obvious that anyone could have stumbled on it. A small income from his dead wife's estate enabled him on his return from Europe to settle at Concord—a small village seventeen miles from Boston amid the quiet New England fields and woods. Here he bought a 'plain square wooden house with horse chestnuts around it,' where, as he wrote, 'the north-west wind, with all his snows, took me in charge and defended me from all company in winter, and the hills and sand-banks that intervened between me and the city kept guard in summer.' Here he remarried and had children and lived for nearly fifty years a peaceful, regular, domestic life, keeping open house for all comers and looked upon as the principal gentleman of the place. Here he wrote and prepared his lectures, and took solitary walks, crowned in thought, through the still half-tamed American wilderness. 'It was good to meet him in the woodpaths,' wrote his neighbour, Hawthorne, ' with that pure intellectual gleam diffusing about his presence like the garment of a shining one; and he, so quiet, so simple, so without pretension, encountering each man alive as if expecting to receive more than he would impart. . . . It was impossible to dwell in his vicinity without inhaling more or less the mountain atmosphere of his lofty thought.'

Yet Emerson was not content with a cloistered and fugitive virtue : he had found a great truth, enlarging the sum total of human happiness, and felt it his duty to give it to others. Preaching, after all, was his hereditary craft. Not possessing the pulpit of his forefathers, he made himself a new one as it were out of bare boards. He set up as a lecturer, touring the little 'Lyceums' and meeting halls of New England, competing with nigger minstrels and shilling concerts, and drawing to himself, by that precarious and arduous calling, an audience of the young in body or heart. It was not a very imposing platform from which to preach the regeneration of man, but it was a free and unrestricted one, and that in Emerson's eyes was everything. ' I am always haunted,' he wrote, ' with brave dreams of what might be accomplished in the lecture-room,—so free and so unpretending a platform,—a Delos not yet made fast.'

He prepared his lectures in the summer and delivered them in the winter. He started by talking on such titles as ' Water,' and the ' Relation of Man to the Globe,' and gradually passed on to ' Michael Angelo,' ' The Doctrine of the Soul,' ' Love,' ' Genius ' and ' Demonology.' But in everything he said the same theme recurred—the heritage that was awaiting man in his own soul and the importance of spiritual self-reliance. Somehow he made it intelligible to his neighbours. They had few pleasures and liked to tramp, lantern in hand, through the winter snow to hear him. ' We are very simple people and can understand no one but Mr. Emerson,' wrote one of them.

After a time he became the apostle of culture to his countrymen and contemporaries. Because they wanted it, he wrote out his lectures in rough essay form and published them. There was little literary style about them, nor much continuity or logic, but he pretended to none. He saw himself solely as a preacher, revealing the obvious. ' I write,' he told Carlyle, ' with very little system, and, as far as regards composition, with most fragmentary result— paragraphs incomprehensible, each sentence an infinitely repellent particle.' He was just, he explained, an incorrigible, spouting Yankee.

And his mission was as plain as a pikestaff—to make man, and above all man in America, aware of his own spiritual stature. In one of his lectures, delivered at the Second Continental Anniversary of his own Concord, he spoke of the simple but to him intensely moving annals of American self-government. It was the story of the victory of the plain man and his virtues in a hard-fought battle. ' If the good counsel prevailed, the sneaking counsel did not fail to be suggested; freedom and virtue, if they triumphed, triumphed in a fair field. And so be it an everlasting testimony for them, and so much ground of assurance of man's capacity for self-government.'

But if in politics the Jeffersonian dream of the ordinary man's capacity to rule himself had been vindicated, in the world of the spirit the American was still strangely timorous and submissive. Sensitive Americans in search of culture crossed the Atlantic and, turning their backs on their own country, worshipped slavishly at the altars of the past in London and Florence. American scholars, instead of interpreting the history and philosophy of their own land, wasted their activities in meaningless pursuit of the tag-ends of European knowledge. It was time to frame a new Declaration of Independence—for the soul. ' Thus far,' Emerson told a gathering of American scholars, ' our holiday has been simply a friendly sign of the survival of the love of letters amongst a people too busy to give to letters any more. As such it is precious as the sign of an indestructible instinct. Perhaps the time is already come when it ought to be, and will be, something else; when the sluggard intellect of this continent will look from under its iron lids and fill the postponed expectations of the world with something better than the exertions of mechanical skill. Our day of dependence, our long apprenticeship to the learning of other lands, draws to a close. The millions that around us are rushing into life cannot always be fed on the sere remains of foreign harvests. Events, actions, arise, that must be sung, that will sing themselves. Who can doubt that poetry will revive and lead in a new age, as the star in the constellation Harp, which now flames in our zenith, astronomers announce shall one day be the pole-star for a thousand years ? '

It was therefore foolish to spend one's days fumbling reverently among the fragments of ancient European art and culture when the eternal treasure house out of which they were made was at one's hand. ' All American manners, language, and writing are derivative. We do not write from facts, but we wish to state facts after the English manner. It is the tax we pay for the splendid inheritance of English literature. We are exonerated by the sea and the Revolution from the national debt, but we pay this, which is rather the worse part.' The great books of the past were all very well, but they should not blind men to the fact that whatever inspiration there may have been in them remained equally available to any true man who was prepared to seek it direct.

' The power which they communicate,' he wrote, ' is not theirs. When we are exalted by ideas, we do not owe this to Plato, but to the idea, to which also Plato was debtor.' The letter availed nothing and was only made to bind the mind of the living. ' Instantly the book becomes noxious: the guide is a tyrant. The sluggish and perverted mind of the multitude, slow to open to the incursions of reason, having once so opened, having received this book, stands upon it and makes an outcry if it is disparaged. Colleges are built on it. Books are written on it by thinkers, not by Man thinking ; by men of talent, that is, who start wrong, who set out from accepted dogmas, not from their own sight of principle. Meek young men grow up in libraries, believing in their duty to accept the views which Cicero, which Locke, which Bacon have given; forgetful that Cicero, Locke, and Bacon were only young men in libraries when they wrote these books.'

The time had come for the world to realise this, and the American, who had taught her one great lesson, could teach her another. But first he must learn to stand on his own feet in the world of the spirit as he had already done in that of politics. ' Why then goest thou,' Emerson asked of his countryman, ' as some Boswell or literary worshipper to this saint or to that ? That is the only lese-majesty. Here art thou with whom so long the universe travailed in labour; darest thou think meanly of thyself whom the stalwart Fate

brought forth to unite his ragged sides, to shoot the gulf, to
reconcile the irreconcilable ? '

Such were the oracles which Emerson uttered on dark
wintry evenings in the village Lyceums of New England.
Man was born to be free. Everyone inherited the whole
past. 'He that is admitted to the right of reason is made
freeman of the whole estate. What Plato has thought, he
may think; what a saint has felt, he may feel; what at any
time has befallen any man, he can understand.' Each man
had it in him to rise to the highest heights of the spirit.
'Trust thyself! every heart vibrates to that iron string.
Accept the place the Divine Providence has found for you,
the society of your contemporaries, the connection of events.
Great man have always done so, and confided themselves
childlike to the genius of their age; betraying their perception that the Eternal was stirring at their heart, working
through their hands, predominating in all their being. And
we are now men, and must accept in the highest spirit the
same transcendent destiny; and not pinched in a corner,
not cowards fleeing before a revolution, but redeemers and
benefactors, pious aspirants to be noble clay plastic under
the Almighty effort, let us advance and advance on chaos
and the dark ! '

This was destiny enough for any nation. 'All these
great and transcendent properties are ours . . . let us
find room for this great guest in our small houses. . . .
Where the heart is, there the muses, there the gods sojourn,
and not in any geography of fame. Massachusetts, Connecticut River, and Boston Bay, you think paltry places, and the
ear loves names of foreign and classic topography. But
here we are, and if we will tarry a little we may come to
learn that here is best. . . . The Jerseys were handsome
enough ground for Washington to tread, and London streets
for the feet of Milton. . . . That country is fairest which is
inhabited by the noblest minds.' And just as the early
pioneers had eschewed all cowardly, backward-longing
glances to Europe, and struck westward into the unknown,
so Emerson would have his countrymen find a new frontier

of the spirit. Here they would find the ' soul of the world, free from all vestige of tradition. . . . Here in our America is the home of man; here the promise of a new and more excellent social state than history has recorded.'

But lecture as Emerson might, he could never arouse America to a proper sense of her opportunity. What was needed was a great poet to make it plain: ' all that we call sacred history attests that the birth of a poet is the principal event in chronology.' For once he almost became one himself in the intensity with which he besought the gods to fire his sober Muse.

> Bring me wine, but wine which never grew
> In the belly of the grape,
> Or grew on vine whose tap-roots reaching through
> Under the Andes to the Cape,
> Suffer no savor of the earth to 'scape.
>
> .   .   .   .   .
>
> Wine that is shed
> Like the torrents of the sun
> Up the horizon walls;
> Or like the Atlantic streams which run
> When the South Sea calls.
>
> Water and bread;
> Food which needs no transmuting,
> Rainbow-flowering, wisdom-fruiting;
> Wine which is already man,
> Food which teach and reason can.
>
> Wine which Music is;
> Music and wine are one;
> That I, drinking this,
> Shall hear far Chaos talk with me;
> Kings unborn shall walk with me;
> And the poor grass shall plot and plan
> What it will do when it is man.
> Quickened so, will I unlock
> Every crypt of every rock.

EMERSON AND WHITMAN

I thank the joyful juice
For all I know;
Winds of remembering
Of the ancient being blow,
And seeming-solid walls of use
Open and flow.

Pour, Bacchus! the remembering wine;
Retrieve the loss of me and mine!
Vine for vine be antidote,
And the grape requite the lote!
Haste to cure the old despair,
Reason in Nature's lotus drenched,
The memory of the ages quenched;—
Give them again to shine.
Let wine repair what this undid;
And where the infection slid,
A dazzling memory revive.
Refresh the faded tints,
Recut the aged prints,
And write my old adventures with the pen
Which, on the first day drew
Upon the tablets blue
The dancing Pleiads, and eternal men.

Emerson was a humble man and knew that, for all this sudden flight, he could never be that poet. The friend and aider of all those who would live in the spirit, as Matthew Arnold called him, he lacked the essential fire that achieves revolution. There was something about him which he himself once described as the ' porcupine impossibility of contact with men.' The glow of flesh and blood was not his. In a lecture hall he convinced by his manifest sincerity, his simplicity of speech and manner, and his sweet and winning gentleness. On paper vitality was lacking, for there was nothing in his actual being by which it could be communicated. It is still recalled in New England how once in the midst of some furniture moving operations at his home Emerson was suddenly noticed sitting in a chair gazing in helpless embarrassment at the active bustle about him; he

115

had been there, it appeared, for over an hour watching his wife and neighbours and unable to take any other part but that of a passive though sympathetic spectator. ' Take care, papa,' said his small son as he witnessed his father's unwonted intervention in the garden, ' or you will dig your leg.' There were times when his habit of always eating pie for breakfast seemed the only human thing about him.

It was this absence of passion from his life that disqualified Emerson from fulfilling his task of awakening his countrymen to a sense of their spiritual capacity. He was conscious of his limitations. ' When I see how much work is to be done,' he wrote, ' what room for a poet, for any spiritualist, in this great, intelligent, sensual, and avaricious America,—I lament my fumbling fingers and stammering tongue.' For a time he tried to find what was needed in queer coteries and brotherhoods of kindred souls and fellow reformers, united by a ' common impatience of routine thinking,' like the Boston Transcendentalists and the Brook Farm Community. But such gatherings produced little else but a crop of impracticable cranks, of wild, mild young men who lived on parched corn, eschewed workaday attire and refused to pay taxes. Their precious abstractions and readymade designs for Utopias could never arouse a young, full-blooded and passionate nation like America. Emerson, who in the midst of their excesses preserved his usual gentle sanity, knew this and soon despaired of finding in their feeble ranks the master poet and prophet whom he was seeking.

> Thy trivial harp will never please
> Or fill my craving ear;
> Its chords should ring as blows the breeze,
> Free, peremptory, clear.
> No jingling serenader's art
> Nor tinkling of piano-strings
> Can make the wild blood start
> In its mystic springs;
> The kingly bard
> Must smite the chords rudely and hard.

When that bard at last appeared, this was precisely what he did. The man whom Emerson was seeking was as rough as the American frontier. In Walt Whitman, born in 1819 of working-class parentage on a farm in Long Island, he was to find his miracle incarnate—'not only the grateful and reverent legatee of the past, but the born child of the New World.'

Walt Whitman, like Joseph, was a carpenter. He had been in turn an errand boy, a clerk and a poor journalist, and in his younger days had moved a good deal about the States. He had thus been able to observe to the full the life of the American people. He was largely self-taught and, like the bulk of his countrymen, both ignorant of and un-trammelled by the traditions and cultural forms of the past. By every instinct he was a poet—observant, hypersensitive, and passionately impetuous.

In the summer of 1855, after some years of passive re-cuperation from an unhappy and tempestuous love affair, he published a small volume of poems called 'Leaves of Grass.' The verse and language was crude, original and forceful. Its purpose, manifest on the first page, was to sing the divinity of the everyday man, what its author called the 'divine average.'

> Of Life immense in passion, pulse, and power,
> Cheerful, for freest action form'd under the laws divine,
> The Modern Man I sing.

Nothing quite like it had ever appeared before. Here, at last, was an ordinary man—ordinary, that is, in the sense of class, upbringing and environment—telling the truth about himself:

> Walt Whitman, a kosmos, of Manhattan the son,
> Turbulent, fleshy, sensual, eating, drinking and breeding,
> No sentimentalist, no stander above men and women or apart
>   from them,
> No more modest than immodest.

What was so satisfactory was that this new bard was entirely American in his outlook: he could not possibly have belonged to any other place or people. Other American poets, like Longfellow and Bryant, wrote excellent verses, but verses that might just as easily have been written in London or Rome. But there was no mistaking Whitman's western accents and the high nasal confidential voice in which they were uttered.

Me imperturbe, standing at ease in Nature,
Master of all or mistress of all, aplomb in the midst of irrational things,
Imbued as they, passive, receptive, silent as they,
Finding my occupation, poverty, notoriety, foibles, crimes, less important than I thought,
Me toward the Mexican sea, or in the Mannahatta or the Tennessee, or far north or inland,
A river man, or a man of the woods or of any farm-life of these States or of the coast, or the lakes or Kanada,
Me wherever my life is lived, O to be self-balanced for contingencies,
To confront night, storms, hunger, ridicule, accidents, rebuffs, as the trees and animals do.

In his roughly hammered, unrhymed, strident-metred verses Whitman made the image of a new great nation in all its free diversity.

I hear America singing, the varied carols I hear,
Those of mechanics, each one singing his as it should be blithe and strong,
The carpenter singing his as he measures his plank or beam,
The mason singing his as he makes ready for work, or leaves off work,
The boatman singing what belongs to him in his boat, the deckhand singing on the steamboat deck,
The shoemaker singing as he sits on his bench, the hatter singing as he stands,
The wood-cutter's song, the ploughboy's on his way in the morning, or at noon intermission or at sundown,
The delicious singing of the mother, or of the young wife at work, or of the girl sewing or washing,
Each singing what belongs to him or her and to none else.

EMERSON AND WHITMAN

Above all Whitman said just what Emerson had wanted his American poet to say :

I say no man has ever yet been half devout enough,
None has ever yet adored or worship'd half enough,
None has begun to think how divine he himself is, and how
certain the future is.

I say that the real and permanent grandeur of these States
must be their religion.

By looking inward and discovering the boundless opportunity in his own spirit, he had widened the frontier of the human soul. Whitman was not in the least dependent on the past or on books or on the thoughts of dead men : he stood, as he said, in his own place in his own day. He saw himself, *homo Americanus*, inheriting everything that had gone before and knocking at the door of an illimitable future. And he was glad to be just himself.

One's self I sing, a simple separate person.

He did not even mind contradicting his own past words and thoughts; that to which his spirit prompted him at the moment was everything. Emerson himself had defined consistency as the hobgoblin of little minds, and here was this rough untaught genius drumming out the same thought:

Do I contradict myself?
Very well, then I contradict myself;
(I am large, I contain multitudes).

There were plenty of faults in Whitman's work—hasty work, absence of critical sense, repetition, crudeness of rhythm—and the critics, so far as they noticed the book at all, fastened on them eagerly. The *Boston Intelligence* went so far as to ascribe the poems to an escaped madman. Very few read them, and the great masses for whom its author intended them never so much as gave them a thought; with their betters ignoring or condemning them, it is difficult to see how they could have done so. The publication was a failure, and the carpenter remained at his bench.

But it so happened that a copy found its way to Emerson's hands. He immediately recognised it as the thing for which he had been waiting. ' I am not blind,' he wrote to its author, ' to the worth of the wonderful gift of the " Leaves of Grass." I find it the most extraordinary piece of wit and wisdom that America has yet contributed. I am very happy in reading it, as great power makes us happy. . . . I give you joy of your free and brave thought. I have great joy in it. I find incomparable things said incomparably well. . . . I greet you at the beginning of a great career.' Authors of established reputation, like other men, are usually jealous of younger aspirants who surpass them at their own craft. Emerson was above such infirmity. Instead he joyously acclaimed the coming of the new bard. ' Americans abroad,' he wrote, ' may now come home: unto us a man is born.'

Walt Whitman, the carpenter, was naturally delighted at this unexpected recognition, at the very moment when his hopes were lowest, by the acknowledged leader of American culture. And when a later edition of ' Leaves of Grass ' was published, he printed the letter as part of it without even the formality of obtaining Emerson's consent. This act caused a major literary sensation, for Whitman had also added to his work some very frank poems on the natural relations of the sexes which but for Emerson's recommendation would have been little noticed, but were now read in successive astonishment, incredulity and horror in every refined North American home. For a time faith in even the sage of Concord was shaken. It was felt that the master had taken leave of his senses.

But this unfortunate occurrence did not shake Emerson's faith in his protégé. A great poet expressing his own essential manhood, he argued, must necessarily sometimes infringe the decorums. Yet before Whitman's next publication he did his best to get the rude genius to tone down some of the more offensive expressions. He did not have the least success: the single man planted himself indomitably on his

own instincts and there abode. After two hours' fruitless
argument, the sage suggested that they should go to dinner,
and there the matter ended. Whitman continued to shock
the cultured public, and the cultured public continued to do
its best to ignore him.

None the less, in the essence of the matter Emerson
was right. Whitman was a great poet who saw the truth in
a new light and told his fellow men of it. A year later the
American Civil War broke out, and, though for a time
with the sublime egoism of his kind Whitman contrived to
ignore it, in the end that great storm of national emotion
carried him away. His experiences in the military hospitals
of the Northern armies enhanced both his manhood and
his verse. His whole being went out into the sufferings
of those whom he nursed and comforted, and he comprehended the full story of why they were there—their proud
virility, their courage, their helplessness when stricken
down, their greatness in surrendering self to an idea that
was greater than self. Not since Homer had anyone
written of actual warfare with such understanding.

> Pass, pass, ye proud brigades, with your tramping sinewy legs,
> With your shoulders young and strong, with your knapsacks
>   and your muskets;
> How elate I stood and watch'd you, where starting off you
>   march'd.

Only those who have had experience of war can appreciate
the fidelity of Whitman's description of the carnage and
desolation of the battlefield.

> Look down fair moon and bathe this scene,
> Pour softly down night's nimbus floods on faces ghastly,
>   swollen, purple,
> On the dead on their backs with arms toss'd wide.

There, in less than thirty words, is the face of war.
Yet Whitman was too great a poet to fall into the fault
of smaller men and see nothing in war but its horror. It

was not the captains and kings who conquered by their trumpery victories, but the plain man who redeemed this world's failure by his own triumph over himself. Behind war's hideous visage was still the shining beauty of human heroism and devotion, of love of comrade for comrade, of forgiveness of enemies and the spirit conquering the bruised flesh, and God's tender and inexorable tool, time, giving all tired things rest and making all things new.

> Word over all, beautiful as the sky,
> Beautiful that war and all its deeds of carnage must in time be
>   utterly lost,
> That the hands of the sisters Death and Night incessantly softly
>   wash again, and ever again, this soil'd world.

In the last resort, after every horror and defilement had been endured and admitted, earth remained good and eternally pure in the renewal of her own youth.

Never did Whitman come nearer to this divine truth than in the commemorative ode which he wrote after Lincoln's death, describing the passage of his body westwards across the States to his home at Springfield. The whole poem is raised above the bitterness and trivialities of contemporary politics and feeling by the great enduring emotions— of the millions mourning the loss of their leader and father, of the pageantry of associated man in all its solemn pomp and poetry and, running through it like a lovely thread, the miracle of recurring nature. On that theme the poem begins and ends; the lilac over the farm doorways, the western star hanging low in the spring sky and the hermit thrush singing in the awakening wilderness.

> When lilacs last in the dooryard bloom'd,
> And the great star early droop'd in the western sky in the night,
> I mourn'd, and yet shall mourn with ever-returning spring.

> Ever-returning spring, trinity sure to me you bring,
> Lilac blooming perennial and drooping star in the west,
> And thought of him I love.

EMERSON AND WHITMAN

O powerful western fallen star !
O shades of night—O moody, tearful night !
O great star disappear'd—O the black murk that hides the star !
O cruel hands that hold me powerless—O helpless soul of me !
O harsh surrounding cloud that will not free my soul.

In the dooryard fronting an old farm-house near the white-
    wash'd palings,
Stands the lilac-bush tall-growing with heart-shaped leaves of
    rich green,
With many a pointed blossom rising delicate, with the perfume
    strong I love,
With every leaf a miracle—and from this bush in the dooryard,
With delicate-color'd blossoms and heart-shaped leaves of rich
    green,
A sprig with its flower I break.

In the swamp in secluded recesses,
A shy and hidden bird is warbling a song

Solitary the thrush,
The hermit withdrawn to himself, avoiding the settlements,
Sings by himself a song.

Song of the bleeding throat,
Death's outlet song of life (for well dear brother I know,
If thou wast not granted to sing thou would'st surely die).

Thus the cortege passes slowly in front of the natural
setting, from which, like the dead man in its midst, it takes
its dignity and significance.

Over the breast of the spring, the land, amid cities,
Amid lanes and through old woods, where lately the violets
    peep'd from the ground, spotting the gray debris,
Amid the grass in the fields each side of the lanes, passing the
    endless grass,
Passing the yellow-spear'd wheat, every grain from its shroud
    in the dark-brown fields uprisen,
Passing the apple-tree blows of white and pink in the orchards,
Carrying a corpse to where it shall rest in the grave,
Night and day journeys a coffin.

123

Coffin that passes through lanes and streets,
Through day and night with the great cloud darkening the land,
With the pomp of the inloop'd flags, with the cities draped in black,
With the show of the States themselves as of crape-veil'd women standing,
With processions long and winding and the flambeaus of the night,
With countless torches lit, with the silent sea of faces and the unbared heads,
With the waiting depot, the arriving coffin, and the sombre faces,
With dirges through the night, with the thousand voices rising strong and solemn;
With all the mournful voices of the dirges pour'd around the coffin,
The dim-lit churches and the shuddering organs—where amid these you journey,
With the tolling tolling bells' perpetual clang,
Here, coffin that slowly passes,
. I give you my sprig of lilac.

Never once in this great ode does the poet mention directly the subject of his elegy. Only, with simple restraint, he describes that which the dead statesman loved, and so says all.

O what shall I hang on the chamber walls ?
And what shall the pictures be that I hang on the walls,
To adorn the burial-house of him I love ?

Pictures of growing spring and farms and homes,
With the Fourth-month eve at sundown, and the gray smoke lucid and bright,
With floods of the yellow gold of the gorgeous, indolent, sinking sun, burning, expanding the air,
With the fresh sweet herbage under foot, and the pale green leaves of the trees prolific,
In the distance the flowing glaze, the breast of the river, with a wind-dapple here and there,
With ranging hills on the banks, with many a line against the sky, and shadows,
And the city at hand with dwellings so dense, and stacks of chimneys,
And all the scenes of life and the workshops, and the workmen homeward returning.

124

EMERSON AND WHITMAN

It is not till the long elegiac has ended in its scented close, that the poet permits himself at last, with effect a hundredfold enhanced, to speak of Lincoln himself.

O Captain! my Captain! our fearful trip is done,
The ship has weather'd every rack, the prize we sought is won,
The port is near, the bells I hear, the people all exulting,
While follow eyes the steady keel, the vessel grim and daring;
        But O heart! heart! heart!
            O the bleeding drops of red,
                Where on the deck my Captain lies,
                    Fallen cold and dead.

O Captain! my Captain! rise up and hear the bells;
Rise up—for you the flag is flung—for you the bugle trills,
For you bouquets and ribbon'd wreaths—for you the shores
    a-crowding,
For you they call, the swaying mass, their eager faces turning;
        Here Captain! dear father!
            This arm beneath your head!
                It is some dream that on the deck,
                    You've fallen cold and dead.

My Captain does not answer, his lips are pale and still,
My father does not feel my arm, he has no pulse nor will,
The ship is anchor'd safe and sound, its voyage closed and done,
From fearful trip the victor ship comes in with object won;
        Exult O shores, and ring O bells!
            But I with mournful tread,
                Walk the deck my Captain lies,
                    Fallen cold and dead.

Whitman's poems on the American Civil War, for all his frequent and sometimes appalling defects of style and taste, place him among the great spiritual adventurers who have enlarged the boundaries of human perception. Yet much of his work was peculiar to his own country. No man ever better expressed American aspirations or understood better the meaning of American history. Alone of the poets of his country in the nineteenth century he looked at life from a purely Western standpoint. For the ideal of the old

125

exclusive gentlemanly refinement of Europe he set before his countrymen an ideal of culture whose essence was that it embraced everybody. He told them that no one could ever gain anything by being better off than his fellows: that so long as any man was in suffering and pain, they were all in suffering and pain: that it was what he shared that ennobled man, not that which he kept to himself.

By his glorification of the divine average Whitman gave new significance to the rough, manly, equalitarian ideal of America. Nobody before but Lincoln had thought that there was anything poetic about it. Whitman saw it as the very soul of romance. Just as the medieval ballad singers had transformed feudal bullies and marauders into the chivalrous kings and nobles of an ideal, so Whitman transformed that shrewd materialist Uncle Sam. This is what a great poet does, he makes the commonplace sublime. A nation's culture only begins when this process has been accomplished.

Over the wide horizons and ever-expanding frontiers of America Whitman cast his spell.

> Lo, body and soul—this land,
> My own Manhattan with spires, and the sparkling and hurrying tides, and the ships,
> The varied and ample land, the South and the North in the light, Ohio's shores and flashing Missouri,
> And ever the far-spreading prairies cover'd with grass and corn.

Land and people he knew and loved them, for he could see into their soul.

> Come my tan-faced children,
> Follow well in order, get 'your weapons ready,
> Have you your pistols? have you your sharp-edged axes?
> Pioneers! O pioneers!

> For we cannot tarry here,
> We must march my darlings, we must bear the brunt of danger,
> We the youthful sinewy races, all the rest on us depend,
> Pioneers! O pioneers!

We primeval forests felling,
We the rivers stemming, vexing we and piercing deep the mines
within,
We the surface broad surveying, we the virgin soil upheaving,
Pioneers! O pioneers!

.   .   .   .   .

All the hapless silent lovers,
All the prisoners in the prisons, all the righteous and the
wicked,
All the joyous, all the sorrowing, all the living, all the dying,
Pioneers! O pioneers!

This is the verse of a great patriot, of one who is moved to
wonder and reverence in the contemplation of his country.
So the child, seeing the star-spangled banner, turns in
wonder and adoration to his parent.

O father it is alive—it is full of people—it has children,
O now it seems to me it is talking to its children.

The heart of American patriotism was that every man
must be true to himself. America was great because, alone
among the nations, she recognised the greatness of man.
She did not try to cramp him, to mould him into a single
groove, to subordinate him to his fellows. All she asked of
him was that he should live his life to the full and make of
it the very utmost of which he was capable. Out of that
her own strength arose.

I swear I begin to see the meaning of these things,
It is not the earth, it is not America who is so great,
It is I who am great or to be great, it is You up there, or any one,
It is to walk rapidly through civilizations, governments, theories,
Through poems, pageants, shows, to form individuals.

Underneath all, individuals,
I swear nothing is good to me now that ignores individuals,
The American compact is altogether with individuals,
The only government is that which makes minute of individuals,
The whole theory of the universe is directed unerringly to one
single individual—namely to You.

.   .   .   .   .

THE AMERICAN IDEAL

O I see flashing that this America is only you and me,
Its power, weapons, testimony, are you and me,
Its crimes, lies, thefts, defections, are you and me,
Its Congress is you and me, the officers, capitols, armies, ships,
    are you and me,
Its endless gestations of new States are you and me,
The war (that war so bloody and grim, the war I will henceforth
    forget), was you and me,
Natural and artificial are you and me,
Freedom, language, poems, employments, are you and me,
Past, present, future, are you and me.

I dare not shirk any part of myself,
Not any part of America good or bad,
Not to build for that which builds for mankind,
Not to balance ranks, complexions, creeds, and the sexes,
Not to justify science nor the march of equality,
Nor to feed the arrogant blood of the brawn belov'd of time.

I am for those that have never been master'd,
For men and women whose tempers have never been master'd,
For those whom laws, theories, conventions, can never master.

I am for those who walk abreast with the whole earth,
Who inaugurate one to inaugurate all.

I will not be outfaced by irrational things,
I will penetrate what it is in them that is sarcastic upon me,
I will make cities and civilizations defer to me,
This is what I have learnt from America—it is the amount, and
    it I teach again.

Democracy, while weapons were everywhere aim'd at your
    breast,
I saw you serenely give birth to immortal children, saw in
    dreams your dilating form,
Saw you with spreading mantle covering the world.

This is Whitman's creed, and he is America's greatest poet
because, under all the superficialities that so easily mislead
the foreigner, it is America's creed also.

128

EMERSON AND WHITMAN

Emerson lived almost to the age of eighty, dying in April 1882. He remained to the end the same gentle, sympathetic, considerate and tolerant creature. Nor were his hopes of the future in any way dimmed. For all the perilous tendencies that were threatening her during his closing years, he still believed his country, the last found, to be ' the great charity of God to the human race.' His burial at Concord was attended by all the learned and famous of America.

His protégé outlived him by ten years, and nobody much attended his funeral. He also never despaired of the future. It seemed to him very good. ' Think of the United States to-day—the facts of these thirty-eight or forty empires solder'd in one—sixty or seventy millions of equals, with their lives, their passions, their future—these incalculable, modern, American, seething multitudes around us, of which we are inseparable parts ! Think, in comparison, of the petty environage and limited area of the poets of past or present Europe, no matter how great their genius. Think of the absence and ignorance, in all cases hitherto, of the multitudinousness, vitality, and the unprecedented stimulants of to-day and here. It almost seems as if a poetry with cosmic and dynamic features of magnitude and limitlessness suitable to the human soul, were never possible before. It is certain that a poetry of absolute faith and equality for the use of the democratic masses never was.' But it happened that he had written it.

CHAPTER IV

THE American dream was first conceived by the English, but the English are a practical race. Impelled by the urgent necessity of extracting a livelihood from the climate and soil of New England, those of them who settled in the more northerly regions of America concentrated with ever-increasing intensity on the business of earning their daily bread. Hard work, a sense of the means requisite to practical ends and the accumulation of money came to be regarded as the principal civic virtues. By these alone could the wilderness be made to flower. And as the English have never excelled at thinking of more than one thing at once and have always tended at any given time to pursue a single purpose to the exclusion of all others, seeking wealth became the normal mode of life of the strenuous people of New England, New York and Pennsylvania. The quicker this process could be achieved the better, subject to the limitations of the Ten Commandments. And as these limitations were sometimes an impediment, it was natural that after a while the Ten Commandments began to seem less important.

With the industrial revolution in the early nineteenth century the possibilities of exploiting nature to increase wealth and employment were enlarged. The British were the first in the field, but their American kinsmen were quick to follow. As early as 1801 Josiah Quincy found a hundred little girls at work in a cotton mill at under 25 cents a day, and was pained to notice a ' dull dejection in the countenances of all of them.' Mills and factories sprang up all over the North, and black waggons, called ' slavers,' paraded the farms of Vermont and New England in search of young females to swell the ranks of the army of wealth.

But in America the rank and file of the race who in Britain flocked into the factories proved harder to catch. Wages could not tempt men who had only to tramp west into the wilderness to be their own masters. They preferred the promise of the Frontier to the capitalist's sooty gold cage. The manufacturers turned elsewhere for the hands they needed. These the overcrowded lands of the Old World offered in abundance. From the poorest and most wretched homes in Europe flowed an inexhaustible stream of immigrants, who crossed the Atlantic as the slaves of the Congo had done a century before. In the twenty years after Jefferson's death two and a half million aliens arrived in America, mostly penniless. As soon as they landed the factory gates closed behind them.

These newcomers were not free men in Jefferson's sense. They did not own their own land or the tools by which they earned their livelihood. They did not share the traditions or comprehend the self-governing institutions of the ruling race who employed them. They had been bred in the lowest servitude of feudal Europe and accepted the new despotism of the men of capital without remark. They were herded in slums around the factories they served and constituted in all but name a race apart. As the negro slaves had supported the culture of the South, so Slav, German, Latin and Irish helots shouldered the rising wealth of the North. Another shadow fell across the sunshine of the American dream.

Yet such was the force of their generous vision that the political formula of the Republican Fathers did not deny the newcomers as it had the slaves. The Europeans of the factory towns entered the constitution on terms of theoretical equality with the masters who employed them. This at least was something, though in every other respect the two remained divided by a vast gulf. For it admitted of hope for the future and left intact the essential faith of America that one day the burden might be lifted from the shoulders of all men.

The entry, however, of the foreign factory hand into the constitution introduced a new danger into the structure of democracy. For the intelligent suffrages of free men, accustomed to the use of independent judgment, was substituted the manipulated mass vote of a city mob, bred in the ways of slavery and too poor and ill-educated to value freedom above a mess of pottage. It was this class that Lincoln had foreseen might form a new basis for servitude within the American Union unless the legal state of slavery were abolished. After his death and the triumph of his cause, its existence still offered to men, who did not even comprehend the meaning of democracy, a chance to establish a new despotism under the outward forms of freedom.

The decade after the death of Lincoln saw the American dream perverted and defiled. The self-sacrifice and idealism of the Civil War was followed by a reaction towards everything that was base. With Lincoln's restraining hand removed, the politicians of the North gave the signal for an orgy of plunder and vengeance. The South was treated like a conquered country overrun by barbarians, and handed over to the rule of negroes, poor whites and carpet-bag politicians, supported by Federal bayonets. The decent elements in the defeated states were ruined.

Meanwhile the nation as a whole, exhausted by the war, returned with feverish haste to its private concerns. Politics were left to professional politicians and to a swarm of pseudo-generals and colonels who then, as after every war, lived loose on society. They were quick to find that there were better paymasters than the public.

For those who knew how to manipulate figures and exploit the labour of others the second half of the nineteenth century was a golden time. The growth of the factory system, the development of railways and of cheap, rapid transport and the accessibility of the resources of a virgin continent offered opportunities such as had never existed before. They were used without morality or scruple. There was no Church in America, no aristocracy and no ancient and established institutions. The only obstacles in the way of the profiteers were the democratic constitution and the elected representatives of the people.

These the men of money proceeded to purchase and to turn, like everything else, to the production of more wealth. In the general lethargy and eclipse of public conscience that followed the Civil War it proved easy. All that the rich had to do was to subscribe liberally to the funds of both parties in return for a *quid pro quo* from the professional politicians. This was easily afforded, as there was half a continent to give away. In the course of little more than a generation the virgin resources of North America—land, forest, oil, coal, iron and precious minerals—were divided by successive governments among a few profiteers who proceeded to waste and exploit them with a total disregard both of the public's welfare and of the future. These resources were so vast that for a time their distribution was carried out unobserved, for almost everyone on a humble scale was doing the same. In the meantime the politicians retained the outward appearance of democracy by bandying about popular parrot-cries about liberty, while they organised the factory hands of the new industrial cities to vote as they were told.

Thus, during the quarter-century after the end of the Civil War, American politics became a thoroughly dirty game, and by the end of that period educated people knew it to be such and accepted it as inevitable. The Presidents who succeeded Lincoln were slight, unmeritable men who were elected merely because they were acceptable to the hard-faced ' bosses ' who ran the political parties. Nor did anyone much mind, neither the urban poor who knew no better nor the well-to-do who were busy coining money in a period of unlimited expansion. The only people who protested were the scattered farmers of the West, who found that the economic policy imposed on the nation by the bankers and industrialists of the East was bad for agricultural prices.

Thus, with the degradation of democratic machinery and

the growth of vast agglomerations of wealth, mostly owned by a few rich men in the names of artificial persons called Trusts, the old America seemed to be fast vanishing. In 1873 the Chief Justice of a Western state painted the picture of that change in ominous words. 'There is looming up,' he said, ' a new and dark power. I cannot dwell upon the signs and shocking omens of its advent. The accumulation of individual wealth seems to be greater than it ever has been since the downfall of the Roman Empire. The enterprises of the country are aggregating vast corporate combinations of unexampled capital, boldly marching, not for economic conquests only, but for political power. For the first time really in our politics, money is taking the field as an organized power. . . . The question will arise, . . . " Which shall rule—wealth or man; which shall lead—money or intellect; who shall fill public stations—educated and patriotic free men, or the feudal serfs of corporate capital ? " '

Into this world of declining morals and rising wealth was born, in 1858, Theodore Roosevelt. His father was a New York citizen of credit and renown, descended from a long line of Dutch merchants who for generations had lived and thrived on Manhattan Island. His mother was a member of an old Georgian family whose brothers fought valiantly for the South. The boy, however, was brought up in the Northern traditions of his father, and sometimes, when he had been naughty and was threatened with punishment, would vex his mother, whom he adored, by praying loudly for the annihilation of the Confederates.

His home life was as happy as an affectionate, well-ordered family, comfortable means, foreign travel and eager intellectual pursuits could make it. He grew up without any knowledge of poverty, restraint and persecution. But, though born with a silver spoon in his mouth, he suffered one serious handicap : his health was exceptionally delicate. His eyesight was bad, his speech defective and his frame racked with asthma, so that his earliest memories were of lying gasping in bed while his father and mother tried to ease and comfort him.

His father was wise enough to teach the boy to help himself. He told him to 'make his body,' and little Teddie set himself to do so. Long, boring hours with dumb-bells, horizontal bars and boxing gloves overcame the constitutional infirmities of his frame. Later he grew to be strong and vigorous, though he could never quite rid himself of the sense of physical inferiority induced by his early humiliations. Though he became robust and even burly and excelled at boxing, swimming and field sports, he always had about him something of the weakling's over-clamorous insistence on the importance of physical strength.

His conquest over the frailties of his own body strengthened his self-confidence and increased the already marked vehemence of his character. Even in his boyhood's diary he would alternate between passionate extremes of enthusiasm and despondency.

I am by the fire with not another light but it. . . . It is now after 5. All was dark except the fire. I lay by it and listened to the wind and thought of the times at home in the country when I lay by the fire with some hickory nuts. Again I was lying by the roaring fire (with the October wind shrieking outside) in the cheerful lighted room and I turned around half expecting to see it all again and stern reality forced itself upon me and I thought of the time that could come never, never, never.

The same gusto marked his youthful love of natural history—another result of his constitutional weakness, for debarred as a boy from games, he took to the collection of scientific specimens and pursued it, like everything else, with breathless zest. 'I picked up a salamander (*Diemictylus irridescens*). I saw a mouse . . . which I should judge to be a harvester mouse (*Hesperomys myoides*). We saw a baldheaded eagle (*Halietus leucocephalus*) sailing over the lake.' 'The loss to science ! the loss to science !' he was once heard moaning round the house after two dead mice had been removed to the dustbin from a wardrobe drawer in which he had secreted them.

At eighteen he went to Harvard—a little fellow, five foot

135

and a half high, with bright eyes and thin legs like pipestems. At first his oddities and exuberance made him something of a joke: at a time when it was considered bad form among undergraduates to move at more than a saunter, Roosevelt was always running. But before long the charm of that boundless vitality, joined as it was with a warm heart and a generous credulity and frankness, had its effect on his contemporaries. His boxing exploits, which he pursued with a reckless disregard of his spectacles, his dashing dogcart, his zest for amateur dramatics, all made him a man of mark. He might be little, but no one could help noticing him.

He gave himself to his work with the same enthusiasm, reading furiously and omnivorously. He was so busy acquiring knowledge, that it seemed doubtful whether he ever had time to think. For a while he proposed to make science a career, but gave it up when he found it entailed too much dry-as-dust detail: he had no desire, he said, to be a microscopist or a section-cutter. Instead he took to history and began a spirited work on the Naval War of 1812.

But his most conspicuous enthusiasm at Harvard was for a young lady. He met her through a College friend in the October of 1878, and loved her as soon as he saw ' her sweet, fair, young face.' Her name was Alice Lee and she lived at Chestnut Hill, Massachusetts. ' See that girl,' he told a friend, ' I am going to marry her. She won't have me, but I am going to have *her* ! '

And have her he did. At first she was a little alarmed and rather amused by his furious talk about his boxing and the living zoological specimens—snakes and reptiles—which he kept in his College rooms. But no woman could resist that impetuous wooing for long. They became engaged, and, though Roosevelt seemed to be in a constant fear that someone would run away with her before the happy day and was always threatening his fellow undergraduates with duels, he married her as soon as he had taken his degree. He was twenty-two at the time and she nineteen.

THEODORE ROOSEVELT

Roosevelt's father died when he was still at the University, leaving him heir to an income of nearly ten thousand dollars a year. After a trip with his bride to Europe, he settled down at New York with the idea of studying law. But he never got far with it, for he had found a new enthusiasm. For a young man of his position, it was a sufficiently strange one. Debased as was the state of federal politics in the post-Civil War epoch, that of state and municipal politics was far worse. These were regarded by the well-to-do and educated classes as a kind of scavenging work, performed in their interests by saloon keepers, liquor dealers and Irish, Italian and German hirelings, who took their orders from Party Bosses and lived on the corrupt by-products of city government. Such men manipulated the votes and controlled the administrative background of the ignorant alien herds who populated the slums of the big cities and fed the factory machines. Occasionally some particularly notorious piece of corruption would acquire the magnitude of a public scandal, and the rich would have to intervene to hush the matter up, but on the whole the system worked quietly and the business community was left in peace to pursue the wealth it coveted. The only thing it had to do to keep politics sweet was to subscribe to Party funds.

So, when young Theodore Roosevelt announced to his relations that he was going into local politics in order to help the cause of better government in New York city, there was something of a sensation. The machinations of the ' Tweed Ring ' and Tammany had long made New York a byword for corruption : and for a well-to-do young man of culture to concern himself in such a cesspool was as good as announcing he was going to work in the drains. It was, indeed, as a kind of sewage system that the business community viewed city politics—necessary, no doubt, but unsavoury.

But Roosevelt had made up his mind and it was impossible to deter him. His relations expostulated and declared that such an occupation was incompatible with member-

137

ship of the ruling class. He replied that those who refused to concern themselves with politics were not a ruling class, and that for his part he was not going to be done out of his rights as a self-governing citizen.

Roosevelt's ' break ' into ' peanut politics ' was as much a sensation to the politicians as it was to his relations. Into the underworld of ' Bosses ' and ' Heelers ' there marched a rich young man with an eye-glass, an evening dress and a Harvard voice. The party hucksters were convulsed with laughter : ' a joke, . . . a dude, the way he combed his hair, the way he talked, the whole thing ! ' But Roosevelt was not in the least put off by the coldness of his reception, for in the heat of his own enthusiasm he scarcely noticed it.

He went right through the mill. He started by attending the Twenty-first District Republican Club, then under the leadership of Jake Hess, a German. The club met in a low-ceilinged, smoke-filled room, reeking with liquor and furnished with wooden benches and spittoons. Its members were saloon keepers, ward heelers and sharks on the loose. But Roosevelt liked them as he liked or hated everyone : to him they were just human beings. And after a while, though they had been annoyed by his intervention, they began to like him.

After a year's apprenticeship he had a stroke of luck. A quarrel between two bosses and the friendship of an Irish party manager, named Joe Murray, who could not resist his eager vitality and charm, gave him an unlooked-for chance. He was nominated as a Republican candidate for the State Legislature, and elected. His success seems to have been due more to his backers than to his own methods of canvassing, according to Joe Murray's subsequent account.

We started in a German lager-beer saloon on Sixth avenue. . . . The saloon keeper's name was Carl Fischer. Hess was well acquainted with him. I knew him slightly. We had a small beer and Hess introduces T. R. to Fischer and Fischer says, ' By the way, Mr. Roosevelt, I hope you will do something for

138

us when you get up to Albany. We are taxed much out of our proportion to grocers, etc., and we have to pay $200 for the privilege.'
' Why that's not enough ! ' said T. R.
After we got out on the sidewalk we came to the conclusion that we had better stop the canvass right then and there. I says, ' Mr. Roosevelt, you go see your personal friends. Hess and I will look after this end. You can reach your personal friends, we can't.'

On January 2, 1882, Roosevelt took his place in the New York State Legislature at Albany. When he arose to address the Chairman with a high determined ' Mr. Speak-ah, Mr. Speak-ah ! ', delivered in the vernacular of the first families of New York, the house rocked. The press was equally entertained. ' Young Roosevelt of New York, a blond young man with eye-glasses, English side-whiskers and a Dundreary drawl in his speech, made his maiden effort as an orator . . . he said that it was a family quarrel . . . and the Republicans ought not to interfere. . . . He had talked with conspicuous men in commercial and financial circles, he said, and they did not care whether the deadlock was broken or not. " In fact," he said, " they felt r a w t h e r r e l i e v e d." ' So wrote the New York *Sun*. Yet here also the young man's charm and enthusiasm soon overcame initial dislike and made him one to be watched. He rose like a rocket.

Within three months he had thrown his first political bombshell, insisting on an enquiry into a well hushed-up scandal that concerned a former Attorney-General. His speech was received with indignant silence and he was warned of his folly. But with complete fearlessness he returned to the attack again and again, until in the end he carried his point. The ex-Attorney-General was, of course, exonerated, but Roosevelt had made his mark. Like all dudes he was a reformer, but unlike the rest of the species, a resolute, fearless and pertinacious one. And young as he was, he managed to focus the limelight on everything he did.

At the next election, though the tide was running strongly against the Republicans, Roosevelt was returned to Albany with an enormous majority. His Party flattered him by nominating him for the Speakership of the Assembly, though with the Democrats in a majority it was only an empty honour. But it was sufficient to turn his head a little, for he seems to have lost his sense of perspective for a while and even to have come a mild cropper. He put himself forward as the champion of sweated labour in the over-crowded New York tenements and spoke of carrying ' private morality into public office.' When in December 1883 the Party chiefs chose a new candidate for the Speakership, they passed his name over. ' This will not be a happy New Year to the exquisite Mr. Roosevelt,' wrote the New York *Sun*.

It was not. At this time he was in the habit of going home on Friday evenings for the week-end to New York, where his wife and mother were sharing a house. His married life was ideally happy, and on these occasions there would always be a joyful shout from Alice to the rest of the household, ' Teddy's here ! Teddy's here ! Come and share him.'

At the beginning of 1884 Alice was expectant, and on Tuesday, February 12, a little before her time, a child was born. Late next night, in a thick fog, Theodore arrived back from Albany, full of high spirits, to greet his wife and daughter. He found his mother dying of typhoid fever and his wife scarcely able to recognise him. The following day the two beings he loved most were dead.

He took his medicine of sorrow like a man and went back to his work. Six days later he moved the passage of a Bill in the Assembly at Albany. In the summer he went to Chicago as a delegate to the National Convention of the Republican Party, then at its lowest moral ebb after its quarter-century monopoly of political power in the pay of Big Business. At that time the leaders of the Party were cynically trying to nominate a notoriously dishonest politician as candidate for the approaching Presidential election. Roosevelt was one of a little group of younger Republicans—

contemptuously nicknamed 'Mugwumps' by the professional Bosses—who were anxious for a return to cleaner politics. They protested at this shameless imposition on the public and tried to substitute a better candidate. But the Caucus was triumphant and its candidate was nominated. 'The voice of the people might be the voice of God in fifty-one cases out of one hundred,' wrote Roosevelt sadly to his sister, ' but in the remaining forty-nine it is quite as likely to be the voice of the devil, or what is still worse, the voice of a fool.'

The election, in which the Democrat, Cleveland, was returned to the White House, proved him right: the Republican choice had been too much for the country to swallow. But unlike his fellow Mugwumps Roosevelt refused to 'bolt' his Party and remained a Republican. He had too much practical sense of the importance of long political association and too much of that fine natural affection for tried comrades which is the sweetest fruit of Party collaboration to do otherwise. But he could not bring himself to return to politics and after the election went off to the far West to nurse his shattered heart and mourn for Alice in solitude.

His rough friends of Albany and the Twenty-first District Club understood. 'You could not talk to him about it,' one of them said, ' you could see at once that it was a grief too deep. . . . There was a sadness about his face that he never had before. . . . He did not want anybody to sympathize with him. . . . He hiked away to the wilderness to get away from the world. . . . He went out there a broken-hearted man.' In the solitude of the bad lands of Dakota he wrote his wife's memorial.

She was born at Chestnut Hill, Massachusetts, on July 29, 1861. I first saw her on October 18, 1878, and loved her as soon as I saw her sweet, fair young face. We were betrothed on January 25, 1880, and married on October 27th of the same year. We spent three years of happiness such as rarely comes to man or woman. On February 12, 1884, her baby girl was born; she kissed it, and seemed perfectly well. Some hours afterward she, not knowing that she was in the slightest danger, but thinking only that she was falling into a sleep, became insensible, and died at two o'clock on Thursday afternoon, February 14, 1884, at 6, West Fifty-seventh Street, in New York. She was buried two days afterward, in Greenwood Cemetery.

She was beautiful in face and form, and lovelier still in spirit; as a flower she grew, and as a fair young flower she died. Her life had been always in the sunshine; there had never come to her a single great sorrow ; and none ever knew her who did not love and revere her for her bright, sunny temper and her saintly unselfishness. Fair, pure, and joyous as a maiden; loving, tender, and happy as a young wife; when she had just become a mother, when her life seemed to be but just begun, and when the years seemed so bright before her—then by a strange and terrible fate, death came to her.

And when my heart's dearest died, the light went from my life for ever.

Thereafter Roosevelt never referred to her again, but tried to put her loss out of his mind, as he had once set himself to overcome his childhood's weakness.

He settled down to a new, vigorous life on a cattle ranch in the Dakota bad lands. ' Black care rarely sits behind a rider whose pace is fast enough,' he gallantly told himself. Dakota was still the real West in those days, a ' land of vast silent spaces, of lonely rivers, and of plains where the wild game stared at the passing horseman.' It was inhabited by buffaloes, Red Indians and a quaint community of cowboys, roughriders, straight-shooters and melodrama sheriffs. It pleased Roosevelt, the sheltered child of New York and of Harvard, to make himself one of them. He did so with his customary gusto.

For 52,000 dollars he bought himself two ranches and stocked them with cattle. ' You would be amused to see me,' he wrote to a political friend, ' in my broad sombrero hat, fringed and beaded, buckskin shirt, horse-hide chaparajos or riding trousers, and cowboy boots, with braided bridle and silver spurs.' The wags of the local cowboy fraternity christened him ' Four Eyes ' on account of his spectacles. To them, as to the New York politicians, he was at first something of a joke, and the saloons of that wild land shook with laughter at tales of how the Harvard ranchman had attended cattle roundings with shrill cries of ' By Godfrey ! ' and ' Hasten forward quickly there ! ' But after a time they, too, learnt to love him and accepted him as one of themselves.

As for Roosevelt, he thoroughly enjoyed himself. For one who had been a weak, sickly child, it was wonderful to become a leading member of a hard-riding, straight-shooting community, to associate with dangerous characters like Hell-Roaring Bill Jones, to act as Deputy Sheriff and round up dangerous malefactors, to hold his own by virtue of his Harvard-learnt love of fisticuffs with daredevils and outlaws. He had become just what every healthy American boy wished himself to be—a hero of romance and a manly power for righteousness in a wild land.

And the land itself was good. It gave him health, and revived and quickened his boyish sense of beauty. ' In the spring when the thickets are green,' he wrote, ' the hermit-thrushes sing sweetly in them; when it is moonlight, the voluble, cheery notes of the thrashers or brown thrushes can be heard all night long. . . . Sometimes, in the early morning, when crossing the open, grassy plateaus, I have heard the prince of them all, the Missouri skylark [which] sings on the wing, soaring overhead and mounting in spiral curves until it can hardly be seen, while its bright, tender strains never cease for a moment.' In the winter the northern gales blew from the snow spaces of Canada and the Arctic. ' They roar in thunderous bass as they sweep across the prairie or whirl through the naked canyons; they shiver the great brittle cottonwoods, and beneath their rough touch the icy limbs of the pines that cluster in the gorges sing like the chords of an Aeolian harp. . . . All the land is granite; the great rivers stand still in their beds, as if turned to frosted steel. In the long nights there is no sound to break the lifeless silence. Under the ceaseless, shifting play of the Northern Lights, or lighted only by the brilliance of the stars, the snow-clad plains stretch out into dead and endless wastes

143

of glimmering white.' Here for Roosevelt was the source of the American dream, the frontier in which his country renewed its spirit in each generation, the land ' of scattered ranches, of herds of long-horned cattle, and of reckless riders who unmoved looked in the eyes of life or of death.'

His sojourn in the wilderness lasted for two years. Then the terrible winter of 1886–87 killed off his cattle, involving him in a loss of about 50,000 dollars. But the experience had been well worth it. He sold his ranches, bade farewell to the bad lands of Dakota, and returned to the East. After an unsuccessful attempt to re-enter New York politics he married his childhood's friend, Edith Carow, and built a home for her at Oyster Bay on Long Island. She set his happy-go-lucky financial affairs in order, gave him a peaceful and happy background to his life, and brought him five children whom he adored. He was ready now to begin his real career.

For a short while he experimented with literature: published in quick succession three books on hunting and ranching and a couple of biographies, and began a six-volume history on ' The Winning of the West.' It amused him to play the rôle of a man of letters. ' Mind you,' he told a friend, ' I'm a literary feller, not a politician, nowadays.' He became an active partner in the publishing firm of Putnams, and turned the business upside down with his theories as to how it should be run. Yet all this was only a side show, and when the chance came he returned joyously to politics.

In 1889 the Republicans were restored to power. Roosevelt asked to be employed and was appointed to a seat on the United States Civil Service Commission. It was a cynical move on the part of the Caucus men, for the efforts of aspiring reformers to substitute the merit system for the spoils system of appointment to the Civil Service were regarded as a harmless joke, and the Commission had been devised solely to deflect their activities into academic channels. By sending Roosevelt to this despised backwater they supposed that they had heard the last of him. But in fact their troubles were only beginning. For Roosevelt brought to the Commission the same dæmonic energy that he applied to everything else. Onto this quiet department of administration there now poured the limelight of that dazzling publicity which accompanied his whole career. Almost at once he got himself uproariously involved in a widely advertised dispute with the Postmaster-General, John Wanamaker, who in defiance of the principles of Civil Service Reform had just replaced 30,000 fourth-class Democratic Postmasters by good Republican supporters. Wanamaker was the leading ' fat cat ' of the Party and became extremely angry when opposed by a youthful Civil Service Commissioner. ' Then damn John Wanamaker,' said Roosevelt explosively and made Civil Service Reform a headline matter. The pressmen were delighted to find a politician who never minced his words and brought the breezy atmosphere of the prairies even into state despatches. ' Cleveland's postmaster at Milwaukee,' he reported of one political appointee, ' is about as thorough-paced a scoundrel as I ever saw—an oily-gammon, church-going specimen.' The reporters served him up, indiscreet phrases and all, piping hot to an enchanted public.

Roosevelt remained a member of the Commission for six years, the greater part of the time as its Chairman. By the publicity he gave to the ' merit system ' of recruiting the Civil Service he brought this hitherto neglected question before the general public, who thus for the first time began to appreciate its advantages. The Party Bosses were, of course, furious, for the spoils system was the life-blood of their organisation. But they found that they could do little against a man who met every criticism with a rejoinder, which generally received far better press publicity than their original charge. When angry members of Congress tried to avenge themselves by cutting down the appropriations for Civil Service examinations, Roosevelt retaliated by omitting to hold examinations in their electoral districts and so got them into trouble with their own constituents. By appealing to the people over the heads of the politicians he let a new breath of democracy into the vitiated public life of America.

When the Democrat, Grover Cleveland, was re-elected President, Roosevelt retained his office, but resigned it in 1895 to take up an appointment offered him by a reforming Mayor of New York on the bipartisan Police Board of that city. Bright as was the limelight which had been centred on the Civil Service Commission, it was nothing to what now became the lot of the New York Police Board. The Service was riddled with corruption, and the police, encouraged by their political chiefs, had grown accustomed to treat the law solely as a means of extracting money from law-breakers. For every crime there was a recognised tariff, known to all the saloon keepers, prostitutes, gamblers and gangsters of New York.

This was just the kind of underhand dealing against which Theodore Roosevelt loved to pit himself: here was a man's work to his hand. Jubilantly he told a friend that he was about to assail some of the ablest and shrewdest men in the city, who would soon have to fight for their lives. He was as good as his word. Before long the people of New York, who did not love their police, were thrilled to hear that erring patrolmen were being visited on their rounds at night by a sturdy figure with glasses and gleaming teeth. 'Sing, heavenly muse,' exulted the New York *World*, 'the sad dejection of our poor policemen. We have a real Police Commissioner. . . . His teeth are big and white, his eyes are small and piercing, his voice is rasping. He makes our policemen feel as the little froggies did when the stork came to rule them. His heart is full of reform, and a policeman in full uniform, with helmet, revolver and night club, is no more to him than a plain, every day human being. . . . The new commissioner cannot be described as an intellectual type . . . but he does look like a determined man.' Soon 'Teddy the Scorcher' had become the hero of New York.

Having disciplined the City Police, Roosevelt set himself

the harder task of teaching the people to respect the law. This was a less popular occupation. There began an entertaining but sturdily fought duel between the Police Commissioner and the New York public over the enforcement of the liquor laws. According to the law no intoxicating liquor could be consumed within the city on Sunday, but thanks to the levy paid by the saloon keepers to the police the populace had hitherto experienced no difficulty in obtaining its Sabbath drinks. Roosevelt announced his resolve of enforcing the law, however ridiculous or unjust it might be. 'I do not deal with public sentiment,' he declared. 'I deal with the law. . . . I am going to see if we cannot break the licence forthwith of any saloon keeper who sells on Sunday. . . . To allow a lax enforcement of the law means to allow it to be enforced just as far as the individual members of the police force are willing to wink at its evasion.'

Within a few weeks the whole city was in an uproar. The Press was in arms, and protest meetings and giant processions were staged by the workers' organisations and the liquor trade. At one rally the members marched past the Police Commissioner with banners borne before a coffin labelled 'Teddyism,' and followed by German drinking societies pathetically holding up empty beer *steins.* One stout German, peering through his glasses as he marched past, called out angrily, ' *Wo ist der Roosevelt?* ' only to be answered by a grinning Police Commissioner, ' *Hier bin ich.*' His courage and the good humour with which he entered into the spirit of the city's protest did him no harm. The people admired his firmness and liked him the more for it.

His two years' service in the New York Police Commission gave Roosevelt an experience of something that few men of his class knew anything about—the social conditions under which the common people of a great city lived and worked. By temperament and upbringing he had all the traditional American belief in independence and hatred of governmental interference. But now his work, by giving him ' a glimpse of the real life of the swarming millions,' made him realise

147

that the promise of the American dream was not being fulfilled in practice. The alien workers of the industrial underworld were not getting a fair deal either from the state or from the wealth that employed them. He began to see that they needed protection against those whom he had always supposed to be their natural allies.

By the time that he was thirty-six Roosevelt was recognised as a coming man. To a discerning few his wonderful vitality seemed one of the most hopeful factors in America. His circle of intimate friends included many of the most brilliant men of the time. Among them were Taft and Henry Adams, the painter John Sargent, and the Englishmen, Cecil Spring Rice, James Bryce and Kipling. The last has left a picture of Roosevelt's amazing flow of talk, as he took his ease of an evening in the society of his peers, 'until the universe seemed to be spinning around and Theodore was the spinner.'

In 1896 Roosevelt first became involved in a great national issue. It was the year of the agrarian revolution and the free-silver controversy, when the long-suffering farmers of the West, maddened by falling prices and heavy mortgages, stampeded the Democratic Caucus and nominated a golden-voiced young orator from Nebraska named Bryan to lead them against the bankers and industrialists of the East. Bryan's oration at the Democratic Convention at Chicago sent all America into rival camps. ' We are fighting,' he told the delegates, ' in the defence of our homes, our families, and posterity. We have petitioned and our petitions have been scorned. We have entreated, and our entreaties have been disregarded. We have begged, and they have mocked when our calamity came. . . . The great cities are in favour of the gold standard. We reply that the great cities rest upon our broad and fertile prairies. Burn down your cities and leave our farms and your cities will spring up again as if by magic, but destroy our farms, and the grass will grow in the streets of every city in the country. . . . If they dare to come out into the open field and defend the gold standard as a good thing, we will fight them to the

uttermost. Having behind us the producing masses of this
nation and the world, the labouring interests, and the toilers
everywhere, we will answer their demand for a gold standard
by saying to them: You shall not press down upon the brow
of labour this crown of thorns. You shall not crucify
mankind upon a cross of gold ! '

To the business men of the East this cry from the
tortured West was rank heresy. The threat to inflate the
currency with the unlimited coinage of free silver seemed to
them a fundamental dishonesty: it was only theft under
another name. The New York *Tribune* described the
Democratic crusade as a ' malicious conspiracy against the
honour and integrity of the nation,' and Bryan as a ' wretched,
rattle-pated boy, posing in vapid vanity and mouthing
resounding rottenness . . . the vocal leader of the league
of hell.'

Into that historic Presidential Election Roosevelt threw
himself with all the ardour of his temperament. He was
an Easterner, a member of the merchant class, and a
Republican, and the Republicans were the champions of
what was termed ' sound money.' He believed in gold as
passionately and as foolishly as Bryan in silver. The
Republican Caucus did not love Roosevelt, but it was no
moment for picking and choosing supporters. In that
tornado of a campaign every hand was needed. The young
New York Police Commissioner played a notable part in
the oratorical battle of that fall. It ended amid intense
excitement in a Republican victory and Bryan's defeat by
half a million votes.

In the spring, restored to the Party fold, Roosevelt left New
York and returned to Washington as a junior member of
President McKinley's administration. He succeeded in
securing the Assistant Secretaryship of the Navy, a service
in which he had been interested since his youthful work on
the Naval War of 1812. At that moment it happened to be
a most opportune appointment, for it enabled Roosevelt to
do his country a signal service.

For the past two years Cuba, the last outpost of Spain in

the Old World, had been carrying on a desperate rebellion against the mother country. It was one of a long and apparently endless series of conflicts, waged with appalling ferocity on both sides, in which the sympathies of almost every American were with the Cubans. Ever since the promulgation of the Monroe Doctrine the United States had opposed armed intervention by European states in the New World. There seemed no reason why that of Spain in Cuba should any longer be regarded as an exception.

Though most chivalrous young Americans, brought up on tales of their ancestors' heroic rebellion against England, wanted to help expel the Spaniards, President Cleveland, and his Republican successor McKinley, deferred to the demand of the banking and business world and tried to keep the peace. In this attitude, the new Assistant Secretary of the Admiralty did not see eye to eye with the trading community from which he sprang or with his political chiefs. In some recent newspaper articles he had condemned the ' timidity of wealth ' and praised the ' rugged fighting qualities ' by which in the last resort great nations live. He now put himself forward as the representative of an adolescent America grown at last to her full stature between the two oceans, and resolved to play her part in the affairs of a wider world. He told the National Republican Club that he favoured the establishment of a Navy that could sustain the honour of the American flag and uphold the Monroe Doctrine in its entirety against all comers.

As the ' prophet of American preparedness,' Roosevelt was all for intervention in the dispute waging off the American coast. ' I would regard a war with Spain from two viewpoints,' he wrote: ' First, the advisability on the ground both of humanity and self-interest of interfering on behalf of the Cubans, and of taking one more step toward the complete freeing of America from European domination; second, the benefit done to our people by giving them something to think of which isn't material gain, and especially the benefit done our military forces by trying both the Army and Navy in actual practice.' As soon as he came to the Admiralty he began to make preparations, often unknown to his elderly and cautious chief, against a conflict which he regarded as inevitable. The most important of these was to secure the appointment of the brilliant George Dewey, the commodore of the American Asiatic Squadron. When war broke out in April 1898, Dewey, acting on Roosevelt's unauthorised instructions, sent during his chief's absence from the office, was able to enter Manila Bay and destroy the Spanish Pacific Squadron with an almost negligible loss to his own men.

Roosevelt himself, feeling that it would be dishonest in him not to take an active part in a war which he had so strenuously advocated, resigned his Assistant-Secretaryship and to the mingled dismay and amusement of his friends volunteered for active service. He obtained a commission as Lieutenant-Colonel of a regiment of horse. This was the famous corps of Rough Riders, made up of cowboys, ranchmen, athletes and New York City Police, and recruited largely by himself from those whom he had encountered in his varied career.

It was a quaint outfit. 'Pretty nifty, eh, captain,' was the reply of one of its members to an official enquiry from his superior. Roosevelt explained that it was recruited 'from among classes who do not look at life in the spirit of decorum and conventionality that obtains in the East.' One of its officers, who in after years kept its former commander in touch with his old comrades' activities, left some startling reports on its more remarkable products.

I have the honor to report, that Comrade Ritchie, late of Troop G, is in jail at Trinidad, Colorado, on a charge of murder. . . . It seems that our comrade . . . became involved in a controversy . . . and it appears that the fellow he killed called him very bad names, even going so far as to cast reflections on the legitimacy of our comrade's birth. He killed the fellow instantly, shooting him through the heart. . . .

Also have to report that Comrade Webb, late of Troop D, has just killed two men at Bisbee, Arizona. Have not yet received the details of our comrade's trouble . . . but understand that . . . he was entirely justified in the transaction. . . .

THE AMERICAN IDEAL

Comrade Johnson, late of Troop G, has been converted and is now a full-fledged Evangelist, laboring in the Lord's vineyard among the Swedish and Norwegian sailors. . . . One of his illustrations of the presence of Our Savior and of the fact that Our Savior sees everything and knows everything is as follows: ' I tell you boys that Jesus Christ sees us all the time; I tell you boys He has an eye just as sharp as a rat.'

Another of Roosevelt's old comrades-in-arms is reported to have written to him after his elevation to the Presidency in the following touching vein: ' Dear Colonel, I am in trouble. I shot a lady in the eyes, but I did not intend to hit the lady: I was shooting at my wife.'

After a few weeks of preliminary training and some spirited wire-pulling which culminated in the virtual storming of a transport, the regiment was transhipped to the front. Here in an atmosphere of tropical jungle, waving sombreros and enthusiastic press reporters, who found in the picturesque Rough Riders just what they were seeking, Lieutenant-Colonel Roosevelt became the hero of the nation. On July 1, amid universal confusion, he led the charge up San Juan Hill. ' San Juan was the great day of my life. . . . I waved my hat and went up the hill with a rush.' Two days later, when no one was expecting it to do so, Santiago fell. The war was virtually over. The newspaper accounts were such that the American people supposed that it had been won principally by Roosevelt and the Rough Riders.

This did not make him popular with the leaders of the Regular Army, nor did his subsequent sensible but highly insubordinate insistence that the troops should return to their native country instead of lingering on the scene of their victory, as their generals seemed to wish them to do, till they were all dead of malaria. But the disapproval of the Higher Command did not detract from the enthusiasm of the people of America: it only made them the more delighted. After his month's campaigning, Roosevelt came home with almost as great a prestige as Grant had done after winning the Civil War. It was not the first time in the history of the country that military glory had pointed the way to the White House.

152

But whatever the people might desire and Roosevelt himself secretly hope, the Party Bosses had not the slightest intention of letting this dangerously independent man become President. It happened, however, at the moment that they were badly in need of someone who was well thought of by the public to stand as Republican candidate for the Governorship of New York State, where the extravagance and corruption of their late nominee had endangered their hold on the electorate. In the existing state of opinion Roosevelt was the one man whom they could hope to get in. He stood and, accompanied by Rough Riders and buglers, and wearing and waving a gigantic black-rimmed felt hat, won what with any other candidate would have been a hopeless struggle. ' I have played it in bull luck this summer,' he said. ' First, to get into the war; and then to get out of it; then to get elected.'

Having once caught the imagination of the great American public, Roosevelt was too much of an artist ever to let it go. His two years as Governor of New York State were picturesque and full of incident. He proceeded to do what he called introduce the Ten Commandments into the government at Albany. He reformed the Civil Service, enforced the Factory Law and regulated ' sweat shops.' At least he appeared to do these things, for even Roosevelt's power for righteousness in the State politics of the eighteen-nineties did not amount to very much. All the while he kept his eye on the next Presidential Election. So did the American younger generation, who watched his career with pleasure and amusement.

Not so the Party Bosses. They had taken up this dangerously aggressive, hat-waving man for their own purpose, but having done so, they could not get rid of him. He broke all their rules, refused to accept their suggestions (in other words, commands) for appointments, and in the friendliest and frankest manner lectured them on his views about the proper relations between a Party Caucus and the Governor of a State. He would certainly, he told them, confer with them, as with everyone else who seemed to him to have any knowledge of and interest in public affairs, and he would do so in the sincere hope that there might always result harmony of opinion and purpose. But he added that while he would always try to get on well with them, they must with equal sincerity strive to do what he regarded as essential for the public good, because in the last resort, after hearing what everyone had to say, he should have to act in all cases as his own judgment and conscience dictated, since he was the head of the State and not a faction leader.

You say that we must nominate some Republican who ' will carry out the wishes of the organization,' and add that ' I have not yet made up my mind who that man is.' Of one thing I am certain, that, to have it publicly known that the candidate, whoever he may be, ' will carry out the wishes of the organization,' would insure his defeat; for such a statement implies that he would merely register the decrees of a small body of men inside the Republican Party, instead of trying to work for the success of the party as a whole and of good citizenship generally. It is not the business of a Governor to ' carry out the wishes of the organization ' unless these wishes coincide with the good of the Party and of the State. If they do, then he ought to have them put into effect; if they do not, then as a matter of course he ought to disregard them. To pursue any other course would be to show servility; and a servile man is always an undesirable— not to say a contemptible—public servant. A Governor should, of course, try in good faith to work with the organization; but under no circumstances should he be servile to it, or ' carry out its wishes ' unless his own best judgment is that they ought to be carried out. I am a good organization man myself, as I understand the word ' organization,' but it is in the highest degree foolish to make a fetish of the word ' organization ' and to treat any man or any small group of men as embodying the organization. The organization should strive to give effective, intelligent, and honest leadership to and representation of the Republican Party, just as the Republican Party strives to give wise and upright government to the State. When what I have said ceases to be true of either organization or party, it means that the organization or party is not performing its duty, and is losing the reason for its existence.

Such language had never been used by a State Governor to his Party chiefs before. It was this sort of thing that made 'lean rat' Platt, the great Republican Boss, almost beside himself with rage.

The worst of it was that Roosevelt was so outwardly reasonable and even unanswerable, so genial in his address and so confoundedly popular with the most unexpected people. He radiated charm, and, unlike most men of charm, he was an indomitable fighter. The only result of rebuking him was to be rebuked, and generally publicly, in return. For he had a maddening habit of appealing to the public, and often the Party's own supporters, over the Party's head. There seemed to be no way of either getting rid of him or controlling him.

On one thing the Caucus chiefs were resolved: that in no event should Roosevelt receive the Republican nomination for the forthcoming Presidential Election. Fortunately that good, colourless man, McKinley, was ready to serve a second time, and his chief supporter, Mark Hanna of Ohio, got him renominated without opposition. Then Platt had a stroke of inspiration and proposed to nominate Roosevelt for Vice-President. His associates were at first much shocked, but the logic of the plan was tempting. It was the business of Vice-Presidents to preside over the Senate, to entertain largely in the discreet and rarefied air of Washington, to keep out of the noisier streets of politics and generally to be seen and not heard. This was precisely what every good party man wanted Roosevelt to do. Four years of this honourable and dignified seclusion would deprive him of the public ear and enable him to be shelved for ever. The only alternative was to leave him another four years in the Governorship of New York, from which there was no practicable way of removing him and which was universally regarded as a stepping stone to a Presidential nomination. The Party chiefs, scandalised as they were at the prospect of putting Roosevelt in the Vice-President's stately chair, were forced to admit the force of Platt's bold argument.

Of course, Roosevelt, with his eye on the Presidential Election of 1904, at first refused to accept. In fact he issued a declaration to that effect. ' It is proper for me *to state definitely that under no circumstances* could I or would I,' he said, ' accept the nomination for the Vice-presidency. . . . My duty is here in the State whose people chose me to be governor.' But the Party chiefs knew their man's enthusiasm and childlike vanity, and guessed that when the time came he would be unable to resist the reception that they were guilelessly preparing for him at the Republican National Convention. It happened just as they had planned, and as one of Roosevelt's backers prophesied to Mrs. Roosevelt : ' then—just a bit late—you will see your handsome husband come in and bedlam will break loose, and he will receive such a demonstration . . . as no one else will receive. And being a devoted wife you will be very proud and happy. Then, some two or three days later, you will see your husband unanimously nominated for Vice-President of the United States.'

So it came to pass that in the spring of 1900 Roosevelt was nominated for the Vice-Presidency of the United States, and in the autumn duly elected. During the election he bore the brunt of the Republican campaign against Bryan, making 673 speeches in 567 towns and cities and showing himself to over three million of his fellow citizens in a journey of over 21,000 miles. He had become even more of a national figure than before. ' Don't any of you realize,' said Mark Hanna, who had never approved of Platt's plan, ' that there's only one life between this madman and the White House ? '

For the Caucus had taken a risk. By the Constitution of the United States, should the President die in office, the rest of his term is filled by the Vice-President. But McKinley was not an old man and there was no reason to think he would die. In the spring of 1901, when he entered upon his second term of office, everything seemed to be going according to plan. The new Vice-President settled down to his harmless duties in the chair of the Senate, and did nothing more startling than enrol himself as a student at the Washington Law School in order to polish up his knowledge of constitutional practice. It began to look as though they had done with him for ever. But one of Roosevelt's friends remarked, ' I would not like to be in McKinley's shoes. He has a man of destiny behind him.' And another, an Englishman, observed, ' Theodore Roosevelt is the hope of American politics.'

A Polish anarchist did the rest. That autumn McKinley was shot while attending the Pan-American Exhibition at Buffalo. The news reached Roosevelt on Lake Champlain, where he was spending a sporting holiday. He hurried to his chief's side, only to find him recovering favourably and apparently out of all danger. After discussing affairs with him, he returned to his holiday. Then a second and more serious message came. A breakneck journey of four hundred miles brought him once more to McKinley's side. But Mark Hanna's McKinley was dead and Theodore Roosevelt, at forty-two, became President of the United States.

When this sanguine, open-hearted, courageous man, with the mind of a boy and the heart of a lion, assumed the supreme office of the Western world, the democratic experiment seemed to many observers to be at its last gasp. Throughout recorded time it had always been so: Greece, Rome, Holland, seventeenth-century England had each tried this appealing, elusive form of government, and each had failed in the same way. Human nature proved too weak to rule itself: old tyrants arose under new names, and under cover of the letter of the democratic law cynically defied the spirit. In America a brazen-faced plutocracy, by utilising the forms of self-government in a way that would have made a dog laugh, had concentrated all real power in their own hands. Vast artificial corporations, creating monopolies in the articles which they sold to the public, were solemnly recognised by the Law as individual persons and secured in their liberties as if they were human beings. The republic of the pigmies had been invaded by giants. No private citizen could stand against the Trusts. They were controlled by men like Rockefeller and Morgan, who sometimes possessed genius but scarcely ever had the slightest respect for democracy. To such men, and their employees, the Party Bosses who worked the political game for them, the Jeffersonian ideal was mere moonshine—the dream of a mugwump. 'The public be damned,' said the great Vanderbilt.

The American earth was the millionaires' and all that belonged to it. 'It matters not one iota,' said one of them, 'what Political Party is in power or what President holds the reins of office. We are not politicians or public thinkers; we are rich; we own America; we got it, God knows how, but we intend to keep it if we can by throwing all the tremendous weight of our support, our influence, our money, our political connections, our purchased senators, our hungry congressmen, our public-speaking demagogues into the scale against any legislature, any political platform, any presidential campaign that threatens the integrity of our estate.' And the politicians were there—the Bosses, the Senators and the Congressmen in their Assemblies and the heelers in their wards and districts—to see that the earth continued to belong to the millionaires. After the defeat of Bryan and the rebellious West, there seemed no reason why it should not remain so.

There arose, to challenge their domination, this glorious, bull-like fool, who did not even seem to know that democracy was dying and acted as if he believed it was still flourishing in its mighty youth, who spoke of reason and righteousness to men like Platt and twinkled friendship out of his gleaming, bespectacled eyes at every scheming rogue that walked the earth. The extraordinary thing about Roosevelt was that by believing a thing he made others believe it too, just as by crediting scoundrels with good as well as evil, he almost made them good. To him the American dream was a reality. Just when his countrymen were losing faith in it he made it seem a reality again.

Roosevelt's Presidency checked the crude materialism that

since Lincoln's death had monopolised American politics. Bribery, corruption, base dealing remained during and after his time, but while he reigned in the White House the Stars and Stripes could be seen again, flapping high in the sky above the misty Washington swamps. To ardent young America he typified all the unspoken aspirations of its spirit, chivalry, generosity and justice. He was every young American in his most expansive moments, only a hundred times more so—great-hearted, roaring, impulsive Teddy. He was the man for whom a great nation shamefully betrayed was waiting. And if the world of actual fact, that measures achievement by the statute book and the balance-sheet, protests, it should be answered that man does not live by bread alone.

But Roosevelt was not merely the blind bull in the china shop that he appeared to his frightened enemies and his old friends the Bosses. There was a method in his madness that made him all the more difficult to resist, even though in the hands of an astute man it could be used to lead him. Believing that there was virtue in all men till he had proved the contrary, he was able to get the best out of them. ' My constant effort,' he once told a friend, ' was to appeal to the side that was decent and to get the man to act rightly. . . . I never broke with any man until I became convinced that it was hopeless to get the good out of him.' This had its practical value.

Nor was he a fanatic. His heart was the most impetuous ever formed, but the bent of his mind was essentially moderate. ' Let us remember,' he loved to say, ' that our success depends upon our not trying to accomplish everything.' He had a curiously shrewd eye for a crank and a mugwump, and, despite his occasional flouting of it, knew how to work with his Party: save for his outbreak in the bitterness of 1912, his bludgeonings of it were always meditated.

His passionate and militant desire to be in the right and prove himself so with a big drum, though often inconvenient, inspired great confidence in his followers, for he was always ready to share his moral glow with them and delighted to take the whole nation crusading with him. The guilty conscience that weakens the action of other men never impeded his, for he never doubted his own integrity, as witness his answers in court under cross-examination:

Query. How did you know that substantial justice was done?

Roosevelt. Because I did it, because . . . I was doing my best.

Query. You mean to say that when you do a thing thereby substantial justice is done?

Roosevelt. I do. When I do a thing I do it so as to do substantial justice. I mean just that.

For every charge against his own good faith and his followers' he had an immediate answer. Somebody once said of him that if the mutilated remains of his grandmother were discovered in his cellar, he would at once have been able to produce a letter proving his innocence of the crime.

His supreme strength lay in the fact that he caused men to love him. Wherever he went he made friends, and enemies too, but the passionate enthusiasm of the former outweighed the hatred of the latter. They were to be found in every walk of life, for throughout his varied career—at Harvard, in the political clubs of New York, in the bad lands of Dakota, at the Admiralty, in the Police and in the Army— he had gathered devoted adherents. In a sense he had identified himself with the whole American nation.

He needed all the strength that this gave him, as well as all the prestige of his great position in the fight against vested interests which was before him. As soon as he became President he countered Wall Street fears and the veiled rumours that were spread about him in the world of high finance, by declaring that he would follow the policy of his predecessor. But his very first message to Congress showed that he was going to attack the Trusts. By announcing that they must be regarded as existing only by permission of the State to administer the riches and power they had received on behalf of the people, he challenged the whole claim of the millionaires to own America. The message sent a thrill of hope through a nation that had begun to despair of ever making any headway against corporate wealth and professional politics. The new President had made it clear that he regarded himself as the leader of the people, and, as such, the enemy of those who had dared to usurp the people's power.

There began a long duel between Roosevelt and the financiers. His first assault was on the monster Trusts, whose powers, vested by the law as they were with the rights of individual persons, were an ironic travesty of the democratic ideal. In November 1901 came the incorporation by the house of Morgan of the Northern Securities Company, with a capital of four hundred million dollars and the virtual monopoly of the railways of the North-west. Roosevelt challenged its legality on the grounds that it transgressed the limitations of the Sherman Act, which had been passed some years before in deference to the popular outcry against the unlimited Trust, but which had been left in abeyance by discreet politicians and judges. But it had never been the new President's way to leave laws in abeyance. Morgan was amazed. 'If we have done anything wrong,' he is reported to have said to the President, 'send your man [meaning the Attorney-General] to my man [naming one of his lawyers] and they can fix it up.' He appeared to regard Roosevelt merely as a big rival operator who was threatening to ruin his interests in order to be bought out.

But Roosevelt could not be bought out. He felt no enmity to the house of Morgan or to any other financial corporation as such, but he had no intention of allowing them to regard themselves as outside the law. They must come inside it or face the implacable opposition of the properly constituted representatives of the people. He demanded and, through the action of the Federal Attorney-General, ultimately secured the dissolution of the Northern Securities Company.

The next phase of the fight between the power of the nation and the power of organised but irresponsible wealth came with the President's intervention in the great Coal

THE AMERICAN IDEAL

Strike of 1902. In the early summer of that year 140,000 miners, who were shamefully paid and treated by the monopolistic federation of mine-owners who employed them, came out on strike in favour of an increase in wages and a shorter working day. They were blindly opposed by their employers, who resisted all attempts at negotiation and, on the doubtful ground that business was ' not a religious, sentimental or academic proposition,' denied them even a hearing. The sublime arrogance of the mine-owners was well expressed by the reply which one of their number, George F. Baer, made to a well-meaning philanthropist who had tried to intervene, that the rights and interests of the labouring man were in the safe and proper keeping, not of labour agitators, but of ' the Christian men to whom God in his infinite wisdom had given the control of the property interests of this country.'

The claim that the Almighty had created the monopoly in anthracite coal was a little too much for American public opinion, and Baer's letter became notorious. With the approach of winter it was plain that the interests of the nation as a whole were about to be compromised by the continuance of the strike. Roosevelt, as President, holding that the dispute ought not to be regarded by the combatants as a mere private affair of their own, resolved to intervene. ' I felt,' he explained, ' that the crisis was not one in which I could act on the Buchanan principle of striving to find some Constitutional reason for inaction, and that the first thing to do was to try to get . . . both sides together to see whether by an appeal to their patriotism I could bring about an agreement.'

Early in October he succeeded in effecting a meeting between the owners and miners. The latter were conciliatory and reasonable, but the owners continued to display the same arrogance that they had shown from the start and refused to yield an inch. The mines, they maintained, were their private property, and it was an impertinence for the President or anyone else to concern himself in their affairs. Baer was so rude that Roosevelt completely lost his temper.

'If it wasn't for the high office I hold,' he told a friend afterwards, 'I would have taken him by the seat of his breeches and the nape of the neck and chucked him out of that window.'

By the Constitution the President possessed no further powers to enforce a settlement on an unwilling party. But the original Constitution had never envisaged a position in which the action of a few individuals could penalise the whole community, and the great position of President had been created to protect the essential rights of the citizens of the United States. He fell back, therefore, on the fundamental rights of government and in the name of the nation invoked 'the old common-law doctrine under which any peasant could take wood that was not his, if necessary for the preservation of life and health in winter weather.' Interference with what appeared to be the rights of private individuals was thus presented in its real guise as a return to the original principles on which the nation was founded. The President called out the Army and announced his intention of taking over and working the mines in the interests of the American people if the mine-owners and their employees could not agree to work them themselves. As soon as they saw that he meant to carry out his word, the 'wooden-headed gentry,' as he privately termed them, climbed down and, after being offered a verbal formula to save their faces, agreed to arbitration.

In this Roosevelt had considerably stretched the authority of President. 'I did not usurp power,' he said, 'but I did greatly broaden the use of executive power.' But it was an extension of presidential action that, however distasteful to sectional interests and to conservative lawyers and politicians, met with the overwhelming approval of the people, for it was undertaken on behalf of the man in the street and the man on the prairie for whom the nation had been founded. It was a return to the ideal of the American fathers, to whose spirit Roosevelt appealed when his enemies were only appealing to its dead letter. Men felt that they were being offered substantial justice instead of warped law, and that the President was acting as Washington or Lincoln would have acted in holding the balance fair between the different elements in the community. ' A man who is good enough to shed his blood for his country,' he declared in a speech at Lincoln's Springfield, ' is good enough to be given a square deal aftcrwards. More than that no man is entitled to and less than that no man shall have.'

Yet in placing himself at the head of the nation in opposition to the sectional and aristocratic interests who were exploiting it, Roosevelt did not act so much as a demagogue as in the authentic tradition of popular kingship. It was like King Richard placing himself at the head of Wat Tyler's leaderless men. In this he followed the steps of all the great American Presidents who had gone before him, from Washington to Lincoln. The action that he took against the Trusts and the irresponsible manipulators of capital was as much, he maintained, in their own interests as that of the nation which he defended against their rapacity. Though they were too blind to see it, failure to take such action could only end in their own ultimate destruction at the hands of an enraged people. And Roosevelt, who himself came from the monied classes, did not wish to see the men of enterprise and capital destroyed: within the framework of the Constitution, though never outside it, they had an important part to contribute to the common weal. ' The labour unions shall have a square deal,' he announced, ' and the corporations shall have a square deal.' Most important of all the nation as a whole should. It was this conservative and even friendly attitude to the very interests which he challenged on behalf of the public that made Roosevelt appear an enigma to persons of purely logical and academic mind. ' Th' trusts,' said the immortal Mr. Dooley in good-humoured mockery of his policy, ' are heejous monsthers built up by th' enlightened intherprise iv th' men that have done so much to advance progress in our beloved country. . . . On wan hand I wud stamp thim undher fut; on th' other not so fast.' Yet it was this very attitude, uninspiring as it may seem to the man of the study, that made Roosevelt so formidable a reformer in his own generation.

Roosevelt based his attack on irresponsible wealth on his support by the people as a whole. He neglected no opportunity of strengthening his position with them. No President, not even Lincoln, ever kept more open house. There was a constant stream to the White House of callers from every part of the nation, who had come, like the three old black-coated farmers of Roosevelt's proudest story, to shake, as they said, that honest hand. The President's youth and boundless vitality enabled him to take this wearing addition to his duties in his stride, and his manifest pleasure in greeting his visitors sent them home delighted. ' That is very kind of you,' he said to an old lady who explained that she had come all the way from Florida just in order to see a live President ; ' persons from up here go all the way to Florida just to see a live alligator.' The Press, whom he could handle as no man living, made his blunt geniality, his robust good humour and self-confidence familiar to the whole nation. Everything about him, America saw with delight, was a hundred per cent. American—his assurance, his cordiality, his beaming grin, his hearty handshake and even his glorious indiscretions. Teddy was something more than a successful politician established for a spell at the White House—he was a national institution.

In nothing was Roosevelt more characteristic of the new America than in his foreign policy. The victory over Spain and the capture of the Philippines had meant an uneasy shifting of the American dream, for America was now no longer responsible only for herself. She had become a world power with world responsibilities. Roosevelt made her conscious of them and of her own strength to shoulder them. Not only did he triumph (perhaps a little brutally) in the Alaska boundary dispute with Canada, and compel Germany to toe the line in her controversy with Venezuela, making her firebrand of a Kaiser ' shinny on his own side of the line,' but he constituted his country policeman of the Western world and of the Pacific. He established sound government and the amenities of civilisation in the unruly islands taken over from Spain, and proclaimed at the same time their ultimate independence so soon as they should show themselves able to rule themselves. He held that it was the business of the United States to assure the same ordered blessings as she enjoyed herself to all the dwellers in the Western world. Further than that his imperialism did not go. 'As for annexing the island,' he remarked of San Domingo, 'I have about the same desire . . . as a gorged boa-constrictor might have to swallow a porcupine wrong-end-to.'

All this was only the natural extension of the Monroe Doctrine proper to an age when America had outgrown her early stature. Her interest, Roosevelt realised, was 'to see all neighbouring countries stable, orderly, and prosperous. . . . Any country whose people conduct themselves well can count upon our hearty friendliness. If a nation shows that it knows how to act with decency in industrial and political matters, if it keeps order and pays its obligations, then it need fear no interference from the United States. Brutal wrong-doing, or an impotence which results in a general loosening of the ties of civilized society, may finally require intervention by some civilized nation, and in the Western Hemisphere the United States cannot ignore this duty.' It was a duty which she could neglect only at the cost of letting the Monroe Doctrine go by default. 'If we are willing to let Germany or England act as the policeman of the Caribbean, then we can afford not to interfere when gross wrong-doing occurs. But if we intend to say " Hands off " to the powers of Europe, sooner or later we must keep order ourselves.' This was not jingoism but plain logic.

Roosevelt's greatest achievement in foreign politics was the securing of a ship canal across Central America to link the two oceans. With a vast coastline to defend on both the Pacific and Atlantic and the rapid growth of rival navies in both, the building of such a canal and its control by the Federal government was a national necessity. Old-fashioned radicals who attacked Roosevelt for his whole-hearted pursuit of the project overlooked the fact that the only alternatives were to maintain two separate fleets or to leave the entire coastline of America at the mercy of any assailant. The expense of the former was prohibitive and the increased mobility of naval forces made the latter too dangerous in an age when the imperialism of every great power was becoming world-wide.

The means which Roosevelt used to attain his ends were more subject to criticism. They received it in ample measure. Yet the very self-assurance with which he pursued his negotiations with the Columbian politicians—' jack-rabbits,' ' blackmailers,' ' Bogotá corruptionists,' as he genially called them—and the boisterous haste with which, when they overreached themselves, he used the forces of the United States to establish the *fait accompli* of the comic opera revolution in Panama, only endeared him the more to the average American of his generation. In after years, when he was being criticised by a younger America, which was reaping the benefits of his *coup d'état*, but which wished to avoid the responsibility for his manner of accomplishing it, he replied contemptuously, ' If I had followed conventional, conservative methods, I should have submitted a dignified state paper of approximately two hundred pages to the Congress and the debate would have been going on yet, but I took the canal zone and let Congress debate, and while the debate goes on the canal does also.' His phrase, ' I took Panama,' outraged precise moralists, but exactly expressed the measure of his hold on a young, arrogant people first finding their feet in the world.

All this was accomplished by Roosevelt when he was President, not in his own right, but in that of the dead McKinley's. But when the Presidential Election of 1904 came round his hold on the nation was such that the Republican politicians, little as they wanted him, had no option but to nominate him again for the Presidency. In his gloomier moments he told his friends that he had no chance: the Caucus intended to down him and he had no machine, no faction, no money. But when it came to the test nothing could stand against his popularity.

His electioneering established a new precedent even in the vigorous political traditions of America. Wherever he went he was received by vast and boisterous crowds to whom he spoke after their own manner. It was characteristic of the man that he enjoyed it more than anybody, describing his experiences afterwards with the zest of a boy. At Butte, Montana, in the Wild West, ' the Mayor led me in or, to speak more accurately, tucked me under one arm and lifted me partially off the ground so that I felt . . . like one of those limp dolls with dangling legs carried around by small children. . . . As soon as we got in the banquet hall and sat at the head of the table, the Mayor hammered lustily with the handle of his knife and announced, " Waiter, bring on the feed ! " Then, in a spirit of pure kindliness, he added, " Waiter, pull up the shades and let the people see the President eat ! " But to this I objected. . . . Of the hundred men who were my hosts I suppose at least half had killed their men in private war. . . . As they drank great goblets of wine, the sweat glistened on their hard, strong, crafty faces. They looked as if they had come out of the pictures in Aubrey Beardsley's " Yellow Book." ' None the less, to Roosevelt these hundred per cent. Americans of the West looked good.

The people returned his love and his understanding. He was elected by 336 to 140 electoral votes and by a popular majority of two and a half millions. ' To-morrow,' he said on the day before his inauguration, ' I shall come into office in my own right. Then watch out for me.'

To the short-sighted men of wealth who viewed America merely as a species of private property this was horribly alarming. ' Darkest Abyssinia,' wrote one of them, ' never saw anything like the course of treatment we received at the hands of the administration following Mr. Roosevelt's election in 1904.' In reality there was nothing more revolutionary about the second term of his Presidency than the first. He made it clear that he would continue to enforce the control of the nation over its component parts. 'Of all forms of tyranny,' he said, ' the least attractive and the most vulgar is the tyranny of mere wealth, the tyranny of a plutocracy.' If the letter of the law enabled that tyranny and so defeated its own spirit, then the law must be changed. ' Neither this people nor any other free people will permanently tolerate the use of the vast power conferred by vast wealth . . . without lodging somewhere in the Government the still higher power of seeing that this power . . . is . . . used for and not against the interests of the people as a whole.' In no other way could the continued existence of a democracy be assured. And believing so passionately in democracy, that is in the right of the common people to govern themselves according to their own standards of justice, he was resolved so to preserve it. ' We do not intend that this Republic shall ever fail as those republics of olden times failed, in which there finally came to be a government by classes, which resulted either in the poor plundering the rich or in the rich . . . exploiting the poor.'

So when the Courts, conservative as ever of the letter of the Constitution rather than the spirit, threatened to declare the federal regulation of Corporations a nullity, Roosevelt again appealed over the heads of the lawyers and politicians to the people and spoke of obtaining a constitutional amendment. When the great corporate interests used their wealth to organise a press campaign against him, he retaliated in kind with his own matchless gifts for publicity. All the while he kept the balance between those who would exploit the state for the sake of individual wealth, and those who would use the popular hatred of such exploitation to plunder the accumulated capital of the nation. In his attack on ' certain malefactors of great wealth,' he was careful to distinguish between those who abused wealth and those who created it.

For it was part of Roosevelt's greatness that for all the blunt and sweeping generalisations by which he gained popularity, he never forgot in his actual contact with men

169

that they were human. He saw the millionaires against whom he fought not as ogres and outlaws, but as fellow mortals who had to be chastised when they did wrong, but were by right comprehended in the broad and catholic union of American citizenship. He had that rare solvent of statesmanship, the historical imagination: he saw the nation, past, present and future, with all its infinite gradations and variations, as a living entity. Among those for whom he kept open house at Washington were the children of his friends and even of his enemies, and he always made it his business to impress them with his own passionate sense of a common nationhood. A cadet of the great house of Vanderbilt has recalled how as a small boy he received an envelope, gloriously marked official, inviting himself and his sister to lunch at the White House, and how when he arrived the President, dismissing his other guests with his own family to the dining-room, announced, 'We men will have our food served here: we have important matters to discuss,' and entertained him alone in the Lincoln Study. There while they ate, facing each other across the presidential desk, ' T. R.' spoke earnestly to his youthful guest of Lincoln and of the splendid vision of America for which he had stood—' that strange figure from the plains of Illinois who spent many a sleepless night in this study standing in front of that window on the right and staring into space, over the leafless trees below and over the dark expanse of the Potomac beyond.' [1] No boy with a grain of imagination was ever likely to forget such a lesson.

Thus the man who presented himself to the common people as ' Teddy the Trust-Buster,' who checked speculators —' the men who seek gain not by genuine work but by gambling '—who fought the growing abuse of railway rebates, never tried to align the *have-nots* against the *haves*. He loved the people too well to be guilty of the easy resort of the hack politician who seeks to establish himself in power by inciting them to commit waste on their own heritage. Roosevelt was always thinking of the future,

[1] Cornelius Vanderbilt, jun., *Farewell to Fifth Avenue*, p. 24.

as well as the immediate present, of the country. One of the most enduring features of his work was his preservation for the nation of the remaining great forests and water systems of the West. By his policy of ' Conservation ' he saved for the young adolescent race, whose trustee he was, at least something of the wherewithal to create a peaceful, happy and progressive future.

Abroad he continued to make America strong and respected as she had never been before. He maintained the policy of the open door for American goods throughout the world, acted as mediator between Russia and Japan and, ignoring the fears of his more timorous countrymen, sent the Fleet round the world to show that America was able to take her place as a leader among the family of nations. Her power for usefulness and what he sincerely called Righteousness depended, he maintained, on her power of implementing her word and her just beliefs. ' Toward all other nations, large and small,' he declared, ' our attitude must be one of cordial and sincere friendship. We must show not only in our words but in our deeds that we are earnestly desirous of securing their good will by acting toward them in a spirit of just and generous recognition of their rights. But justice and generosity in a nation, as in an individual, count most when shown not by the weak but by the strong.' The practical means he took in strengthening the Fleet to maintain this end laid him open to the charges of imperialism and jingoism. Yet the Committee of the Nobel Peace Prize chose him for its award in 1906, holding, and holding rightly, that the man who made democratic America strong was doing nothing but what advanced the permanent order and peace of mankind.

The ruler of so vast a nation could scarcely hope in his seven years of office to escape criticisms and set-backs, and least of all when he was such a man as Roosevelt. His impetuous tongue and overflowing vitality often concealed the ultimate sanity and justice of his vision and got him into many scrapes. ' He was the most indiscreet guy I ever met,' one of his followers recalled in after years.

Half the time . . . George, Billy O'Neill and I used to sit on his coat-tails. Billy O'Neill would say to him: ' What do you want to do that for, you damn fool; you will ruin yourself and everybody else ! '

He was the leader, and he started over the hill, and here his army was, following and trying to keep him in sight.

Yes, trying to keep him from rushing into destruction.

If it had not been for you and Billy O'Neill, he would certainly have done some things most impulsively.

He was the most impulsive human being I ever knew.

To those who knew him only superficially he seemed to be in a perpetual state of mind. To them he appeared like a big boy who had never quite grown up, lovable but dangerous, and far too ready to plunge into every fray and to deliver ' horse-back ' judgments on every conceivable subject. ' You must always remember,' said one of them, ' that the President is about six.'

In much of this there was truth. More than half of the great President never grew up: he was for ever enthusing and had, like a boy with over-abundant spirits, to be in the thick of everything. ' Father never likes to go to a wedding or a funeral,' said one of his small sons whose romps he always led, ' because he can't be the bride at the wedding or the corpse at the funeral.' The learned and genial French Ambassador, Monsieur Jusserand, drew an amusing picture of the same boyish vitality as manifested in the President's post-prandial rambles in Rock Creek, scrambling expeditions in which all his eminent guests, willy-nilly, were involved.

Yesterday President Roosevelt invited me to take a promenade with him this afternoon at three. I arrived at the White House punctually in afternoon dress and silk hat, as if we were to stroll in the Tuileries Garden or in the Champs-Elysées. To my surprise, the President soon joined me in a tramping suit, with knicker-bockers and thick boots, and soft felt hat, much worn. Two or three other gentlemen came, and we started off at what seemed to me a breakneck pace, which soon brought us out of the city. On reaching the country, the President went pell-mell over the fields, following neither road nor path, always on, on, straight ahead! I was much winded, but I would not give in, nor ask him to slow up, because I had the honour of *La Belle France* in my heart. At last we came to the bank of a stream, rather wide and too deep to be forded. I sighed relief, because I thought that now we had reached our goal and would rest a moment and catch our breath, before turning homeward. But judge of my horror when I saw the President unbutton his clothes and heard him say 'We had better strip, so as not to wet our things in the Creek.' Then I, too, for the honour of France, removed my apparel, everything except my lavender kid gloves. The President cast an inquiring look at these as if they, too, must come off, but I quickly forestalled any remark by saying, 'With your permission, Mr. President, I will keep these on, otherwise it would be embarrassing if we should meet ladies.' And so we jumped into the water and swam across.

Excessive energy, especially when exercised in great place, is apt to get its possessor into trouble. 'Power,' wrote Henry Adams, 'when wielded by abnormal energy, is the most serious of facts, and all Roosevelt's friends knew that his restless and combative energy was more than abnormal. Roosevelt, more than any other man living . . . showed the singular primitive quality that belongs to ultimate matter—the quality that medieval theology ascribed to God —he was pure act.' His last years as President were consequently a good deal troubled. Those he had offended joined forces against him, and many of his transient indiscretions came home to roost. He was faced by an unpleasant alliance between the Caucus politicians of his own party and Big Business, and in the summer of 1908 the Judicature invalidated a fine of twenty-nine million dollars imposed on the Standard Oil Company. Such action in the name of the Constitution struck at the very heart of his system, which viewed the Constitution of the United States 'not as a straight-jacket . . . laying the hand of death upon our development, but as an instrument designed for the life and healthy growth of the nation.'

Yet had Roosevelt seen fit to stand again in the Presidential Election of 1908, not all the disgruntled politicians, financiers and lawyers in the nation could have prevented his re-election. The ordinary American saw his seven years as President as seven glorious milestones in the nation's progress towards some indefinable but better goal. He represented the aspirations of his people, and for all his outspoken roughness they loved him for it.

But Roosevelt could not stand again, for he had tied his hands by his impulsive declaration after his election of 1904 that he would respect the spirit of the traditional custom that limited Presidents to two terms of office and would under no circumstances accept another nomination. In doing so, though he had barred his own return to the White House, he had secured his better self and his future historical status from unworthy personal ambition, and had kept trust with the American democratic dream of which he was the representative. All that now remained for him to do was to nominate his successor. This he did, choosing one who was both a member of his Cabinet and one of his closest friends, generous, unassuming William Taft, who possessed almost as great a heart as his own. But his genius Taft did not possess, though even this attribute seemed his to Roosevelt, who saw all his geese as swans. ' You blessed old trump,' he wrote to him before his election, ' I have always said you would be the greatest President bar only Washington and Lincoln, and I feel mighty inclined to strike out the exceptions.'

In March 1909, having seen Taft installed at the White House, Roosevelt retired into private life. He was only fifty, and there seemed nothing left for him to achieve. ' To me there is something fine,' he wrote, ' in the American theory that a private citizen can be chosen . . . to occupy a position as great as that of the mightiest monarch . . . and then leave it as an unpensioned private citizen, who goes back into the ranks of his fellow-citizens with entire self-respect, claiming nothing save what on his own individual merits he is entitled to receive.' But there was tragedy in the position as well. John Morley, visiting America, had been struck by the fact that its two most extraordinary phenomena were the Niagara Falls and President Roosevelt.

Now one of those mighty forces was unharnessed and running to waste.

It was not in Roosevelt's nature to repine at the inevitable. It was his motto that life in all circumstances had compensations. To break the fall and to avoid embarrassing his successor he decided to take a long period of absence from the States and sailed for Africa on a big game hunting expedition. Here he wrote and read assiduously, was known to the astonished natives as ' The Man with the big paunch '—translated for his benefit ' the man with unerring aim '—and shot nine lions, five elephants, thirteen rhinoceroses and seven hippopotamuses—no bad record for a middle-aged man who was blind in one eye. ' There are a great many people,' said Boss Platt, ' who do not think Mr. Roosevelt will ever return from Africa alive. Many who have undertaken the same trip have been stricken by disease or killed by accident. He may be very strenuous and he may be physically strong, but he is taking a long chance.' Perhaps some of Platt's associates would not have been sorry if Roosevelt had never returned: it was rumoured that in certain high political and financial circles a popular toast of the time was ' The Lions.'

But Roosevelt survived and, after a visit to Egypt, appeared in glorious form in England in the spring of 1910. He was received with open arms by a people who richly appreciated his full-blooded American patriotism, though *Punch* politely intimated that the lions in Trafalgar Square were not to be shot. At Oxford he delivered the Romanes Lecture, choosing as subject ' Biological Analogies in History,' and astonishing his learned audience with startling comparisons between extinct animals and the more unprogressive kingdoms of the modern world, likening one to the *megatherium* and another to the *glyptodon*. ' In the way of grading which we have at Oxford,' remarked one of his most distinguished listeners, ' we agreed to mark the lecture "*Beta minus*" but the lecturer "*Alpha Plus*." While we felt that the lecture was not a very great contribution to science, we were sure that the lecturer was a very great man.'

So delighted was John Bull with his visitor that he even permitted him to preach to him on his own deficiencies. In a remarkable speech delivered at the Guildhall on the occasion of his receiving the Freedom of the City, Roosevelt dealt in his downright fashion with the reluctance of the British to assume their responsibilities in Egypt. 'I speak as an outsider, but in one way this is an advantage, for I speak without natural prejudice. . . . In Egypt you are not only the guardians of your own interests: you are also the guardians of the interests of civilization; and the present condition of affairs in Egypt is a grave menace to both your Empire and the entire civilized world. . . . Now, either you have the right to be in Egypt or you have not; either it is or it is not your duty to establish and keep order. If you feel that you have not the right to be in Egypt . . . then, by all means get out of Egypt. If, as I hope, you feel that your duty to civilized mankind and your fealty to your own great traditions alike bid you to stay, then make the fact and the name agree and show that you are ready to meet in very deed the responsibility which is yours.' His hosts were astonished but accepted his straight talks on effete civilisations in good part.

It was a symbol of the place which Roosevelt had won for himself in the estimation of the world that, though now only a private American citizen, he was asked to walk among the Kings and Emperors who followed that May the coffin of King Edward VII in the greatest military pageant of the century. Both then and later in the summer in his travels through Europe he was treated as an equal by the crowned heads he visited. He stayed with the Kaiser and rode by his side when he reviewed his troops and was afterwards presented by him with two photographs, the one labelled in the imperial hand, 'The Colonel of the Rough Riders instructing the German Emperor in field tactics,' and the other, 'When we shake hands we shake the world.' He even managed to rebuke the Pope.

He enjoyed it all enormously and described with great gusto the unfamiliar etiquette which he found himself

176

called upon to observe. 'When I was brought up to the Queen to take her in to dinner,' he wrote of his entertainment at Rome, 'I again thought it was time for me to get rid of my hat. But not a bit of it! I found that I was expected to walk in with the Queen on my arm, and my hat in the other hand—a piece of etiquette which reminded me of nothing with which I was previously acquainted except a Jewish wedding on the East Side of New York.' As in his dealings in the past with New York bosses and heelers, Dakota ranchmen and Wall Street financiers, Roosevelt got the best out of the royalties with whom he associated, because he chose to regard them not as types but as human beings. 'I thoroughly liked and respected almost all the various kings and queens that I met,' he wrote, 'they struck me as serious people . . . devoted to their people and anxious to justify their own positions by the way they did their duty. . . . I doubted whether the sovereigns cared to see me. I am now inclined to think that they did, as a relief to the tedium, the dull, narrow routine of their lives.' Their lives would indeed have been unusually exciting had it been otherwise.

Then, having as usual won all hearts, he returned to his own country. He was greeted with a royal reception as the first citizen of the world. It was rather hard on Taft, who, generous, unseeking soul as he was, could not help contrasting his own comparative neglect with the wild enthusiasm with which Roosevelt was received by his countrymen.

It had not been Roosevelt's intention to take any part in politics on his return to America. But he was unable to help himself. During his absence things had not been going well with the policy he had initiated: the financiers and the trusts were raising their heads again and the politicians were returning to their old ways. The old chasms in the national life which he had sought to bridge were widening ominously. Taft was doing his best to follow in his footsteps, but he was not a strong man and he lacked his dynamic and compelling force. The country was growing restless and, in its bitterness against the millionaires and their allies the bosses, was turning towards strange gods, to the Democrats and William Jennings Bryan and the new saviour whom the unorthodox of that Party were tentatively putting forward, the thin-lipped, doctrinaire, college professor, Woodrow Wilson. It was growing doubtful whether the Republicans, who with two brief and unimportant spells had governed America for over half a century, would win the Presidential Election of 1912.

Under the circumstances it was not surprising that pressure was put on Roosevelt by many of his old followers to return to politics. ' The country is awaiting you anxiously,' one of them had written during his absence, ' not out of mere curiosity to know what your attitude will be, but to lead it, to give it direction. . . . Your personal following is larger to-day than it has ever been.' With no other vent for his vast energies and himself deeply anxious for the future of his country, it was natural enough that Roosevelt gradually, though with many efforts to resist it, succumbed to temptation. Now that his strong hand was withdrawn from the helm it was becoming increasingly obvious that the representative and judicial institutions of the country were proving insufficient to preserve the spirit of American democracy against the forces that were menacing it. More and more Roosevelt felt that the only remedy was a revision of the constitution which would enable the popular will to triumph over the obstacles placed in its way by a corrupt Congress and a subservient and ultra-conservative judicature. ' The whole point of our governmental experiment,' he wrote, ' lies in the fact that it is a genuine effort to achieve true democracy.' It had become necessary to repeat that effort to meet the changed circumstances of a new age.

' I stand for the square deal. But . . . I mean not merely that I stand for fair play under the present rules of the game, but that I stand for having those rules changed so as to work for a more substantial equality of opportunity and reward.' Such was the New Nationalism which Roosevelt began to advocate in the sixth decade of his life and the fourth of his political career. It involved a

178

strengthening of the Federal powers at the expense of the individual States in order to deal with abuses which no State was strong enough to remedy. 'The State must be made efficient for the work which concerns only the people of the State; and the nation for that which concerns all the people. There must remain no neutral ground to serve as a refuge for lawbreakers of great wealth, who can hire the vulpine legal cunning which will teach them how to avoid both jurisdictions. It is a misfortune when the national legislature fails to do its duty in providing a national remedy, so that the only national activity is the purely negative activity of the judiciary in forbidding the State to exercise power in the premises.

'I do not ask for overcentralization; but I do ask that we work in a spirit of broad and far-reaching nationalism when we work for what concerns our people as a whole. . . . The betterment which we seek must be accomplished, I believe, mainly through the national government. The American people are right in demanding that New Nationalism without which we cannot hope to deal with new problems. The New Nationalism puts the national need before sectional or personal advantage. . . . The New Nationalism regards the executive power as the steward of the public welfare. It demands of the judiciary that it shall be interested primarily in human welfare rather than in property.'

It was not unnatural that many of his fellow Conservatives in the Republican Party saw Roosevelt's attempt to restate the Democratic dogma in a plutocratic age as a thinly-veiled species of Socialism, then the fashionable scare in well-to-do and cultured circles. He was accused of being a revolutionary and an incendiary. Roosevelt, whom opposition only stimulated, was not afraid to meet the issue and to advocate Hamiltonian measures to serve Jeffersonian principles. 'We are face to face with new conceptions of the relations of property to human welfare,' he declared. 'The man who wrongly holds that every human right is secondary to his profit must now give way to the advocate of human welfare, who rightly maintains that every man holds his property subject to the general right of the community to regulate its use to whatever degree the public welfare may require it.' To free the government of America from the control of money he was prepared to advocate all devices that would make the representatives of the people more easily and certainly subject to the people's will.

Gradually Roosevelt drifted into the unhappy position first of the leading critic and then of active opponent of his old friend Taft and of the official Republican Party organisation. When the Presidential Election of 1912 approached, he allowed his name to be spoken of for nomination by those who believed that the future of their Party and of the country was endangered by the narrow formalism of the Party machine and the excessive legalism of his successor. Under such circumstances, Taft, whom the Caucus was hoping to see re-elected, abandoned his attitude of long-suffering humility and attacked his former leader. This was too much for Roosevelt and with a cry of ' My hat is in the ring,' he flung himself into the fray.

At the National Republican Convention at Chicago in June 1912, a dramatic struggle took place between Roosevelt's supporters and the Old Guard of the Party. On the side of the latter was the whole elaborate organisation of a great political machine, backed by enormous wealth and resolved at all costs to prevent the nomination of its rebellious champion. Roosevelt was supported by the fanatics who wore his personal colours, right or wrong, by all who were dissatisfied by the excessive conservatism of their Party, and by that section of the primitive West which was not already Democrat. Though he commanded a numerical majority among the rank and file delegates and among the great mass of Republicans in the country, the odds against him were enormous and he knew it. Not all the brass bands and the shouting, hysterical Westerners who kept Chicago resounding with his name could prevail against the cold, ruthless manipulation of the Party machinery by the Caucus chiefs. Roosevelt's delegates were one by one expunged from the roll-call, and the rules of the Convention were so skilfully and unscrupulously used against him that he was defeated by 561 to 107 votes.

In view of his former declaration never to intervene in a presidential election, this was perhaps no more than he deserved. Yet his defeat was a flagrant defiance of the whole principle of democracy. In those States where a Primary Law had permitted a popular expression of opinion, the delegates elected for the Convention had been overwhelmingly in Roosevelt's favour, yet these had been cynically prevented from exercising their votes by a handful of office holders who controlled the so-called National Committee that made up the roll-call of the Convention. To Roosevelt himself it was far more than a death-blow to his career: it was a cruel and heartless repudiation of a religious ideal by its own priests. 'Thou shalt not steal,' he told his defrauded followers. 'Thou shalt not steal a nomination. . . . Thou shalt not steal from the people the birthright of the people to rule themselves.'

This was the real *raison d'être* of the 'Bull Moose' campaign. It was not personal ambition or spite, as his enemies supposed, that made Roosevelt commit the unforgivable crime of American political morality and 'bolt' his Party. To the ordinary politician, who knew of no other motive powers but a selfish careerism and a more noble loyalty to Party, there was only one explanation of his action. A great man had betrayed himself and his cause: proud Lucifer had fallen from Heaven. Those who thought thus could not understand that to Roosevelt there was something dearer either than Party or his own career—an historical and imaginative ideal with which he had identified his whole work and without which life for him would no longer have any meaning.

To many who loved him he seemed to be taking the action of a lunatic. 'Your old friend Theodore,' wrote Henry Adams to Cecil Spring Rice, ' has dropped us all, and has gone in pirating on his own account. . . . I much fear that our dear Theodore is a dead cock in the pit.' And

Roosevelt knew it and was under no delusions. He understood better than any man living the power of Party and all that it implied. But there was something greater in the world than Party, and it had to be stated at whatever cost or go by default. It was his fate to test out that which the patient Lincoln had had to decide, and on a new battlefield. ' So far as I am concerned I am through,' he told his ragged following, ' I went before the people and I won. . . . Let us find out whether the Republican Party is the party of the plain people . . . or the party of the bosses and the professional radicals acting in the interests of special privilege.'

When the National Convention of the newly formed Progressive Party met that August at Chicago to nominate Roosevelt as a third and breakaway Presidential candidate, it seemed to many sober and unimaginative Americans, who had hitherto supported him, a rather hysterical and ridiculous concern. ' We stand at Armageddon and we battle for the Lord,' he thundered at his excited ' Bull Moose ' delegates. But those who knew him saw that he wore his fighting face. For though he realised in his heart that he could not win and that with the Republican Party split the Presidency must go on a minority vote to the Democrat Wilson, he believed himself engaged in a battle that was vital to the future existence of the American ideal. There are moments when it is a good thing for a man to go down fighting. ' The leader for the time being, whoever he may be, is but an instrument to be used until broken and then to be cast aside; and if he is worth his salt, he will care no more when he is broken than a soldier cares when he is sent where his life is forfeit in order that the victory may be won.'

For Roosevelt was fighting for something which the prosperous America of 1912 could not see, but to which a generation later, desperate and at its last gasp, it was to turn that it might be saved from the tyranny of its own past blindness and folly. A great people that disregards its historic principles and chooses to live by greed and materialism must in the end pay the price which greed and materialism exact. A little while before Roosevelt had spoken earnestly to his friends of the need to draw into one dominant stream all the intelligent and patriotic elements in the nation in order to prepare against the social upheaval which must otherwise overwhelm her. His imagination, trained by history, enabled him to see or rather to feel what was coming to America. He wished, by keeping alive her latent idealism, to safeguard her line of retreat.

In doing so he almost lost his own life. Inspired by the virulent Press campaign which his enemies, the bosses and speculators, were waging against him, a half-frenzied man shot him in the breast when he was about to speak at Milwaukee on October 14, 1912. After saving his would-be assassin—'the poor creature'—from the crowd that tried to lynch him, he insisted against the entreaties of his doctors on making his speech. 'It may be the last one I shall ever deliver,' he said, ' but I am going to deliver this one. It takes more than that to kill a bull-moose.' Only after he had spoken for an hour and a half and his strength was manifestly failing, did he allow himself to be taken to hospital for an operation.

He did not die, but he was defeated. Yet he polled 4,126,020 popular votes, half a million more than Taft, the nominee of the official Republican Party, and a Democratic President, Woodrow Wilson, the Princeton Professor, went to the White House on a minority vote. Roosevelt took his defeat with equanimity, for he had established, deep in the public consciousness, the principle for which he had fought. ' I accept the result with entire good humour,' he said. ' As for the Progressive cause, I can only repeat . . . [that] the cause in itself must triumph, for this triumph is essential to the well-being of the American people.' For the rest his sword was broken. ' I thought you were a better politician,' he told one of his followers. ' The fight is over. We are beaten. There is only one thing to do and that is to go back to the Republican Party. You can't hold a party like the

Progressive Party together . . . there are no loaves and
fishes.'

Then once again he went off into the wilderness. At
fifty-five he led an exploring expedition by canoe through
the heart of the Brazilian forest down a river which no
white man had ever traversed before. He suffered from
jungle fever and abscesses and nearly perished in the rapids.
When he came back to America he suffered worse things—
false and cruel libels and the shame of seeing Wilson
hand over twenty-five million dollars to the Colombian
politicians who had tried to trick America out of the
Panama Canal. He consoled himself by remembering his
uncle Jimmy Bulloch, who had fought for the South and
become in his old age a British citizen and a most rabid
Tory. 'He was one of the best men I have ever known,' he
wrote, ' and when I have sometimes been tempted to wonder
how good people can believe of me the unjust and impossible
things they do believe, I have consoled myself by thinking
of Uncle Jimmy Bulloch's perfectly sincere conviction that
Gladstone was a man of quite exceptional and nameless
infamy in both public and private life.'

The World War of 1914–18 brought Roosevelt one last
campaign, though it was not the one he sought. At first
his attitude to the events of Europe was the characteristic
American one: nothing but the clearest advantage of his
country should be allowed to draw her into that inferno of
warring nations. But as soon as he realised the issues at
stake his view changed. He had never believed that his
country could afford to stand outside the moral comity
of mankind. There could be no real safety or morality on
earth so long as one nation could attack a civilised, in-
offensive and entirely guiltless people like the Belgians with
impunity. At the Hague Convention America had given her
adherence to certain canons of conduct between the nations
which had been flagrantly outraged. She would not now
evade a plain duty by insisting on the benefits to herself of
peace. 'The kind of neutrality,' he said, 'which seeks
to preserve " peace " by timidly refusing to live up to our

184

plighted word and to denounce and take action against such wrong as that committed in the case of Belgium is unworthy of an honourable and powerful people.'

For the next two years Roosevelt was the chief protagonist of American intervention. After the sinking of the *Lusitania*, his contempt for President Wilson and what he termed his ' cult of cowardice ' became measureless. In one famous speech he spoke of the ghosts of murdered and unavenged Americans that must haunt the home of a President who was ' too proud to fight ' and too afraid of his people to lead instead of following them. ' There should be shadows now at Shadow Lawn; the shadows of the men, women and children who have risen from the ooze of the ocean bottom and from graves in foreign lands; the shadows of the helpless whom Mr. Wilson did not dare protect lest he might have to face danger; the shadows of babies gasping pitifully as they sank under the waves; the shadows of women outraged and slain by bandits. . . . Those are the shadows proper for Shadow Lawn; the shadows of deeds that were never done; the shadows of lofty words that were followed by no action; the shadows of the tortured dead.' It is not surprising that words like these were never forgiven by the man of whom they were spoken.

When Wilson at last descended from his lofty tower and, at the eleventh hour of dying Europe's agony, proclaimed the American crusade for freedom and civilisation, Roosevelt approached him with open arms. He was received with cold unconcern. It had been his hope to be allowed to lead a division of American troops to France and, in a cause in which he believed with his whole heart, once more to bear arms as a soldier. It was denied him. Clemenceau himself wrote in vain to Wilson to beg that the great American might be permitted to come.

His name is the ' one . . . which sums up the beauty of American intervention. . . . He is an idealist, imbued with simple, vital idealism. . . . You are too much of a philosopher to ignore that the influence on the people of great leaders of men often exceeds their personal merits, thanks to the legendary halo

185

surrounding them. The name of Roosevelt has this legendary force in our country. . . . You must know, Mr. President, more than one of our *poilus* asked his comrade: " But where is Roosevelt ? " '

The request only hardened the idealogue's refusal. ' It is a very exclusive war,' Roosevelt observed sadly.

Denied the opportunity of active service, he devoted himself to helping to rouse his vast country to a sense of the urgency of the occasion that she might put her full forces into the field before it was too late. The swiftness with which the volunteer armies of America took their place beside the hard-pressed veterans of France and Britain was in some measure due to the superb energy with which he threw himself, already a dying man, into the campaign which he conducted in every part of the country. He saw his four sons leave for France and bore with proud constancy the death of the youngest, Quentin, in aerial combat. Into that hour of sacrifice all his life's philosophy went. ' Only those are fit to live,' he wrote, ' who do not fear to die; and none are fit to die who have shrunk from the joy of life. Both life and death are parts of the same Great Adventure. Never yet was worthy adventure worthily carried through by the man who put his personal safety first. . . . In America to-day all our people are summoned to service and to sacrifice. Pride is the portion only of those who know bitter sorrow or the foreboding of bitter sorrow. But all of us who give service, and stand ready for sacrifice, are the torch-bearers. We run with the torches until we fall, content if we can then pass them to the hands of the other runners. The torches whose flame is brightest are borne by the gallant men at the front, by the gallant women whose husbands and lovers, whose sons and brothers are at the front. These men are high of soul, as they face their fate on the shell-shattered earth, or in the skies above or in the waters beneath; and no less high of soul are the women with torn hearts and shining eyes; the girls whose boy-lovers have been struck down in their golden morning, and the mothers and wives to whom word has been brought that henceforth they must walk in the shadow. These are the torch-bearers; these are they who have dared the Great Adventure.'

On November 11, 1918, Armistice Day, Roosevelt was taken ill with abscesses in the thigh and ears. He refused to yield to the physicians and for a while seemed to be holding his own. Young Cornelius Vanderbilt, who to his joy had run away from his sheltered home to enlist and had served in France, was present at an Armistice dance at his house and sought the old man out to speak to him of his own dreams and aspirations. The boy told him of his disillusionment and fears for America and impulsively confided his belief that the country was overrun with bankers and railway executives. ' Is it ? ' said Roosevelt sadly. ' You must be better informed about the country than I am, Neil. In all my born years, boy and man, Rough Rider and President, I have never met a banker or railroad executive. All I saw were promoters and stockbrokers.' And when the boy questioned him further he added : ' Ever read Disraeli's speeches ? . . . He was by far the cleverest man produced by the nineteenth century. Here's what he said of life : "Youth is a blunder, maturity a struggle, old age a regret." . . . There's the answer to all your queries. Now go and dance and stake your claim to blunder while the staking is good.' [1]

For the boy in Roosevelt had died at last, and he could not survive him. He was tired and ready to depart. An operation was found to be imperative. ' Serene and high of heart,' he wrote with a spark of the old flame, ' we must face our fate and go down into the darkness.' He died in hospital in the cold of January 1919, carrying his wounds and scars with him and leaving his courage and skill to those that could get them.

[1] Cornelius Vanderbilt, jun., *Farewell to Fifth Avenue*, pp. 64–5.

CHAPTER V

IN the ruined South there grew up, in the years after the American Civil War, a boy called Walter Page. He was born in 1855, the son of an enterprising citizen of North Carolina and of his wife, who mingled French with English blood in her veins. His earliest memories were of the sights and sounds of war—of helping his mother sew up rags for wounded soldiers, of the coffins that passed the door and of that memorable day when Sherman's victorious army marched past from dawn till nightfall, leaving havoc in its wake. Next day there were bodies lying beside the roads, and the old negress servant of the house declared indignantly that all Yankees were chicken thieves, whether they brought freedom or no.

Walter Page's father, like most of his neighbours, was ruined by the war. The boy, whose love of books was inordinate, went to a small Southern college. Here he had the happy fortune to come under the influence of a great teacher, Professor Price, the apostle of good English in America, whose daily prayer it was: ' O great Apollo, send down the reviving rain upon our fields; preserve our flocks; ward off our enemies and—build up our speech ! ' He taught the boy to express himself and gave him his sense of all that was best in literature.

Young Page had another stroke of luck to counteract his father's misfortunes. When he was twenty-one he was selected, on Price's recommendation, as one of the twenty undergraduates chosen from all America to be the first *alumni* of the new Johns Hopkins College. ' Gentlemen,' said President Gilman in his opening address, 'you must light your own torch.' Page was enabled to light his with the help of one of the greatest classical scholars America has ever produced, Professor Gildersleeve, one of whose five original Grecians he became.

The Johns Hopkins College did more for Walter Page than turn him into a good scholar. It made him an American. When most of his fellow Southerners were bewailing the vanished past and nursing a justifiable but sterile hatred against their Northern conquerors, he became alive to the aspirations of the nation as a whole. Refusing to embrace either of the alternative professions of young Southerners of education—teaching or the Church—he insisted on striking out on a line of his own, and being mostly interested in 'that one of the main tenses which we call the Present,' became a journalist.

Finding little scope for his profession in the moribund South, he answered an advertisement for a post as general job-reporter on a small Middle-West paper. Succeeding, he borrowed fifty dollars for his journey and spent a highly educative year or two reporting the price of cattle and the small gossip of a Western agricultural community. Later he served as reporter on the New York *World*, which sent him all over the United States. It was a great education. Everyday contact with his countrymen gave him an understanding of the common man and of the 'divine average,' and filled him, as it had done Lincoln, with a deep love for democracy.

Being an able young man with plenty of courage and industry, he did well in his profession. At thirty-two he was chosen editor of a small national journal, *The Forum*. In eight years he raised its circulation from a few thousands to over thirty thousand. He established a new conception of editorship, which superseded the pompous high priest of letters aloof in his sanctum by the wide-awake and sympathetic man of the world. 'An editor,' he said, 'must know men and be out among men.' He made it his task to get in touch with his contributors, to draw them out and make them talk of their knowledge and interests, then to advise and inspire their writing.

At forty-three he became editor of the *Atlantic Monthly*, the most important cultural journal in North America. Into this also he transfused new life, gathering round him nearly all the most vigorous minds of his age and country. He also became attached to the great publishing house of Harper, whose then confused affairs he helped to restore, and later founded the independent publishing firm of Doubleday, Page & Co. He brought to publishing the same originality and enthusiasm that he did to journalism. In all he did he was an educator and a leader of public opinion.

Such a man being American could not fail to be interested in politics, and he took the fullest part in them that his profession admitted. By virtue of his Southern traditions he was a Democrat, but that did not prevent him from sympathising strongly with Theodore Roosevelt's New Nationalism and enrolling him among his contributors. Like Roosevelt he wished to see America take her proper place for good in the world, viewed the Spanish War as a necessary act of surgery for the health of civilisation, and greatly shocked the Boston anti-Imperialists by avowing it by bringing out the *Atlantic Monthly* with the American flag all over its cover.

It was because he felt so strongly the need of the nation to realise itself and saw its great opportunities that he engaged in a journalistic venture of his own and founded a new magazine, the *World's Work*. Its theme was the every-day work of mankind and of American democratic man in particular. ' There is *one* new subject, to my thinking worth all the old ones: the new impulse in American life, the new feeling of nationality, our coming to realize ourselves. To my mind there is greater promise in democracy than men of any preceding period ever dared dream of—aggressive democracy—growth by action.' For to Page Democracy was something far greater than the mere right to vote, which all too often the Caucus politicians, relying on the ordinary man's ignorance, rendered a worthless thing. To him it was rather the right to share in all the best and noblest that life offered. It was not so much a form of government as a ' scheme of society.'

It was on national education, therefore, that Page pinned his political hopes. ' The fundamental article in the creed of the American democracy,' he once said, ' is the unchanging and unchangeable resolve that every human being shall have his opportunity for his utmost development—his chance to become and do the best he can.' He carried this creed into the prosaic business of professional democratic politics. The enthusiasm with which he preached it, in and out of season, presently made him a leading light in the New York Reform Club.

He first turned his attention to his own South. Here among the poor whites of his native state, North Carolina, he found an appalling illiteracy: it was reckoned that over a quarter of them, for all their full democratic citizenship, could neither read nor write. In 1897 at the State Normal College for Women Page made a great speech. He pointed out that the South was ruled by ' Mummies '—by the dead hand of the Confederate Dead, of Religious Orthodoxy, of the fear of Negro Domination. While a little stagnant aristocracy, obsessed by fears, lived on the memories of the past, the present and future of the race was forgotten.

Then he used a phrase that struck the imagination of his countrymen. In their midst was ' the Forgotten Man.' The forgotten man was the uneducated cultivator of the South who was content to be forgotten. He lived wretchedly, but was told by the stump politicians that he was a fine fellow and the backbone of the best State in the Union, and was fool enough to believe them. He resisted all change for his own betterment, because he was assured that what was good enough for his fathers was good enough for him. He was a dupe, shamefully neglected and ignorantly thankful for being neglected.

Beside the ' forgotten man ' was the ' forgotten woman,' like him cheated and deprived of her heritage. ' Thin and wrinkled in youth from ill-prepared food, clad without warmth or grace, living in untidy houses, working from daylight till bedtime at the dull round of weary duties, the slaves of men of equal slovenliness, the mothers of joyless children—all uneducated if not illiterate.' In the light of that grim picture, verifiable by anyone who was prepared to look outside his own gates, American civilisation was a failure.

Instead of a useless memory of a tragic past Page offered the Conservative South a great work in the present and a great hope for the future. Then in resounding phrases he announced his Credo.

I believe in the free public training of both the hands and the mind of every child born of woman.

I believe that by right training of men we add to the wealth of the world. All wealth is the creation of man, and he creates it only in proportion to the trained uses of the community; and the more men we train the more wealth everyone may create.

` I believe in the perpetual regeneration of society, and in the immortality of democracy and in growth everlasting.

The South tried to shout down the maker of the speech as a renegade, but the conscience of the nation as a whole, and particularly of its youth, was aroused. Page continued his crusade. During the closing years of the nineteenth century and the opening years of the twentieth he helped to complete work which Lincoln had hoped to perform for the regeneration of the South. He was the motive force behind the ' Educational Awakening,' the appointment of the Southern Education Board, and the gradual recognition of the State's liability to give every child a fair intellectual start in life. Side by side, and actively fostered by Page's enthusiasm, was Booker Washington's campaign for the education and self-improvement of the Southern negro.

Page did not confine his work for the South only to the realm of the mind. He employed his remarkable powers of moulding public opinion in reviving Southern agriculture and helped to obtain the Rockefeller grants for Dr. Knapp's demonstration work. Even more important was his courageous championship of Dr. Stiles's discovery that the proverbial dullness and inertia of the average Carolina agriculturist was caused by the hookworm that destroyed the red blood corpuscles in his body and produced chronic anæmia. Page's passionate advocacy of Stiles's discovery gradually transformed a stock vulgar jest into a proper public awareness of a terrible plague. By securing the backing of Rockefeller's money for the endowment of an International Health Commission he enabled the plague to be fought, and not only brought new hope into the future of the South but of the tropics throughout the world.

All this, out of the ordinary run of politics though it was, made Page an important force in the Democratic camp. Too modest to be a public figurehead and too unassuming to seek office, his very detachment enhanced his power. It was not in his nature to make himself king, but he became a kingmaker.

In the course of his work as a journalist Page had been deeply impressed by the intellectual brilliance of a University lecturer, Woodrow Wilson, the President of Princeton. In a young and raw country like America such brilliance was still a sufficiently rare phenomenon to be remarkable. Rightly or wrongly he read into Wilson's genius for political generalisation something of his own passionate idealism, and saw him as the prophet of a restored Democracy who would build America anew and give the disinherited their inheritance. The fatal defects of character, that Wilson's great intellectual gifts concealed, Page did not as yet see.

He encouraged Wilson to write and speak on political subjects, brought his name before the public and the Party, and assiduously nursed his self-confidence. The chiefs of the Democratic Caucus were looking for a figurehead with an idealistic appeal, who could steal the thunder that Roosevelt had brought to the Republicans, and so focus on their Party all the vague discontent and aspirations of the average American. The inspired college professor, so aloof, so manifestly virtuous and so perpetually preaching, was just what they wanted. They offered to nominate him for the Governorship of New Jersey, and Page persuaded him to stand. Later he induced him to make a speaking tour of the West and brought him into contact with the great Colonel House of Texas. And in due course, when the Bull Moose campaign split the Republican Party, the Princeton Professor became President of the United States.

That was in 1912, and a great hope filled Page's heart. He wrote eagerly to the friend whom his advocacy had set on the throne about the Era of Great Opportunity upon which America was now entering: 'It is hard to measure the extent or the thrill of the new interest in public affairs and the new hope that you have aroused in thousands of men who were becoming hopeless under the long-drawn-out reign of privilege.' The new President alone of men would be able to restore the Jeffersonian dream, to raise the countryman to his proper stature so that he could combat the servile power of the boss-led urban masses, to put Democracy into real practice. As yet most people did not even know what it was. 'I find among men the very crudest ideas of government or of democracy. They have not thought the thing out. They hold no ordered creed of human organization or advancement. They leave all to chance and think, when they think at all, that chance determines it. And yet the Great Hope persists.' For Wilson would teach them.

Yet even at this moment Page had his fears. He saw Wilson isolated and lonely and hemmed in by hard, unimaginative men who could not understand his dreams. 'The political managers who have surrounded him these six months have now done their task. *They* know nothing of this Big Chance and Great Outlook.' His awful office was so great that it tended to oppress and change its holders. Could Page be quite sure of the man he had chosen? 'I have a new amusement, a new excitement, a new study . . .' he confided, ' a new hope, and sometimes a new fear; and its name is Wilson. I have for many years regarded myself as an interested, but always a somewhat detached, outsider, believing that the democratic idea was

194

real and safe and lifting, if we could ever get it put into action, contenting myself ever with such patches of it as time and accident and occasion now and then sewed on our gilded or tattered garments. But now it is come—the real thing; at any rate a man somewhat like us, whose thought and aim and dream are our thought and aim and dream. That's enormously exciting! I didn't suppose I'd ever become so interested in a general proposition or in a governmental hope. Will he do it? Can he do it? Can anybody do it? How can we help him do it? Now that the task is on him, does he really understand?'

For already Page could see the chink in Wilson's armour. ' I wonder if he quite knows himself. Temperamentally very shy, having lived too much alone and far too much with women (how I wish two of his daughters were sons!) this Big Thing having descended on him before he knew or was quite prepared for it, thrust into a whirl of self-seeking men even while he is trying to think out the theory of the duties that press, knowing the necessity of silence, surrounded by small people—well, I made up my mind that his real friends owed it to him and to what we all hope for, to break over his reserve and to volunteer help.' Page tried to do so.

There were many who hoped that the publisher who had discovered the new President and blazed his trail to power would become his Secretary of State. But when the Cabinet was formed there was no place for Page, nor did he ask for any. A marvellous advocate for others, he quietly effaced himself. But one day in April the telephone rang, and Colonel House addressed him as ' Your Excellency.' ' What the devil are you talking about?' asked Page. His friend, the College Professor, had appointed him American Ambassador to Great Britain.

The London Embassy had always been the chief diplomatic post of the United States. It had not been an easy one. During its early history as a legation its holders had had to struggle against every sort of difficulty and prejudice. Though George III had greeted the earliest of them with the assurance that as he had been the last man in his dominions to recognise the American nation, so he was happy to be the first to welcome its envoy, the British people did not follow their sovereign's example. They seemed to be engaged in a tacit conspiracy to deny all corporate existence to the presumptuous kinsmen who had discarded their government. So far as the envoys of America were noticed by the British at all, they were abused by the vulgar and offensively patronised by the rich.

They had other difficulties. The poverty of their country and their own rather aggressive republican ideals forbade them the exercise of that lavish hospitality which the richest and most aristocratic city in the world expected of its official visitors. John Adams lived in suburban lodgings at Ealing and kept his office in rooms in Harley Street, over a sign announcing that hot and vapour baths could be had at the establishment. Such conditions greatly increased the difficulty of the fight for recognition which the early American diplomats had to maintain long after the political independence of their country had been accepted.

It was not till Richard Rush became Minister to the Court of St. James's, in the years following the Anglo-American War of 1812–14, that a real improvement occurred in the diplomatic relationships between the two countries. Rush was a charming creature with an open, unjealous nature, ready to appreciate all that was best in the character of his hosts, and he was more than met half-way by the English Foreign Secretary, Castlereagh. By that time, too, the bitterness of past defeat was beginning to disappear, and a new generation of British statesmen had grown up who could view the events of the War of Independence as mere history. Henceforward the natural affinities between the two races began to reassert themselves and even to triumph over their political differences.

For as Burke had said before the break between the Anglo-Saxon peoples, there were ties between them light as air yet strong as links of iron. Not the least of these was that they spoke the same language, even though they did not always share the same thoughts. And of that common speech, it was the noblest products that were peculiarly the legacy of both peoples. The great classics of the age of Elizabeth and the seventeenth century belonged to them equally, and every cultured American and Englishman would feel with Wordsworth:

> We must be free or die, who speak the tongue
> That Shakespeare spake; the faith and morals hold
> Which Milton held.—In every thing we are sprung
> Of Earth's first blood, have titles manifold.

This union, based on common culture, was the better cemented because, whatever might be said of English visitors to America during the nineteenth century, America sent Britain of her very best. The line of American Ministers [1] at the Court of St. James's included many of her finest minds and more than one distinguished man of letters. ' It should be the exulted ministry of literature,' wrote Washington Irving, who himself served at the American Legation in London, ' to keep together the family of human nature.' It helped to preserve the spiritual unity of the Anglo-Saxon race.

There was another bond between the best minds of Britain and America. The American dream of Democracy had never been an exclusive one: it was based in Jefferson's famous formula on the common rights of mankind, and existed in the highest expression of its purpose, that the burden might be lifted from the shoulders of all men. Americans who visited Britain were often shocked by the divisions that existed between class and class: ' there is such a thing,' wrote one of them, ' as being civil without being servile, but it struck me that the bow of a poor man in England to a gentleman was rather too low to be made to a being of the same order in the creation as himself.' The rigidity of rank and social formality and the absence of any broad bottom of freemen owning their own land distressed them. But they viewed it less as a matter of exultation than of regret, and in the hearts of all the noblest Americans who crossed

---

[1] Prior to 1893 the U.S.A. had only a Legation in London.

the Atlantic was a perennial desire to assure something of their own free social heritage to the people of the proud, feudal island from which they derived their origin.

This wish coincided with a growing desire among the more liberal elements in Britain itself to attain to a more natural and less untrammelled mode of society. These found a sympathetic understanding from the distinguished Americans who visited their country as Ministers and Ambassadors. The best American plenipotentiaries at the Court of St. James's were more than diplomatic agents: they were the representatives of the Western democratic ideal in the Old World. In return they absorbed and took back to their own country something which it needed of the maturer civilisation of England: the grace of ancient manners, art and literature to lighten the drab curse of mediocrity that long weighed on the raw young republic of the West.

Many things in common had struck the representatives of America when they came to England. 'Think,' an American lieutenant had said to Richard Rush as his ship bore him up the Channel, 'we may be in the track of the Armada.' History was in the very air that filled the Minister's unaccustomed lungs, and he found in every acre of the island's small green fields and narrow streets classic ground. 'No language,' he wrote, 'can express the emotion which almost every American feels when he first touches the shores of Europe. This feeling must have a special increase, if it be the case of a citizen of the United States going to England. Her fame is constantly before him. He is accustomed to hear of her statesmen, her orators, her scholars, her philosophers, her divines, her patriots. In the nursery he learns her ballads. Her poets train his imagination. . . . In spite of political differences, her glory allures him. In spite of hostile collision, he clings to her lineage.'

But there were other aspects of the Old World that Britain revealed to the children of the New. As they approached her shores they saw the bristle of guns from the forts and heard the shrill sound of bugles. Other contrasts tended to lessen with time, such as the accumulated wealth and splendour of display which amazed the primitive republicans who visited London in the early nineteenth century but made small impression on the sophisticated New Yorker of the twentieth. But the sense of warlike preparation remained a constant source of comment to the traveller from the Western world. That, and the strength of antique tradition in the English ruling classes that manifested itself in such pageants as the changing of the Guard and the Royal Procession at Ascot, and, even more pervading, the brume and darkness of the land. ' I am tempted to ask,' wrote Rush in 1817, ' how the English become great with so little daylight.' It was an insoluble mystery.

In the succession of these observers, and in pursuit of the same cementing mission, came Walter Page in the early summer of 1913. He was unacquainted with either the island or its people, though he knew its literature better than most. The race struck him even before he arrived, for he observed its characteristics on the boat. ' There are three titled Englishmen who sit at the table with me on this ship,' he wrote in the earliest of the brilliant letters that tell the story of his embassy to Britain, ' one a former Lord Mayor of London, another a peer, and the third an M.P. Damn their self-sufficiencies ! They do excite my envy. *They* don't shoulder the work of the world; they shoulder the world and leave the work to be done by somebody else. Three days' stories and political discussion with them have made me wonder why the devil I've been so industrious all my life. They know more than I know : they are richer than I am ; they have been about the world more than I have ; they are far more influential than I am ; and yet one of them asked me to-day if George Washington was a born American ! I said to him, " Where the devil do you suppose he came from— Hades ? " And he laughed at himself as heartily as the rest of us laughed at him, and didn't care a hang ! '

Almost as soon as he landed Walter Page endeared himself to this strange people. He was asked by a reporter, who had read some garbled report of his words in an

American paper, whether it was true that he was to wear knee-breeches, and he replied, in the open fashion of his country, that the existence of an ass in the United States ought not necessarily to require the existence of a corresponding ass in London. The delighted reporter printed it. The quick humour of the answer was a better passport to the hearts of the islanders than all the formal verbiage of his official credentials.

Page found London much as his predecessors had done. There was no ambassadorial residence provided by his country and he had to spend three months at the Coburg Hotel while he transacted official business in a depressing Chancery in Victoria Street, dingy with twenty-nine years of dirt and darkness and wedged ' between two cheap stores, with the same entrance that the dwellers in cheap flats above used—I knew that Uncle Sam had no fit dwelling there.' ' The offices of the United States Government in London,' he wrote home, ' ought at least to be as good as a common lawyer's in a country town in a rural state of our Union.' The King of England, the first monarch he had ever seen, when he spoke to him at his audience, sympathised : ' it is not fair to an Ambassador,' he said and spoke most earnestly. Page, ever forward to defend his country, explained that the United States had so many absorbing domestic tasks and so comparatively few foreign problems, that she had only recently begun to develop an international consciousness.

He got his embassy—a fine house in Grosvenor Square— and was able in his letters home to impress on the President the importance of America's presenting a proper appearance in her dealings with other powers. ' Our Government, though green, isn't young enough to plead its youth. It is time that it, too, were learning Old World manners in dealing with Old World peoples.' After all an inward and spiritual grace demanded an outward and visible form.

The country he had come to quickly impressed itself on Page's mind. There were vast houses with powdered footmen and a queer half-stilted, half-intimate society in which confusion was intensified for a foreigner by nobody ever introducing anybody to anybody. The most extra-ordinary customs survived : pots of herbs placed on the desk of every court of law in London, because of the days of Defoe or thereabouts they had been supposed to keep the Plague off; a company of soldiers each night in the Bank of England, because two centuries before someone had tried to rob it; flowers every anniversary on the statue of King Charles I in Trafalgar Square. The towels were always folded in the way they had always been folded, the coal fires were laid in the grates as they had always been laid, and a second grace was said before dessert instead of at the end of dinner, because some generations back the parson had generally vanished under the table before that consummation could be reached. The very Boots refused to leave off blacking the soles of one's shoes because they had blacked in that way from time immemorial.

Then there was the climate. ' The winter has come—the winter months at least. But they have had no cold weather. . . . But the sun has gone out to sea—clean gone. We never see it. A damp darkness (semi-darkness at least) hangs over us all the time. But we manage to feel our way about.' Yet the people who lived in these depressing conditions had a genius for gardens and good living: in the summer they entertained one under ancient trees on wonderful green lawns, blazing with flowers. Only they resisted new conveniences with a fierce, unyielding opposition almost as though they were a kind of disease. ' They don't really like bathrooms yet. They prefer great tin tubs, and they use bowls and pitchers when a bathroom is next door. The telephone—Lord deliver us !—I've given it up. They know nothing about it. . . . You can't buy a newspaper on the street, except in the afternoon. Cigar-stores are as scarce as hen's teeth. Barber-shops are all " hair-dressers "—dirty and wretched beyond description. You can't get a decent pen; their newspapers are as big as tablecloths. In this aquarium in which we live (it rains every day) they have only three vegetables and two of them are cabbages.'

Yet antiquated as were their institutions and absurd their prejudices, the people were good. They abhorred the smart in talk, were gentle, cultivated and, after their first frigidity, good mannered, had wit and were frank and genuine. For all the talk of national decay, there was nothing degenerate about them: under the surface Page recognised that they were fighters to a man.

But they had terrible handicaps—slums and an idle class and another class of servants and parasites who depended on the rich. That struck him as the worst disability of all. ' To an American democrat,' he wrote, ' the sad thing is the servile class. Before the law the chimney sweep and the peer have exactly the same standing. They have worked that out with absolute justice. But there it stops. The serving class is what we should call abject. It does not occur to them that they might ever become—or that their descendants might ever become—ladies and gentlemen.' These Britishers seemed to suppose that forms and ceremonies were more important than human beings. And they thought as much of the once-a-year ceremony of opening their courts of law as they thought of the even justice that they dispensed : the justice was made to depend on the ceremony. Their whole lives appeared to be formulas.

Yet even in their worship of flummery Page recognised a certain method in their madness. The servants sat at table in a rigid order, and his wife's English maid wouldn't yield her precedence to a mere housemaid for any mortal consideration any more than a royal person would yield to one of a lower rank. A real democracy seemed as far off as Doomsday. ' So you argue, till you remember that it is these same people who made human liberty possible—to a degree—and till you sit day after day and hear them in the House of Commons, mercilessly pounding one another. Then you are puzzled. Do they keep all these outworn things because they are incapable of changing anything, or do these outworn burdens keep them from becoming able to change anything ? I daresay it works both ways. Every venerable ruin, every outworn custom, makes the King more secure; and the King gives veneration to every ruin and keeps respect for every outworn custom.'

When all was said and done the world never saw a finer lot of men than the best of their ruling class, men like Sir Edward Grey, Lord Morley and Mr. Harcourt, with whom Page associated in his daily work. And he met such men everywhere—gentle-bred, high-minded, physically fit, intellectually cultivated, patriotic. 'If the devotion to old forms and the inertia which makes any change almost impossible strike an American as out-of-date,' he wrote, 'you must remember that in the grand old times of England, they had all these things and had them worse than they are now. I can't see that the race is breaking down or giving out.'

Yet over the whole of this remarkable country, so like America in some respects, so utterly unlike in others, brooded the shadow of fear. Among those in high place there was an atmosphere of strain that amounted almost to hysteria. Somehow it reminded Page of the tense days of the slavery controversy before the Civil War. Its cause wasn't in the political bitterness that divided the rulers of the nation into two mutually exclusive and angry camps: it lay deeper than that. For all the assurance of their ancient wealth and pomp of power, these proud islanders were afraid. They, and all their neighbours, were awaiting something terrible. Every now and then the Ambassador got glimpses of what it was.

For the men of the Old World felt that they were living on a powder magazine. One evening at dinner Page sat next to an officer from the Admiralty named Sir John Jellicoe, who told him that he never slept out of reach of the telephone. Page asked him if it ever rang. 'No,' replied Jellicoe, 'but it will.' For their very bread and meat these islanders depended on the unshaken ability of their armed ships to hold the seas: even now they were frantically laying down dreadnoughts, two keels to one. And across the North Sea a great military and naval power was watching them jealously and preparing, it seemed, to strike. All over Europe men were waiting and watching, ready to fly at one another's throats because they were afraid. ' Everything is lovely and the goose hangs high. We're having a fine time. Only, only, only—I do wish to do something constructive and lasting. Here are great navies and armies and great withdrawals of men from industry— an enormous waste. Here are kings and courts and gold lace and ceremonies which, without producing anything, require great cost to keep them going. Here are all the privileges and taxes that this state of things implies—every one a hindrance to human progress. We are free from most of these. We have more people and more capable people and many times more territory than both England and Germany; and we have more *potential* wealth than all Europe. They know that. They'd like to find a way to escape. The Hague programmes, for the most part, just lead them around a circle in the dark back to the place where they started. Somebody needs to *do* something. If we could find some friendly use for these navies and armies and kings and things—in the service of humanity—they'd follow us. We ought to find a way to use them in cleaning up the tropics under our leadership and under our code of ethics—that everything must be done for the good of the tropical peoples and that nobody may annex a foot of land. They want a job. Then they'd quit sitting on their haunches, growling at one another.'

So Page diagnosed the evil that lay over Europe. A way had to be found out of this stagnant watching. Otherwise a way would have to be fought out of it, and a great European war would set the Old World, and perhaps the New World too, a long way back, and thereafter the armed watching would only begin again. And no one but his own beloved country, the Ambassador argued, could find it. ' We are in the international game—not in its Old World intrigues and burdens and sorrows and melancholy, but in the inevitable way to leadership and to cheerful mastery in the future; and everybody knows that we are in it but us. It is a sheer blind habit that causes us to continue to try to think of ourselves as aloof. They think in terms of races here, and we are of their race, and we shall become the strongest and the happiest branch of it.'

For there lay the best promise of the future. ' The great economic tide of the century flows our way. *We* shall have the big world questions to decide presently. Then we shall need world policies; and it will be these old-time world leaders that we shall then have to work with, more closely than now.' And England, though the time had not yet come for her to admit it, would presently welcome American leadership towards peace. ' A civilization, especially an old civilization, isn't an easy nut to crack. But I notice that the men of vision keep their thought on us. They never forget that we are 100 million strong and that we dare do new things; and they dearly love to ask questions about—Rockefeller ! Our power, our adaptability, our potential wealth they never forget. They'll hold fast to our favour for reasons of prudence as well as for reasons of kinship. And, whenever we choose to assume the leadership of the world, they'll grant it—gradually—and follow loyally. They cannot become French, and they dislike the Germans. They must keep in our boat for safety as well as for comfort.'

Yes, the future of the world lay with America. A man with two economic eyes in his head needed to live in England but a very little time to become aware of it. The English were spending their capital. ' We're making History, and these people here know it The trade of the world, or as much of it as is profitable, we may take as we will. The over-taxed, under-productive, army-burdened men of the Old World—alas ! I read a settled melancholy in much of their statesmanship and in more of their literature. The most cheerful men in official life here are the High Commissioners of Canada, Australia, New Zealand, and such fellows who know what the English race is doing and can do freed from uniforms and heavy taxes and class feeling and such like.' Soon the leadership of the Anglo-Saxon race and with it of mankind must pass to American hands. What was she going to do with it ?

But little more than a year after Page's arrival in England

it became doubtful whether mankind was to have any future at all, beyond a shambles. With dramatic suddenness the crash he had foretold came about. At one moment it seemed he was living in the high midsummer pomps of the Alice-in-Wonderland world of the London season—Courts and Palace garden parties, dinners and evening receptions with stars and orders glittering beneath ancient pictures and candelabra, and week-ends in graceful ancestral homes where all the greatest men and smartest women of the land congregated—and the next the whole world was standing on its head while the guns thundered across the Channel. Page, like others, remembered the first week of the War as a series of nightmare glimpses—the Embassy crowded with stranded Americans clamouring for money, lost relatives and immediate transport across the Atlantic, the Austrian Ambassador almost crazy in his pyjamas despairingly reiterating, ' My dear colleague, my dear colleague,' and the King of England throwing up his hands and breaking out in simple and unanswerable staccato, ' My God, Mr. Page, what else could we do ? '

Page's first reactions to the tragedy were purely American. Thank God, he thought, for the Atlantic ocean ! ' You are in a peaceful land,' he wrote to his son, ' the war is a long, long way off. You suffer nothing worse than a little idleness and a little poverty. They are nothing. I hope (and believe) that you get enough to eat. Be content, then. Read the poets, improve a piece of land, play with the baby, learn golf. That's the happy and philosophic and fortunate life in these times of world-madness. As for the continent of Europe—forget it. We have paid far too much attention to it. It has ceased to be worth it. And now it's of far less value to us—and will be for the rest of your life—than it has ever been before. An ancient home of man, the home, too, of beautiful things—buildings, pictures, old places, old traditions, dead civilizations—the place where man rose from barbarism to civilization—it is now bankrupt, its best young men dead, its system of politics and of government a failure, its social structure enslaving and tyrannical—it has little help

for us. The American spirit, which is the spirit that concerns
itself with making life better for the whole mass of men—
that's at home at its best with us. The whole future of the
race is in the new countries,—our country chiefly. This
grows on one more and more and more. The things that
are best worth while are on our side of the ocean. . . . For
fifty years the continent won't be worth living on. My
heavens ! what bankruptcy will follow death ! '

And it would all end, in whatever else, in America's being
stronger and more assured of the future than ever. ' It will
revive our shipping. . . . The United States is the only great
Power wholly out of it. The United States, most likely,
therefore, will be able to play a helpful and historic part at
its end. It will give President Wilson, no doubt, a great
opportunity. It will probably help us politically and it will
surely help us economically. . . . I walked out in the night
a while ago. The stars are bright, the night is silent, the
country quiet—as quiet as peace itself. Millions of men are
in camp and on warships. Will they all have to fight and
many of them die—to untangle this network of treaties and
alliances and to blow off huge debts with gunpowder so that
the world may start again ? '

For the rest Page like everybody else was absorbed in the
frantic improvisation of those first days. ' Upon my word,
if one could forget the awful tragedy, all this experience
would be worth a lifetime of common-place. One surprise
follows another so rapidly that one loses all sense of time;
it seems an age since last Sunday. I shall never forget
Sir Edward Grey's telling me of the ultimatum—while he
wept; nor the poor German Ambassador who has lost in
his high game—almost a demented man. . . . Along with
all this tragedy come two reverend American peace delegates
who got out of Germany by the skin of their teeth and
complain that they lost all the clothes they had except what
they had on. " Don't complain," said I, " but thank God
you saved your skins." Everybody has forgotten what war
means—forgotten that folks get hurt. But they are coming
around to it now. A United States Senator telegraphs me:

" Send my wife and daughter home on the first ship."
Ladies and gentlemen filled the steerage of that ship—not a
bunk left; and his wife and daughter are found three days
later sitting in a swell hotel waiting for me to bring them
stateroom tickets on a silver tray ! '

That was the first mood. But when the time came for
reflection Page realised that he was not merely a spectator.
What was taking place concerned the whole future of
the human race, and neither America nor any other people
could stand aside from it. For here was no mere dog-
fight between jealous nations, but a struggle between
certain great principles of right and wrong. Whatever the
fears that had made the tragedy first possible its issues had
been dictated by the nature of the German challenge. The
King of England had been right: when Belgium had been
invaded in cynical defiance of every sacred promise and
canon of civilisation, what else could his country have done ?

For Page, living on the spot, saw what the great mass of
his countrymen, cut off by the ocean, could not see, that
there was a fundamental difference in the position of the
combatants. If there was any such thing as public morality
and decency and good faith between nations, Germany was
in the wrong. The issue had got to be fought now to the
finish, horrible though the cost must be. It was unavoidable.
' No, no, no,' Page wrote to House, ' no power on earth
could have prevented it. The German militarism, which is
the crime of the last fifty years, has been working for this for
twenty-five years. It is the logical result of their spirit and
enterprise and doctrine. It *had* to come. . . . We've got
to see to it that this system doesn't grow up again. That's all.'

Therefore, her Ambassador held, America could not rid
herself of the issue. In the end it must affect her as much as
any nation—nay, more, for her whole ideal of human society
was at fundamental loggerheads with the conception of
Prussian militarism. ' If sheer brute force is to rule the
world, it will not be worth living in. If German bureaucratic
brute force could conquer Europe, presently it would try to
conquer the United States; and we should all go back to

208

the era of war as man's chief industry and back to the domination of kings by divine right.' In that event the Monroe Doctrine would be shot in two and America would have to get out of her place in the sun to make room for some new German demand. Somehow, therefore, the Hohenzollern idea must be strangled.

In stating this view, Page indicated the position that was to be occupied after two and a half bitter years by his own President and the people of his country. At the moment he was almost in it. There was no immediate likelihood or even possibility of America's abandoning her natural and highly profitable neutrality. All he could do was to devote himself to the heavy and wearing task of representing her at the seat of war, keep the President and his advisers informed of what was really happening, and contemplate the grim spectacle of the island race among whom his lot had been cast fighting for their existence and the future of mankind.

He could not help being deeply moved by what he saw, and no Englishman who reads his letters to-day can do anything but be grateful to this American that he saw it. Many years before when he visited her, Emerson had pronounced that England was never greater than in the day of adversity. The truth of his dictum was now being proved before Page's eyes. ' Even a fortnight ago,' he wrote home, ' the people of this Kingdom didn't realize all that the war means to them. But the fever is rising now. The wounded are coming back, the dead are mourned, and the agony of hearing only that such-and-such a man is missing— these are having a prodigious effect. The men I meet now say in a matter-of-fact way: " Oh, yes ! we'll get 'em, of course; the only question is, how long it will take us and how many of us it will cost. But no matter, we'll get 'em." Old ladies and gentlemen of the high, titled world now begin by driving to my house almost every morning while I am at breakfast. With many apologies for calling so soon and with the fear that they interrupt me, they ask if I can make any inquiry in Germany for " my son," or " my nephew "—

" he's among the missing." They never weep; their voices do not falter; they are brave and proud and self-restrained. It seems a sort of matter-of-course to them. Sometimes when they get home, they write me polite notes thanking me for receiving them. . . . And at intervals they come all day. Not a tear have I seen yet. They take it as a part of the price of greatness and of empire. You guess at their grief only by their reticence. They use as few words as possible and then courteously take themselves away. It isn't an accident that these people own a fifth of the world. Utterly unwarlike, they outlast anybody else when war comes. You don't get a sense of fighting here—only of endurance and of high resolve.'

And as he watched his generous American heart could not help expanding with pride. The daughter had not strayed so far from the mother after all. ' I see these British at close range, full-dress and undress; and I've got to know a lot of 'em as well as we can ever come to know anybody after we get grown. There is simply no end to the silly sides of their character. But, when the real trial comes, they don't flinch; and (except the thoroughbred American) there are no such men in the world.'

' Turning from the awful spectacle on land and sea, it is inspiring to watch this nation—sad, dead-earnest, resolute, united—not a dissenting voice—silent. It will spend all its treasure and give all its men, if need be. I have never seen such grim resolution.'

Feeling as he did, Page's task at the capital of the chief of the allied belligerents was anything but easy: it would have been hard enough under any circumstance. American shipping and business interests were presented with a golden harvest by the war, and the way to it was being constantly barred by the British Fleet, whose part it was to deprive Germany of the raw materials which she needed for the struggle. All the old questions of contraband that had brought England and America to blows in 1812, and had nearly done so again during the Civil War, once more became acute. The tempers of American traders and of hard-pressed British Admiralty officials were constantly aroused, and both tended to vent their wrath on the Ambassador. His difficulties were increased by the pettifogging inhumanity of the departmental lawyers at Washington who persisted, after the manner of their kind, in presenting the complaints of their injured countrymen in the most exacting and offensive form of which they were capable, without making the slightest allowance for the overwhelming difficulties of the British Foreign Office. ' The lawyer-way in which the Department goes on in its dealings with Great Britain is losing us the only great international friendship that we have any chance of keeping or that is worth having. . . . I sometimes wish there were not a lawyer in the world.'

In his telling and human way Page put the nature of his problem to House. ' Suppose the postman some morning were to leave at your door a thing of thirty-five heads and three appendices, and you discovered that it came from an old friend whom you had long known and greatly valued—this vast mass of legal stuff, without a word or a turn of courtesy in it—what would you do ? He had a grievance, your old friend had. Friends often have. But instead of explaining it to you, he had gone and had his lawyers send this many-headed, much-appendiced ton of stuff. It wasn't by that method that you found your way from Austin, Texas, to your present eminence and wisdom. Nor was that the way our friend found his way from a little law-office in Atlanta, where I first saw him, to the White House. More and more I am struck with this—that governments are human. They are not remote abstractions, nor impersonal institutions. Men conduct them; and they do not cease to be men.' In such realisation, as Page like Lincoln before him had always seen, was the gist of all good government.

Fortunately, Page had as his *vis-à-vis* at the British Foreign Office a man, human and sympathetic as himself. He and Sir Edward Grey, sometimes in the teeth of the temporary impatience of their countrymen, made their own understanding of one another the measure of Anglo-American relationships at one of the most difficult moments of their history. Nor was there any lack of frankness between them. ' I have, in fact,' Page related, ' stood up before Sir Edward's fire and accused him of stealing a large part of the earth's surface, and we were just as good friends afterward as before. But I never drew a lawyer's indictment of him as a land-thief: that's different.'

The nature of that alliance between the English country gentleman and the American journalist and publisher is illustrated by a curious story told in Mr. Hendrick's brilliant life of Page. At a moment when matters were dangerously strained between the two nations, a German vessel, which had been lying at her wharf in Port Arthur, Texas, since the outbreak of the War, was purchased by an American, admitted to American registry, laden with cotton and openly despatched for Germany. Those in America who were hostile to Britain, and they were at that time many, regarded it as a ' dare,' and the British Admiralty made matters still more tense by announcing their intention of taking up the ' dare.' About the time the *Dacia* sailed, Page called at the Foreign Office, and, after bidding him good morning, asked the astonished Sir Edward Grey if he had ever heard of the British Fleet. ' Yes,' the American Ambassador went on, ' we've all heard of the British Fleet. Perhaps we've heard too much about it. Don't you think it's had too much advertising ? '[1] And when Grey, supposing his friend had gone mad, asked him what he meant, Page demanded if he had ever heard of the French Fleet. ' France,' he said, ' has a Fleet too I believe.' The friendly hint was taken, and the *Dacia* was seized by the French, not the British Fleet, and promptly condemned by a French prize court. Nor did anybody in America, recalling Lafayette, complain.

There were other ships beside the *Dacia*, and worse injuries done to vital American interests than any a harassed,

[1] Burton J. Hendrick, *The Life and Letters of Walter H. Page*, vol. i. p. 394.

reluctant Britain offered. In May 1915 the *Lusitania* was torpedoed by a German submarine off the coast of Ireland and over a hundred American citizens went down with her. It was one of a long and seemingly endless series of wrongs and insults done by Germany to the United States. The State Department at Washington answered them with a succession of notes and President Wilson announced that he was too proud to fight. Others took a different view of America's attitude. ' War with America? Ach no ! ' said a German staff officer to an American correspondent. ' Not war. If trouble should come, we'd send over a platoon of our policemen to whip your little army.' ' As for being kicked by a *sauerkraut* case,—O Lord give us backbone ! ' was Page's mournful comment.

Even the English, painfully and pathetically anxious as they were to retain America's friendship, began after a while to express bewilderment and then contempt at the President's attitude. ' They say that the American democracy since Cleveland's day,' Page wrote, ' has become a mere agglomeration of different races, without national unity, national aims, and without courage or moral qualities.' The man in the street was humorously and undisguisedly contemptuous: American neutrality and the infinite capacity of the American President for accepting insults became the stock popular joke with which they cheered themselves at a time when jokes were hard to come by. The more serious classes politely refrained from comment and avoided the subject when they spoke with the Ambassador: but in talk among themselves expressed the belief that Wilson's reliance on notes had reduced America to the status of a third or fourth-rate power, and even spoke of spheres of German influence in the United States as though she were another China.

Page, who loved his country and her great ideals as passionately as Jefferson or Roosevelt, felt the shame of it intensely. He, who was so fond of boasting of the greatness of American democracy, and who loved so much to mix with his fellow men, ceased almost entirely to engage in social intercourse lest he should hear America ill spoken of or feel

213

the slur implied by the silent consideration of his hosts. Many of his countrymen, reading his letters superficially, have marvelled at their open support of England at that tragic period of his life, and have set him down as an amiable but unAmerican Anglo-maniac. But Page's desire for American intervention was not based on love for England, though he did understand and love her as few strangers have done, but on his far deeper love for his own country. Like Theodore Roosevelt on the other side of the Atlantic, he was praying that she would be true to herself and to her own innermost ideal before it should be too late to save, as she alone could save, the world's doomed democracy.

His was a sad and perplexed sojourn. All round him the death agonies of the Old World intensified, as he saw France and Britain fighting with their backs to the wall for the future of the democratic ideal. He seemed to stand altogether alone. His communications to Washington were unanswered, and his secret despatches were even given to the Press by the State Department he was supposed to represent. His faith in the President he had made was gone, though he still wrote him long, friendly and amazingly frank letters. He had come at last to see that this man of whom he had hoped so much was not a leader but a mere stubborn phrase-maker. In London Page did not care any more to have friends. ' It's the loneliest time I've had in England,' he confided, ' there's a tendency to avoid me.' All the while he bore the burden of a ceaseless labour that was slowly killing him. He was only saved by his wonderful gift for sleep. But sometimes he would not sleep: only sit beside his bed long into the night in silent and solitary communing.

But he never lost his faith in the ultimate unity of creed between England and America nor ceased to pursue his patient purpose to bring about their ultimate understanding. It was the farthest future that he was thinking of. ' Since I have lived here I have spent my days and nights, my poor brain, and my small fortune all most freely and gladly to get some understanding of the men who rule this Kingdom, and of the women and the customs and the traditions that rule these men—to get their trick of thought, the play of their ideals, the working of their imagination, the springs of their instincts. It is impossible for any man to know just how well he himself does such a difficult task—how accurately he is coming to understand the sources and character of a people's actions. Yet, at the worst, I do know something about the British: I know enough to make very sure of the soundness of my conclusion that they are necessary to us and we to them. Else God would have permitted the world to be peopled in some other way.'

Nor even at his darkest moment did he doubt that somehow he would achieve his purpose. He sought it by a patient courtesy, which he believed to be the infallible solvent between nations and the only sovereign method of all diplomacy—the opposite end of the pole, in fact, to war. ' I have found out that the first step toward that end is courtesy, that the second step is courtesy, and the third step courtesy.' And the reward, if it ever came, would be such an understanding between the two nations as should henceforward make each other's security under every circumstance certain. ' For this reason every day that I have lived here it has been my conscious aim to do what I could to bring about a condition that shall make sure of this—that, whenever we may have need of the British Fleet to protect our shores or to prevent an aggressive war anywhere, it shall be ours by a natural impulse and necessity—even without the asking.' And there would be more to it even than that. For if the American and British fleets could only learn to shoot the same language, there would be assured a permanent peace in the world and an end of wars of aggression. Nor was any other permanent peace-basis worth talking about— by those who knew how the world was governed.

Through the long waiting agony of 1916 and the opening months of 1917 Page ploughed his hard and lonely furrow. Fortunately his sense of humour saved him from the less serious horrors of his position. 'Six American preachers,' he wrote, 'pass a resolution unanimously " urging our Ambassador to telegraph our beloved, peace-loving President to stop this awful war "; and they come with simple solemnity to present their resolution. Lord save us, what a world ! ' Such delegations were growing phenomena at the Embassy. ' Daughters of the Dove of Peace and Sons of the Olive Branch come every week. The latest Son came to see me to-day. He said that the German Chancellor told him that he wanted peace—wants it now and wants it bad, and that only one thing stood in the way—if England would agree not to take Belgium, Germany would at once make peace ! This otherwise sensible American wanted me to take him to see Sir Edward to tell him this, and to suggest to him to go over to Holland next week to meet the German Chancellor and fix it up. A few days ago a pious preacher chap (American) who had come over to " fix it all up," came back from France and called on me. He had seen something in France—he was excited and he didn't quite make it clear what he had seen ; but he said that if they'd only let him go home safely and quickly he'd promise not to mention peace any more—did I think the American boats *entirely* safe ? So, you see, I do have some fun even in these dark days.'

They came to an end. For nearly three years the President appeared to see the war only as a bloody consummation of the economic rivalries of Germany and England and told the people of America to follow the tempting, easy course and wash their hands of the whole business. To Page it seemed that, shut up in his study, the air currents of the world never ventilated his mind. But at last they began to reach the American people, and the time came when the President had only to raise a finger to bring his country into the war. That was the moment that the Potsdam Government chose to commence an unrestricted submarine campaign against neutral shipping and to make overtures to Mexico and Japan for an attack on the United States. The President raised his finger and at the eleventh hour America entered the war.

It is arguable that in doing so the President showed consummate statesmanship in exactly gauging the feeling of the country and leading her into the conflict at the precise moment when she was ready for it. But this argument presupposes that not by any act of leadership or word of counsel from its own elected chief could the nation have been impelled a step nearer war prior to the spring of 1917. From the time of Washington each of the great American Presidents, through Andrew Jackson and Lincoln to Theodore Roosevelt, had followed the brave and honourable practice of giving the nation a definite lead in time of crisis. And the nation had always responded. Between August 1914 and April 1917 Wilson gave the country no lead whatever, except for his declaration that a country could be too proud to fight and a certain degree of public self-congratulation that he had kept her out of war. Yet if it was right to enter the war on behalf of freedom in 1917, it had been equally right in 1914: the issues of the conflict had not changed. The delay prolonged the struggle, and vastly increased the casualty lists at the time and the price of bitterness and suffering to be paid later. For that delay the American people cannot be blamed: it was in their President's power and not in theirs to advocate a policy of vigorous action. If on the other hand, as many Americans now believe, the intervention of the United States was wrong, Wilson showed even less capacity for leadership in failing to prevent it.

A few evenings before the President's decision was announced to the world, Page, breaking his rule at last, dined at a friend's house. During the meal one of the guests so far forgot himself as to make a sneering reference to America's delay. The Ambassador made no comment. But when the ladies had left the room, he turned to a young English diplomat, now a famous man of letters,[1] who was in the secret and said quietly, ' Well, Mr. Nicolson, I think that you and I will drink a glass of wine together.' ' Mr. Page is perhaps the greatest gentleman I have ever known,' was Mr. Nicolson's subsequent comment.

For the Ambassador's heart was full with thankfulness.

[1] The Hon. Harold Nicolson.

A week later, on the day after America's declaration of war, an English friend met him in the street and, seeing his beaming face, greeted him with a ' Thank God that there is one hypocrite less in London to-day. I mean you,' he added, ' pretending all this time that you were neutral.' At the moment Page was probably the happiest man in London.

But his work was almost done, and his life too. For a further year, and more, though he had brought himself to the very end of his reserves of strength, he continued at his post, unflagging in his labours to cement the alliance of the two peoples and to assist the tremendous effort which his country-men were now putting forth under the leadership of their President to win the war. And in that wonderful corre-spondence with his friends he continued to pour out the treasures of his observation, which in days to come will constitute one of the chief records of what those last months of the war were like.

One of his pictures stands in the mind.

I was at a dinner of old Peers at the Athenæum Club—a group of old cocks that I meet once in a while and have come to know pretty well and ever to marvel at. I think every one is past seventy—several of them past eighty. On this occasion I was the only commoner present. The talk went on about every imaginable thing—reminiscences of Browning, the years of good vintages of port, the excellence of some court opinions handed down in the United States by quite obscure judges—why shouldn't they be got out of the masses of law reports and published as classics ?—wouldn't it have been well if the King had gone and spent his whole time at the front and on the fleet,—what's an English King for anyhow ?—then a defence of Reading; and why should the Attorney General or the Lord Chief Justice be allowed out of the Kingdom at all at such a time ?

' Call in the chief steward. . . . Here, steward, what's that noise ? '

' A hair raid, milord.'

' How long has it been going on ? '

' Forty minutes, milord.'

' I must be deaf,' said the old fellow, with an inquiring look at

218

the company. Everybody else had heard it, but we've learned to take these things for granted and nobody had interrupted the conversation to speak of it. Then the old man spoke up again. 'Well, there's nothing we can do to protect His Excellency. Damn the air raid. Pass the port.'

The man who wrote thus was already dying of nephritis. 'Quit your job and go home,' the doctors told him, 'your life will be forfeit otherwise.' 'I have only one life to lay down,' he answered. 'It's quitting on the job. I must see the war through. I can't quit until it's over.' Not till his worn-out frame collapsed beneath him did he surrender. The grateful people, whose friend he had been in their hour of need, surrounded him with kindness, and as he lay helpless at Sandwich he could hear the guns across the Channel sounding the final crisis and approaching victory. Then the *Olympic* bore him across the Atlantic, with her engines driven at breakneck speed, that he might see his own western land before he died.

'History,' his biographer has written, 'will indeed be ungrateful if it ever forgets the gaunt and pensive figure, clad in a dressing gown, sitting long into the morning before the smouldering fire at 6, Grosvenor Square, seeking to find some way to persuade a reluctant and hesitating President to lead his country in the defence of liberty and determined that, so far as he could accomplish it, the nation should play a part in the great assize that was in keeping with its traditions and its instincts.' [1] Yet his real service to America was not that he persuaded the President, but that he left behind in the hearts of the noblest Englishmen a great love and a new understanding and the recollected realisation of a fragrant and beautiful dream.

[1] Burton J. Hendrick, *The Life and Letters of Walter H. Page*, vol. ii. pp. 319-20.

CHAPTER VI

TWO AMERICAN POETS OF THE TWENTIETH CENTURY

IN the last resort a nation lives not by what it does—by its conquests and acquisitions—but by what it is. And the best measure of what a nation is, is to be found in its art and its poetry. Modern America is vast and powerful, she has been rich and will probably be so again, for her material resources are gigantic. But wealth and power are only consequences, and arise as a result of certain spiritual qualities—courage, energy, vitality—in the race which creates them. If those qualities are lost, wealth and power may continue to subsist for a time but will inevitably pass.

' All that we call sacred history,' wrote Emerson, ' attests that the birth of a poet is the principal event in chronology.' Alan Seeger was born on June 22, 1888, at New York, of New England descent on both sides of his family. The first ten years of his life were spent on Staten Island, at the entrance to New York harbour, ' the gateway to the Western Hemisphere,' and the very quintessence of the passing beauty and glamour of the modern age. When he was twelve his family moved to Mexico, so that his childish eyes, which had learnt to take in one form of earthly loveliness, the perfection of great machines moving through northern waters under the shadow of New York's gigantic cliffs, were now presented with another—of the dreaming South that had haunted Whitman's early manhood and which Seeger himself in later years was to sing.

TWO AMERICAN POETS

Star of the South that now through orient mist
At nightfall off Tampico or Belize
Greetest the sailor rising from those seas
Where first in me, a fond romanticist,
The tropic sunset's bloom on cloudy piles
Cast out industrious cares with dreams of fabulous isles—

Here he passed two pregnant years.

Where tinted coast-towns gleam at close of day,
Where squares are sweet with bells, or shores thick set
With bloom and bower, with mosque and minaret.

Later Seeger, with his mind already stored with the images
of a poet, was sent to a school at Tarrytown in New
York State, overlooking the Hudson. Thence he went to
Harvard, where he ransacked, for his own benefit and
glory, the whole American heritage, reading furiously in
the Boston Library, translating Dante and Ariosto and
playing a leading part in the social life of the University.
Then with comfortable means, many friends and an almost
boundless capacity for enjoyment, he plunged into the life of
New York.

But the bustle and calculated self-seeking of pre-war New
York could not satisfy the deepest needs in Seeger's nature.
In 1912 he obtained his parents' consent to go to Paris, and
here in *appartements* near the Musée de Cluny he found the
fulfilment he was seeking—

A law that's sane, a Love that's free, and men of every birth
and blood
Allied in one great brotherhood of Art and Joy and Poverty . . .

In the Quartier Latin he shared the life of his fellow artists,
wrote and worked, cemented friendships, made love and
followed beauty in all its transient, earthly forms. In the
immature verses which he wrote at this time and called his
Juvenilia he tried to paint the life he lived and the world
of Paris that was its background.

221

THE AMERICAN IDEAL

Oh, go to Paris. . . . In the midday gloom
Of some old quarter take a little room
 That looks off over Paris and its towers
From Saint-Gervais round to the Emperor's Tomb,—

So high that you can hear a mating dove
Croon down the chimney from the roof above,
 See Notre-Dame and know how sweet it is
To wake between Our Lady and our love.

And have a little balcony to bring
Fair plants to fill with verdure and blossoming,
 That sparrows seek, to feed from pretty hands,
And swallows circle over in the Spring.

There of an evening you shall sit at ease
In the sweet month of flowering chestnut-trees,
 There with your little darling in your arms,
Your pretty dark-eyed Manon or Louise.

And looking out over the domes and towers
That chime the fleeting quarters and the hours,
 While the bright clouds banked eastward back of them
Blush in the sunset, pink as hawthorn flowers,

You cannot fail to think, as I have done,
Some of life's ends attained, so you be one
 Who measures life's attainment by the hours
That Joy has rescued from oblivion.

It was a simple, pagan existence, not very serious, un-
checked by puritanical inhibitions, and infinitely removed,
it seemed, from the ordinary struggles and problems of a
harsh world. His attitude towards it was that of the pure
artist, neither condemning nor questioning, but enjoying
every moment of it and its ever-changing vitality and
loveliness. And even in what many would condemn as its
unblushing immorality there was nothing morbid, for it was
all joyous and alive with the spirit of youth.

Here Mimi ventures, at fifteen, to make her *début* in romance,
And join her sisters in the dance and see the life that they
   have seen.

.   .   .   .   .   .

Uncorseted, her clinging dress with every step and turn betrays,
In pretty and provoking ways her adolescent loveliness,

.   .   .   .   .   .

Each turn a challenge, every pose an invitation to compete,
Along the maze of whirling feet the grave-eyed little wanton
   goes,

And, flaunting all the hue that lies in childish cheeks and
   nubile waist,
She passes, charmingly unchaste, illumining ignoble eyes. . . .

For it is the sense of wonder, and of adoration arising from
that wonder, which poetry and religion have in common. As
yet it was only the outward world of the senses that commanded Seeger's worship.

In the Bohemian day-by-day existence of Paris, Seeger
accepted the joy and exultation of living as an outward
manifestation of the beauty that was his religion. Long
before the post-war writers had made it commonplace this
young American, characteristic of so much that was best
and most adventurous in his race, restored to literature
without fuss or humbug the physical and emotional intimacies
of early life of which the nineteenth century had deprived it.
He approached the forbidden subject not as a thing brutal
and unclean but as the threshold to some greater perception
and understanding.

    I bless the spot, and hour, and circumstance,
    That wed desire to a thing so high.

Believing as he did, he was perfectly frank in his avowal of
it. It was a frankness which it will be recalled the blameless
Emerson had recommended to his countrymen.

But Seeger was too much of a poet to rest content with any
purely material perfection. Behind it, as yet only dimly

perceived, he saw the shrine of some higher beauty, divorced from the limitations of the body and the outward form.

> Then on the soul from some ancestral place
> Floods back remembrance of its heavenly birth,
> When, in the light of that serener sphere,
> It saw ideal beauty face to face
> That through the forms of this our meaner Earth
> Shines with a beam less steadfast and less clear.

For, poet's poet that he was, he was already haunted by the ever-recurring Platonic dream.

For the moment it was enough for him to live and to sum up all youthful experience, never flinched and taken with both hands, in Keats' creed ' I loved.'

> I loved illustrious cities and the crowds
> That eddy through their incandescent nights.
> I loved remote horizons with far clouds
> Girdled, and fringed about with snowy heights.
> I loved fair women, their sweet, conscious ways
> Of wearing among hands that covet and plead
> The rose ablossom at the rainbow's base
> That bounds the world's desire and all its need.
> Nature I worshipped, whose fecundity
> Embraces every vision the most fair,
> Of perfect benediction. From a boy
> I gloated on existence. Earth to me
> Seemed all-sufficient, and my sojourn there
> One trembling opportunity for joy.

And the sadness of love came as well as the happiness, the bitterness and the ache—this also he sang.

> And the tower-clock tolls five, and he admits at last,
> She will not come, the woman that he waits.

But it was worth it.

> Farewell, dear heart, enough of vain despairing !
> If I have erred I plead but one excuse—
> The jewel were a lesser joy in wearing
> That cost a lesser agony to lose.

I had not bid for beautifuller hours
  Had I not found the door so near unsealed,
Nor hoped, had you not filled my arms with flowers,
  For that one flower that bloomed too far afield.

If I have wept, it was because, forsaken,
  I felt perhaps more poignantly than some
The blank eternity from which we waken
  And all the blank eternity to come.

And I betrayed how sweet a thing and tender
  (In the regret with which my lip was curled)
Seemed in its tragic, momentary splendour
  My transit through the beauty of the world.

Rejoicing, he drank the whole passionate, intoxicating, bitter-sweet draught of it—everything except love's sad satiety. That he never knew, for the Gods slay those whom they love young.

When Seeger was twenty-six, his love of living and beauty was suddenly tested. His creed had taught him to live to the full and to let no craven fear of consequences detain him from any experience to which his youth and passion for beauty prompted him. Suddenly the life of France, which had given him all he desired, was threatened with destruction. His companions, the young Frenchmen with whom he had shared his pursuit of happiness, had vanished almost in a night to take their place in the armies which alone could save the world he loved. He could not allow his friends to die and continue to take the pleasures purchased by their sacrifice.

Seeger did not hesitate but at once enlisted in the Foreign Legion. In a letter home he explained the motives which had impelled him and other Americans in Paris to such a step. 'I have talked with so many of the young volunteers here. Their case is little known, even by the French, yet altogether interesting and appealing. They are foreigners on whom the outbreak of war laid no formal compulsion. But they had stood on the Butte in springtime perhaps, as Julian and Louise stood, and looked out over the myriad twinkling lights of the beautiful city. Paris—mystic, maternal, personified, to whom they owed the happiest moments of their lives—Paris was in peril. Were they not under a moral obligation, no less binding than [that by which] their comrades were bound legally, to put their breasts between her and destruction ? Without renouncing their nationality, they had yet chosen to make their homes here beyond any other city in the world. Did not the benefits and blessings they had received point them a duty that heart and conscience could not deny ?

' " Why did you enlist ? " In every case the answer was the same. That memorable day in August came. Suddenly the old haunts were desolate, the boon companions had gone. It was unthinkable to leave the danger to them and accept only the pleasures oneself, to go on enjoying the sweet things of life in defence of which they were perhaps even then shedding their blood in the north. Some day they would return, and with honour—not all, but some. The old order of things would have irrevocably vanished. There would be a new companionship whose bond would be the common danger run, the common sufferings borne, the common glory shared. " And where have you been all the time, and what have you been doing ? " The very question would be a reproach, though none were intended. How could they endure it ? '

To take arms at such a moment was the natural fulfilment of Seeger's creed. To count no cost, to give oneself as freely to the call of death as of life, to take no thought for the morrow but rejoice in the moment, that was the way in which a man who was true to himself should live. And death was the consummation of life, as giving was of taking and renunciation of enjoyment.

And in the realisation of this the boy who had tried in vain to express his hours of ecstasy in verse became a great poet. His lips, as Kipling wrote of a young Englishman who trod the same path, were touched. The mystic meaning of existence became revealed to him in the hour of renuncia-

tion, and the certainty of sacrifice and death only increased
the wonder and loveliness of life. The marching armies
were the letters that spelt that truth, and it was good to be
young to share in their knowledge.

> Comrades in arms there—friend or foe—
> That trod the perilous, toilsome trail
> Through a world of ruin and blood and woe
> In the years of the great decision—hail !
> Friend or foe, it shall matter nought;
> This only matters, in fine: we fought.
> For we were young and in love or strife
> Sought exultation and craved excess:
> To sound the wildest debauch in life
> We staked our youth and its loveliness.
> Let idlers argue the right and wrong
> And weigh what merit our causes had.
> Putting our faith in being strong—
> Above the level of good and bad
> For us, we battled and honored and killed
> Because evolving Nature willed,
> And it was our pride and boast to be
> The instruments of Destiny.
> There was a stately drama writ
> By the hand that peopled the earth and air
> And set the stars in the infinite
> And made night gorgeous and morning fair,
> And all that had sense to reason knew
> That bloody drama must be gone through.
> Some sat and watched how the action veered—
> Waited, profited, trembled, cheered—
> We saw not clearly nor understood,
> But yielding ourselves to the master hand,
> Each in his part as best he could,
> We played it through as the author planned.

There was another feeling : Seeger belonged to the
young, chivalrous America which Theodore Roosevelt had
fired with a sense of its own greatness and moral destiny.
Here was a war in which other peoples were staking their
existence for the ideals in which America believed. An
uneasy feeling assailed him that America, through ignorance

of the issues, was betraying her own beliefs. In the ꞁde
which he wrote in the trenches during the spring of 1916,
to be recited on Decoration Day over the volunteer American
dead of the Foreign Legion, he gave expression to this feeling and to the sense of an ancient national debt to France,
as yet unredeemed.

O friends ! I know not since that war began
From which no people nobly stands aloof
If in all moments we have given proof
Of virtues that were thought American.
I know not if in all things done and said
All has been well and good,
Or if each one of us can hold his head
As proudly as he should,
Or, from the pattern of those mighty dead
Whose shades our country venerates to-day,
If we've not somewhat fallen and somewhat gone astray.
But you to whom our land's good name is dear,
If there be any here—
Who wonder if her manhood be decreased,
Relaxed its sinews and its blood less red
Than that at Shiloh and Antietam shed,
Be proud of these, have joy in this at least,
And cry: ' Now heaven be praised
That in that hour that most imperilled her,
Menaced her liberty who foremost raised
Europe's bright flag of freedom, sòme there were
Who, not unmindful of the antique debt,
Came back the generous path of Lafayette;
And when of a most formidable foe
She checked each onset, arduous to stem—
Foiled and frustrated them—
On those red fields where blow with furious blow
Was countered, whether the gigantic fray
Rolled by the Meuse or at the Bois Sabot,
Accents of ours were in the fierce mêlée;
And on those furthest rims of hallowed ground
Where the forlorn, the gallant charge expires,
When the slain bugler has long ceased to sound,
And on the tangled wires

The last wild rally staggers, crumbles, stops,
Withered beneath the shrapnel's iron showers:—
Now heaven be thanked, we gave a few brave drops;
Now heaven be thanked, a few brave drops were ours.'

In his letters and poems Seeger expressed the experience
and philosophy of the fighting man in the first two years
of the war. The disillusionment and bitterness of its
latter part he never lived to realise. He wrote home to
his mother of the joy he found in the training of those
early months, rising at five and drilling and marching for
twelve hours a day at a sou a day: 'I hope to earn higher
wages than this in time to come, but I never expect to
work harder.' His battalion was quartered at the time in
the south and he described the beauty of the autumnal
scene, with its vineyards and yellow harvest fields and the
peasants and their teams moving about them, the poplars,
little hamlets and church vanes and on the horizon the blue
line of the Pyrenees and its snow-capped mountains. 'It
makes one in love with life, it is all so peaceful and beautiful.
But Nature to me is not only hills and blue skies and flowers,
but the Universe, the totality of things, reality as it most
obviously presents itself to us; and in this universe strife and
sternness play as big a part as love and tenderness, and cannot
be shirked by one whose will it is to rule his life in accordance
with the cosmic forces he sees in play about him. I hope
you see the thing as I do, and think that I have done well,
being without responsibilities and with no one to suffer
materially by my decision, in taking upon my shoulders, too,
the burden that so much of humanity is suffering under, and,
rather than stand ingloriously aside when the opportunity
was given me, doing my share for the side that I think
right. . . .'

With the same joyful sense of dedication he described
in October the approach to the line—the frosty nights and
sunny days on the bare, rolling expanses of Champagne,
with the sound of gunfire growing nearer as his regiment
drew north. 'You have no idea how beautiful it is to

229

see the troops undulating along the road in front of one, in *colonnes par quatre* as far as the eye can see, with the captains and lieutenants on horseback at the head of their companies. . . . To-morrow the real hardship and privations begin. But I go into action with the lightest of light hearts. The hard work and moments of frightful fatigue have not broken but hardened me, and I am in excellent health and spirits. . . . I am happy and full of excitement over the wonderful days that are ahead.' He must have had his weary and depressed moments, but he did not speak of them. ' I am feeling fine, in my element, for I have always thirsted for this kind of thing, to be present always where the pulsations are liveliest. Every minute here is worth weeks of ordinary experience.'

Seeger shared the cold and privations of that first winter in the trenches, before the armies had learnt how to equip themselves for a new mode of warfare. Exposed to all the dangers and discomforts of war with nothing of its legendary excitement, he and his companions found themselves condemned to sit half frozen, like animals in their burrows, while the shells whistled overhead and took toll of their friends. Yet even this stark life offered compensation. ' The sentinel has ample time for reflection. Alone under the stars, war in its cosmic rather than its moral aspect reveals itself to him. . . . He thrills with the sense of filling an appointed, necessary place in the conflict of hosts, and, facing the enemy's crest, above which the Great Bear wheels upward to the zenith, he feels, with a sublimity of enthusiasm that he has never before known, a kind of companionship with the stars.' Whether he was missing the chances of a great career or of success, did not seem to matter : all that he was sure of was that not for anything in the world would he be anywhere but where he was.

Sometimes, of course, there were moments of respite, when Seeger out of the line and on leave refound, in his old haunts in Paris, the joys he had formerly sought. Only they were changed now. For war and renunciation changed all things, petrifying the hours of pleasure and ecstasy and

leaving them, like the figures on Keats' urn, chaste and remote,
yet ever young, to endure for eternity.

Do you remember once, in Paris of glad faces,
The night we wandered off under the third moon's rays
And, leaving far behind bright streets and busy places,
Stood where the Seine flowed down between its quiet quais ?

The city's voice was hushed; the placid, lustrous waters
Mirrored the walls across where orange windows burned.
Out of the starry south provoking rumours brought us
Far promise of the spring already northward turned.

And breast drew near to breast, and round its soft desire
My arm uncertain stole and clung there unrepelled.
I thought that nevermore my heart would hover nigher
To the last flower of bliss that Nature's garden held.

    .   .   .   .

Dear face, when courted Death shall claim my limbs and find
    them
Laid in some desert place, alone or where the tides
Of war's tumultuous waves on the wet sands behind them
Leave rifts of gasping life when their red blood subsides,

Out of the past's remote delirious abysses
Shine forth once more as then you shone,—beloved head,
Laid back in ecstasy between our blinding kisses,
Transfigured with the bliss of being so coveted.

And my sick arms will part, and though hot fever sear it,
My mouth will curve again with the old, tender flame.
And darkness will come down, still finding in my spirit
The dream of your brief love, and on my lips your name.

In a still greater expression of this feeling—emotion
recollected in tranquillity, the joy in earth's loveliness that in
the days of realisation he had been unable to express—Seeger
linked the dead, whose bodies lay thick on the Champagne
battlefield, with the youth and pagan, passionate love which
in life they had sought.

THE AMERICAN IDEAL

In the glad revels, in the happy fêtes,
   When cheeks are flushed, and glasses gilt and pearled
With the sweet wine of France that concentrates
   The sunshine and the beauty of the world,

Drink sometimes, you whose footsteps yet may tread
   The undisturbed, delightful paths of Earth,
To those whose blood, in pious duty shed,
   Hallows the soil where that same wine had birth.

Here, by devoted comrades laid away,
   Along our lines they slumber where they fell,
Beside the crater at the Ferme d'Alger
   And up the bloody slopes of La Pompelle,

And round the city whose cathedral towers
   The enemies of Beauty dared profane,
And in the mat of multicoloured flowers
   That clothe the sunny chalk-fields of Champagne.

Under the little crosses where they rise
   The soldier rests. Now round him undismayed
The cannon thunders, and at night he lies
   At peace beneath the eternal fusillade. . . .

That other generations might possess—
   From shame and menace free in years to come—
A richer heritage of happiness,
   He marched to that heroic martyrdom.

    .   .   .   .   .

There the grape-pickers at their harvesting
   Shall lightly tread and load their wicker trays,
Blessing his memory as they toil and sing
   In the slant sunshine of October days. . . .

I love to think that if my blood should be
   So privileged to sink where his has sunk,
I shall not pass from Earth entirely,
   But when the banquet rings, when healths are drunk,

And faces that the joys of living fill
Glow radiant with laughter and good cheer,
In beaming cups some spark of me shall still
Brim toward the lips that once I held so dear.

So shall one coveting no higher plane
Than nature clothes in colour and flesh and tone,
Even from the grave put upward to attain
The dreams youth cherished and missed and might have
known;

And that strong need that strove unsatisfied
Toward earthly beauty in all forms it wore,
Not death itself shall utterly divide
From the belovèd shapes it thirsted for.

. . . . . .

Honour them not so much with tears and flowers,
But you with whom the sweet fulfilment lies,
Where in the anguish of atrocious hours
Turned their last thoughts and closed their dying eyes,

Rather when music on bright gatherings lays
Its tender spell, and joy is uppermost,
Be mindful of the men they were, and raise
Your glasses to them in one silent toast.

Drink to them—amorous of dear Earth as well,
They asked no tribute lovelier than this—
And in the wine that ripened where they fell,
Oh, frame your lips as though it were a kiss.

In his own happy life nothing had been unfulfilled, and the
knowledge made it easy to go down into the darkness with
a certain faith that what one's own doomed generation had
enjoyed would be enjoyed again by others.

For the rest, individual survival in that inferno of sudden
death seemed to signify very little; so long as one played
one's allotted part, death must certainly find one.

THE AMERICAN IDEAL

I have a rendezvous with Death
At some disputed barricade,
When Spring comes back with rustling shade
And apple-blossoms fill the air—
I have a rendezvous with Death
When Spring brings back blue days and fair.

It may be he shall take my hand
And lead me into his dark land
And close my eyes and quench my breath—
It may be I shall pass him still.
I have a rendezvous with Death
On some scarred slope of battered hill,
When Spring comes round again this year
And the first meadow-flowers appear.

For by 1916 spring had ceased to have its old meaning: it now signified some new 'push,' the massing of troops, awaiting the appointed time of slaughter, the long and crazed hours of preliminary bombardment.

But I've a rendezvous with Death
At midnight in some flaming town,
When Spring trips north again this year,
And I to my pledged word am true,
I shall not fail that rendezvous.

An Arab comrade in the same company of the Foreign Legion helped Seeger to fashion into a ring a piece of twisted metal that he had found lying by a friend's body, and carved on it the Arab word ' Maktoob '—' 'tis written ': Seeger wore it and found comfort in the thought of its meaning. Its simple teaching was being illustrated for the attentive student at every moment of the lunatic carnival that death was holding around him.

So, when the order comes: ' Attack ! '
And the assaulting wave deploys,
And the heart trembles to look back
On life and all its joys;

234

Or in a ditch that they seem near
To find, and round your shallow trough
Drop the big shells that you can hear
Coming a half-mile off;

When, not to hear, some try to talk,
And some to clean their guns, or sing,
And some dig deeper in the chalk—
I look upon my ring:

And nerves relax that were most tense,
And Death comes whistling down unheard,
As I consider all the sense
Held in that mystic word.

And it brings, quieting like balm
My heart whose flutterings have ceased,
The resignation and the calm
And wisdom of the East.

The end was not now far. On July 4, the anniversary
of the Declaration of Independence, Seeger went over
the top with his company at Belloy-en-Santerre. He was
last seen alive, wounded but cheering on his advancing
companions. A few weeks before he had written his
'Ode in Memory of the American Volunteers Fallen
for France,' which he was to have read before the statue
of Lafayette and Washington in Paris on Decoration Day.
Still little known to his countrymen, it stands among the
great and enduring expressions of human triumph over
circumstance, a testimony to what man at his noblest may be.

Ay, it is fitting on this holiday,
Commemorative of our soldier dead,
When—with sweet flowers of our New England May
Hiding the lichened stones by fifty years made gray—
Their graves in every town are garlanded,
That pious tribute should be given too
To our intrepid few
Obscurely fallen here beyond the seas.

235

Those to preserve their country's greatness died;
But by the death of these
Something that we can look upon with pride
Has been achieved, nor wholly unreplied
Can sneerers triumph in the charge they make
That from a war where Freedom was at stake
America withheld and, daunted, stood aside.

By they remembered here with each reviving spring,
Not only that in May, when life is loveliest,
Around Neuville-Saint-Vaast and the disputed crest
Of Vimy, they, superb, unfaltering,
In that fine onslaught that no fire could halt,
Parted impetuous to their first assault;
But that they brought fresh hearts and springlike too
To that high mission, and 'tis meet to strew
With twigs of lilac and spring's earliest rose
The cenotaph of those
Who in the cause that history most endears
Fell in the sunny morn and flower of their young years.

Now, for ever, they rested where they had fallen beside their
French comrades.

There, holding still, in frozen steadfastness,
Their bayonets toward the beckoning frontiers,
They lie—our comrades—lie among their peers,
Clad in the glory of fallen warriors,
Grim clusters under thorny trellises,
Dry, furthest foam upon disastrous shores,
Leaves that made last year beautiful, still strewn
Even as they fell, unchanged, beneath the changing moon;
And earth in her divine indifference
Rolls on, and many paltry things and mean
Prate to be heard and caper to be seen.
But they are silent, calm; their eloquence
Is that incomparable attitude;
No human presences their witness are,
But summer clouds and sunset crimson-hued,
And showers and night winds and the northern star.

Nay, even our salutations seem profane,
Opposed to their Elysian quietude;
Our salutations calling from afar,
From our ignobler plane
And undistinction of our lesser parts:
Hail, brothers, and farewell; you are twice blest, brave hearts.
Double your glory is who perished thus,
For you have died for France and vindicated us.

Nine months later America entered the War.

Vachel Lindsay was a poet of a different kind. Born in Springfield, Illinois, nearly ten years before Seeger, he grew up in the shadow of Lincoln's memory as an early Christian missionary might have grown up at Nazareth. The house he lived in was old by Middle-West standards, and had been formerly occupied by Mrs Lincoln's sister, and in its front parlour a party had been given to Lincoln on the day before he left Springfield for Washington. Sometimes little Vachel Lindsay used to play with his fellow children in the rooms of Lincoln's home.

He inherited the traditions of both the combatants of the Civil War, for though he used to march in his boyhood's games to the battle songs of the North, ' Marching through Georgia ' and ' John Brown's Body,' his mother came from Kentucky and his father was a Southerner who went to the Democratic Convention that elected Grover Cleveland and rode in sash and Democratic hat in the torchlit parade that celebrated that victory for the South. ' The inexplicable Mason and Dixon line, deep-eyed and awful,' he used to say ran straight through his heart. ' My father had filled me with the notion that, way down in Kentucky, once upon a time a certain Abraham Lincoln came, with many soldiers. According to this tale they stole all the horses from my Grandfather Lindsay's estate, drove off all the negroes forever (my grandfather's personal property and mine), burned the crops, and then, in a way not mentioned, stole the farm, and left us all to begin again by studying medicine by a solitary candle. And as for Harriet Beecher Stowe, any one who would read her book was worse than an infidel. This general view of history was challenged by my mother, who, though having many Southern ideas, was all for Lincoln. And I have in many ways agreed with her, but not enough to alter the fact that Mason and Dixon's line runs straight through our house in Springfield still, and straight through my heart. No man may escape his bouncing infancy.'

His parents were of the educated, middle-class leaven, who form the aristocracy of a Middle-West town. Once, in later years, when he was introduced to a Canadian audience as having come from humble and poverty-stricken antecedents, he explained that he was not only sophisticated himself but that all his ancestors had been sophisticated. ' My people were not only important but they were self-important. The family conceit is hereditary from a long way back. It is the hardest thing I have to overcome.'

His father was a doctor and his mother had been a Kentucky college teacher till she met her future husband on a tour of the European art galleries. She had been in the habit of writing plays and oracles and delivering them all over the Middle-West. If the world had only paid heed to them, her son used to say, it would be a kinder, more literary, more sapient, a wittier, a more motherly and a far more resplendent one !

She intended to make Vachel an artist of the pre-Raphaelite sort and bred him up to draw from the life, copy sculpture and imitate Japanese prints, Aubrey Beardsley and Blake. She was a most enlightened and advanced woman. Her husband added to this æsthetic education by reading ' Uncle Remus ' aloud in a musical voice and singing his children asleep with negro melodies. And there was generally a negro servant in the house to chant to them in the sonorous rhythm of his race. Vachel took to the music of words like a duck to water, and did a good deal of serious reading on his own account. One of his chief treasures was an old battered ' Chambers's Encyclopædia of English Literature,' and in it he stumbled on Chatterton and Shelley, Byron, Coleridge and Dryden, all of whom he regarded as his own special discoveries. Another youthful find was Edgar Allen Poe, Emerson's ' jingle-man.'

The boy went to a New York art school, studied at the Metropolitan Museum of Art, and, having been filled with a passionate desire to preach the gospel of beauty, was thus suitably equipped for the battle of life in a materialist country. When he returned to Springfield he joined a little group of earnest Swedenborgians who flourished somewhat exotically in its midst. For some time he sat at their feet, absorbing their peculiar visions, and possibly benefiting by their intellectual discipline. He also made a study on his own account of the science of hieroglyphics. These symbols came to mean a lot to him—perhaps too much for his good as a prospective poet. But he was probably right in supposing that a study of symbols was important to America : the art of all adolescent civilisations tends to be symbolistic, like the pageantry and statuary of medieval Europe, because only by such means can a young, unintellectualised people understand the significance of its national instincts and institutions. The painting of a crown or the carving of a saint established monarchy and Christianity in the hearts of the European peasantry. Some such imagery was needed to unify and civilise young, anarchical America.

With such ideas Lindsay viewed the life of a typical Middle-West town and saw that, though there was much that he loved in it, it was not altogether good. ' Over-eating is indeed a dangerous thing; and on the whole, middle-westerners have too much to eat, too many automobiles, too easy communication, too rich soil, and often an outrageous complacency: they often have the blinking expression that comes after a pious Sunday dinner.' But it was nothing to the expression that these worthy citizens wore when they contemplated Vachel Lindsay. For this young gentleman proceeded to outrage all their deepest convictions. When the chief newspaper of the place offered a prize for the best answer to ' What would you do with a million dollars ? ' he publicly replied, ' I would change them into dimes and have them thrown into the State House yard and anyone who wanted them could come and take as much as he liked.' To Main Street this was as though a man had publicly reviled the Host in a Catholic country. That morning the telephone at his father's house rang continuously.

But Lindsay persisted in his ' merry war with Springfield respectability.' He kept issuing little pamphlets and hieroglyphic drawings, which he called War Bulletins, printing them in gold and distributing them in the streets, and what was far worse, going broke over them. This at least made his enemies take notice of him. ' There is just one way,' he wrote afterwards, ' to convince citizens of the United States that you are dead in earnest about an idea. It will do no good to be crucified for it, or burned at the stake for it. It will do no good to go to jail for it. But if you go broke for a hobby over and over again the genuine fructifying wrath and opposition is terrific. They will notice your idea at least.'

The ' usual Middle-West crucifixion of the artist ' followed, but Lindsay bore it cheerfully. Only every now and then he found he could stand it no more and went off on his own, tramping about without money like a beggar. It was on the same principle as Patrick Henry's ' Give me liberty or give me death ! ' Only the revolt now was not against England but against the United States' own commercial standard— ' a protest against the type of life set forth for all time in two books of Sinclair Lewis: *Babbitt* and *Main Street*. I was told by the Babbitts on every hand I must quit being an artist, or beg. So I said, " I will beg." '

This periodic act of defiance gave Vachel Lindsay the broad American education he needed. To keep body and soul together he worked in a gas-tubing factory in New York City, pushed a truck in the wholesale toy department of Marshall Fields, Chicago, and cut corn with a dollar-a-day gang of roughs on an Illinois farm. He helped to instal a boiler for a public authority and painted signs in Tampa, Florida. Once he was offered the job of ' assistant town sanitarian (as it were) ' for the town of Raton, New Mexico, at seventy-five cents a day, but at this he drew the line. Usually he was driven home after three or four months of roving, but in the spring he would try again. And every time he did so, in the loud language that his young country expects and understands, Lindsay took care to proclaim from the house-tops his rebellion against vulgarity and materialism and everything little and cheap, ' the drab, square-toed, dull, unimaginative America which is gaining on us all.' [1]

His experiences and the confidence bred by his bold revolt taught Lindsay to sing. He discovered that by reciting his crusading verses in lonely farmhouses and inns, where there were few amusements, he could often earn a meal and a night's lodging. He had a rich and powerful voice, with a wonderful range, and a natural sense of rhythm, and his use of them without reserve appeared to entertain his fellow men and women. He therefore started to write songs to recite to ordinary folk about the everyday life of the States, and emulating his mother's earlier experiences, began to build up a professional practice as a reciter of verse in the schools and lecture-rooms of the United States.

It was queer, unorthodox stuff he composed and recited, rather like his own life and the strange medley of the Western American world. It was founded on the primitive elemental songs of the Southern negroes, with the big drum and purposeful force of white America added, and every now and then, strangely unexpected, a touch of the austerity of the Red Indian: Lindsay himself believed that he had Indian blood in his veins. It appealed, like jazz and negro dancing, by rhythm and sheer force of noise straight to the emotions. Often he would make his audience take a part in it themselves. In one of his familiar recitations he would cry in his rich thrilling voice, ' I've been to Palestine,' and his listeners would shout back, ' What did you see in Palestine ? ' And in the margins of his verses, when he printed them, strange

[1] Stephen Graham, *Tramping with a Poet in the Rockies*, p. 40.

communal directions would appear, such as 'Here the audience roars with the leader.'

> King Darius said to the lions:—
> ' Bite Daniel.   Bite Daniel.
> Bite him.   Bite him.   Bite him ! '
>
> Thus roared the lions:—
> ' We want Daniel, Daniel, Daniel,
> We want Daniel, Daniel, Daniel.'
>
> And Daniel did not frown,
> Daniel did not cry.
> He kept on looking at the sky.
> And the Lord said to Gabriel:—
> ' Go chain the lions down,
> Go chain the lions down.
> Go chain the lions down.
> Go chain the lions down.'
>
> And *Gabriel* chained the lions,
> And *Gabriel* chained the lions,
> And *Gabriel* chained the lions,
> And Daniel got out of the den,
> And Daniel got out of the den,
> And Daniel got out of the den.
> And Darius said:—' You're a Christian child,'
> Darius said:—' You're a Christian child,'
> Darius said:—' You're a Christian child,'
> And gave him his job again,
> And gave him his job again,
> And gave him his job again.'

Sometimes, of course, this kind of thing degenerated into mere bombast and repetition, with fantastic idioms which sacrificed sense to sound.   And almost always, when read in silence, his verses offend the taste of the cultured reader bred in the study.   Yet when recited aloud, they are often strangely moving, for Lindsay had a superb ear and a poet's instinct for emotional effect.   He knew how to play on the nerves of sound and, better than most English poets, how to achieve effect by sudden and dramatic contrast—the artist's gift which Shakespeare possessed and most of his great successors of the Anglo-Saxon race have lacked. Nowhere does Lindsay achieve this more triumphantly than in his poem on the Chinese Nightingale, with its introduction to the sinister oriental ironing away in his squalid little shop in San Francisco:

> ' Friend Chang,' I said,
> ' San Francisco sleeps as the dead—
> Ended license, lust and play:
> Why do you iron the night away?
> Your big clock speaks with a deadly sound,
> With a tick and a wail till dawn comes round.
> While the monster shadows glower and creep,
> What can be better for man than sleep?'
>
> ' I will tell you a secret,' Chang replied;
> ' My breast with vision is satisfied,
> And I see green trees and fluttering wings,
> And my deathless bird from Shanghai sings.'
>
> .   .   .   .   .
>
> Chang turned not to the lady slim—
> He bent to his work, ironing away;
> But she was arch, and knowing and glowing,
> For the bird on his shoulder spoke for him.
>
> ' Darling . . . darling . . . darling . . . darling . . .'
> Said the Chinese nightingale.
>
> The great gray joss on a rustic shelf,
> Rakish and shrewd, with his collar awry,
> Sang impolitely, as though by himself,
> Drowning with his bellowing the nightingale's cry:
> ' Back through a hundred, hundred years
> Hear the waves as they climb the piers,
> Hear the howl of the silver seas,
> Hear the thunder.
> Hear the gongs of holy China
> How the waves and tunes combine
> In a rhythmic clashing wonder,
> Incantation old and fine:

THE AMERICAN IDEAL

' Dragons, dragons, Chinese dragons,
Red firecrackers, and green firecrackers,
And dragons, dragons, Chinese dragons.'

.   .   .   .   .

Then sang the bird, so strangely gay,
Fluttering, fluttering, ghostly and gray,

.   .   .   .   .

    ' I have forgotten
    Your dragons great,
    Merry and mad and friendly and bold.
Dim is your proud lost palace-gate.
I vaguely know
There were heroes of old,
Troubles more than the heart could hold,
There were wolves in the woods
Yet lambs in the fold,
Nests in the top of the almond tree. . . .
The evergreen tree . . . and the mulberry tree . . .
Life and hurry and joy forgotten,
Years on years I but half-remember . . .
Man is a torch, then ashes soon,
May and June, then dead December,
Dead December, then again June.
Who shall end my dream's confusion ?
Life is a loom, weaving illusion . . .

.   .   .   .   .

One thing I remember:
Spring came on forever,
Spring came on forever,'
Said the Chinese nightingale.

The sudden break of rhythm and meaning at

    Man is a torch, then ashes soon,

gives the very banality of the preceding lines significance.
It recalls the effect produced by the changes in Lear's
speeches: in both cases a poet, ordinarily far removed from
mysticism, causes an astonished, bewildered sense of recogni-

tion in the reader: surely, the latter reflects, he has visited this place before.

In other poems like ' The Congo ' and ' General William Booth enters into Heaven,' Lindsay won considerable popular fame for himself by the sheer power and repetition of his rhythm. In the first he employs a medium of ' basic savagery ' to explain, as no other medium could, the basic savagery of his theme.

Fat black bucks in a wine-barrel room,
Barrel-house kings, with feet unstable,
Sagged and reeled and pounded on the table,
Pounded on the table,
Beat an empty barrel with the handle of a broom,
Hard as they were able,
Boom, boom, BOOM,
With a silk umbrella and the handle of a broom,
Boomlay, boomlay, boomlay, BOOM.
THEN I had religion, THEN I had a vision.
I could not turn from their revel in derision.
THEN I SAW THE CONGO, CREEPING THROUGH THE BLACK,
CUTTING THROUGH THE FOREST WITH A GOLDEN TRACK.
Then along that riverbank
A thousand miles
Tattooed cannibals danced in files;
Then I heard the boom of the blood-lust song
And a thigh-bone beating on a tin-pan gong.
And ' BLOOD ' screamed the whistles and the fifes of the warriors,
' BLOOD ' screamed the skull-faced, lean witch-doctors,
' Whirl ye the deadly voo-doo rattle,
Harry the uplands,
Steal all the cattle,
Rattle-rattle, rattle-rattle,
Bing.
Boomlay, boomlay, boomlay, BOOM.'

Whether one likes it or not, there is no escaping the rhythmic compulsion of this nor the effectiveness of

Mumbo-Jumbo is dead in the jungle.
Never again will he hoo-doo you.
Never again will he hoo-doo you.

245

In the width of his human sympathies Lindsay occasionally resembles a very different poet, the great Catholic mystic of the pavements, Francis Thompson. Like him he had experienced the underworld of the tramp and the hobo and during his periodic disappearances into the heart of America he had learnt that poetry is to be found in everything. In his ' General William Booth enters into Heaven ' the ragged corps enters.

> Booth led boldly with his big bass drum—
> (Are you washed in the blood of the Lamb ?)
> The Saints smiled gravely and they said : ' He's come.'
> (Are you washed in the blood of the Lamb ?)
> Walking lepers followed, rank on rank,
> Lurching bravos from the ditches dank,
> Drabs from the alleyways and drug fiends pale—
> Minds still passion-ridden, soul-powers frail:—
> Vermin-eaten saints with moldy breath,
> Unwashed legions with the ways of Death—
> (Are you washed in the blood of the Lamb ?)

But above all Lindsay is, like Whitman, an American poet pure and simple. Nobody but an American could possibly have written verse like his. When his friend, Stephen Graham, heard for the first time the ' Rah ! Rah ! Rah ! Rah ! ' of an American school call, Lindsay turned to him with a quick, explanatory, ' There is America ! . . . Most human beings are incapable of understanding anything till they are moved. That's how we do things in America, and go ahead by whoops and yells ! ' [1] To some Englishmen this seems almost shocking.

Like Whitman and every true American, Lindsay believed that the good things of life were meant to be shared, and that without sharing they ceased to be good. His poetry was therefore communal, emotional and scarcely ever intellectual. It was written, like the purple patches of the Elizabethan dramatists, to arouse the feelings of crowded, popular audiences: it deliberately appealed to the groundlings.

[1] Stephen Graham, *Tramping with a Poet in the Rockies*, pp. 173-4.

No American can see that there is anything wrong in doing so. '*Vox populi, vox Dei.*'

Lindsay had a voice like Bryan's, and it carried. Trading rhymes for bread, as he called it, he visited every corner of the nation, as well as Canada and Saskatchewan. But it was not only for bread that he traded rhymes. He had a gospel to preach. Much of his recitation was performed in schools. He has left us a description of it. 'Every new high school auditorium is built to receive the whole school at once, generally two thousand students. It generally has a stage, almost as wide and high as the length of the auditorium the longest way. This is standardization with a vengeance. But there is an innocent and happy glory that goes with it. And there is a secret here, also, that remains unadvertised. As he meets me in the office for the preliminary chat, nearly every principal says: "We had eight hundred students in the old high school building. We built this new school and auditorium for fifteen hundred, and two thousand young men and women came the first day. Therefore they are sitting on the platform, stuffing the balcony, and in the aisles and standing up in the back, and crowding in there at the open doors, and some are out there in the yard trying to find a place to listen. We are now erecting a Junior High School building on the other side of town. Students who were leaving high school in 1912 and heard me then were university seniors in 1916 and heard me then, and are now the people sending for me as the heads of responsible faculty committees in universities. That is, I have seen these young Americans grow up, hundreds of them, all over the United States, unharnessed young Americans.'

All true American poetry is at core political, and Lindsay's is no exception. For a young nation whose whole business has been to plant and create a society in the wilderness, politics is poetry, romance and the source of spiritual inspiration. The birth of a new society is a divine thing. We have seen how the ceaseless discussion of politics was the means of educating Lincoln, who was not only the supreme politician but the supreme poet and prophet of

247

American history. In his day in Springfield, Illinois, politics was the sole topic of intellectual conversation. It was still so in Lindsay's.

How intense was the effect of politics on Lindsay is shown in his poem on the Free Silver Election of 1896. He was only a lad at the time, but he was one of the excited crowd who thronged round the State House at Springfield to hear Bryan, dressed in a coat like a deacon and wearing a black Stetson hat, make one of his famous speeches in his crusade to rouse the Democratic West against the Eastern bankers and Republican bosses. In Lindsay's verse, re-calling in tranquillity the intense emotion of that *annus mirabilis*, the campaign takes on an Homeric quality that lives long after the trumpery differences between the rival camps are forgotten.

> I brag and chant of Bryan, Bryan, Bryan,
> Candidate for president who sketched a silver Zion,
> The one American Poet, who could sing outdoors,
> He brought in tides of wonder, of unprecedented splendor,
> Wild roses from the plains, that made hearts tender,
> All the funny circus silks
> Of politics unfurled. . . .
>
> . . . . .
>
> There were truths eternal in the gab and tittle-tattle.
> There were real heads broken in the fustian and the rattle.
> There were real lines drawn:
> Not the silver and the gold,
> But Nebraska's cry went eastward against the dour and old,
> The mean and cold.

As Bryan's golden voice rang out, all the wild pure things of the West, ' by the dour East oppressed,' were rising in passionate rebellion.

> These creatures were defending things Mark Hanna never
>   dreamed:
> The moods of airy childhood that in desert dews gleamed,
> The gossamers and whimsies,
> The monkeyshines and didoes

Rank and strange
Of the canyons and the range,
The ultimate fantastics
Of the far western slope,
And of prairie schooner children
Born beneath the stars
Beneath falling snows,
Of the babies born at midnight
In the sod huts of lost hope.

The poetry that moves most deeply tells of lost causes.
Bryan was defeated, inevitably, and mankind was again
crucified upon its cross of gold. And for that very reason,
bitterness of it, with all its tragic, sweet regret becomes in
Lindsay's lines as fresh as youth.

Election night at midnight:
Boy Bryan's defeat.
Defeat of western silver.
Defeat of the wheat.
Victory of letterfiles
And plutocrats in miles
With dollar signs upon their coats,
Diamond watchchains on their vests
And spats on their feet.
Victory of custodians,
Plymouth Rock,
And all that inbred landlord stock.
Victory of the neat.
Defeat of the aspen groves of Colorado valleys,
The blue bells of the Rockies,
And blue bonnets of old Texas,
By the Pittsburg alleys,
Defeat of alfalfa and the Mariposa lily,
Defeat of the Pacific and the long Mississippi.
Defeat of the young by the old and silly.
Defeat of tornadoes by the poison vats supreme.
Defeat of my boyhood, defeat of my dream.

There are greater things even than man's struggles and
defeats—the dark, for instance, that swallows them up.
Here is the eternal food of all poetry, Achilles and Hector

249

and the fighters of Greece and Troy going down alike into the shadows from which no man returns. McKinley, the President who won and Mark Hanna, the great boss who made him, the defeated Bryan and brave Altgeld were no exceptions.

Where is McKinley, that respectable McKinley,
The man without an angle or a tangle,
Who soothed down the city man and soothed down the farmer,
The German, the Irish, the Southerner, the Northerner,
Who climbed every greasy pole, and slipped through every
    crack;
Who soothed down the gambling hall, the bar-room, the church,
The devil vote, the angel vote, the neutral vote,
The desperately wicked, and their victims on the rack,
The gold vote, the silver vote, the brass vote, the lead vote,
Every vote? . . .

Where is McKinley, Mark Hanna's McKinley,
His slave, his echo, his suit of clothes?
Gone to join the shadows, with the pomps of that time,
And the flame of that summer's prairie rose.

    .   .   .   .   .

Where is Hanna, bulldog Hanna,
Low-browed Hanna, who said: ' Stand pat ' ?
Gone to his place with old Pierpont Morgan.
Gone somewhere . . . with lean rat Platt.

Where is Roosevelt, the young dude cowboy,
Who hated Bryan, then aped his way?
Gone to join the shadows with mighty Cromwell
And tall King Saul, till the Judgment day.

Where is Altgeld, brave as the truth,
Whose name the few still say with tears ?
Gone to join the ironies with Old John Brown,
Whose fame rings loud for a thousand years.

Where is that boy, that Heaven-born Bryan,
That Homer Bryan, who sang from the West?
Gone to join the shadows with Altgeld the Eagle,
Where the kings and the slaves and the troubadours rest.

As an English critic has pointed out, this poem is at present less moving to an American than to a foreign reader: [1] substitute ' Asquith ' for Bryan, ' Churchill ' for Altgeld, and ' Bonar Law ' for McKinley, and it is easy to see why. But in fifty years the purely factious and irrelevant gloss such names give to the poem will mean no more in America than in England, and they will be as much the stuff of which poetry is made as Homer's catalogue of ships. It is a measure of Lindsay's remarkable achievement.

Lindsay's politics are reflected in his poetry. They are the unchanging politics of the American dream. His love, first and last, is ' the old horse-and-buggy America,' that stood by Jefferson, that sent Andrew Jackson and Lincoln from the wilderness to the White House, that supported Bryan and Roosevelt against the bosses and millionaires, and put Woodrow Wilson into the presidential chair. In one of his prose passages Lindsay describes how during some improvements at Springfield the builders uncovered a pioneer's dwelling buried behind the façade of later additions. ' It was actually a log cabin of the very earliest times, and a two-story log cabin at that. It had been inclosed in sawed boards and fitted with plaster and wall paper, and all modern conveniences; and the logs, almost a foot thick, had been long forgotten; the floors beneath the floors made of hewn logs had been a buried mystery; and the plastered-up fireplace had been a center of incantation long lost. Now all was open. The magnificent walnut logs were there for all to see; and the memory of Sangamon County when it was the rail splitter's Far West, and not a mere Middle West, was before us. Though the wreckers had torn down this log cabin in a week, and though the new brick residence is on the corner now, that log cabin is eternal, and symbol of all we desire.'

All through his poetry Lindsay pleads for the hundred-percent. American tradition, and would have his countrymen accept the full implications of their own free, boisterous past. The rough Lincoln:

[1] Davidson, 'Vachel Lindsay,' *Contemporary American Authors* (ed. J. C. Squire).

A bronzed, lank man ! His suit of ancient black,
A famous high top-hat and plain worn shawl
Make him the quaint great figure that men love,
The prairie-lawyer, master of us all.

and old Hickory before him, prancing high on his horse
before the Capitol with all the wild frontier running behind
him.

Andrew Jackson was eight feet tall.
His arm was a hickory limb and a maul.
His sword was so long he dragged it on the ground,
Every friend was an equal. Every foe was a hound.

Andrew Jackson was a Democrat,
Defying kings in his old cocked hat.
His vast steed rocked like a hobby-horse.
But he sat straight up. He held his course.

' It is only the America that has the courage of her complete
past that can hold up her head in the world of the artists,
priests and sages. It is for us to put the iron dog and deer
back upon the lawn, the John Rogers group back into the
parlor, and get new inspiration from these and from Andrew
Jackson ramping in bronze replica in New Orleans, Nashville
and Washington, and add to them a sense of humor, till it
becomes a sense of beauty that will resist the merely dulcet
and affettuoso.' The American dream was still the best
hope of the future.

Lindsay never stopped preaching it. ' This whole book,'
he wrote of one of his collections, ' is a weapon in a strenuous
battlefield.' It was not merely to the reader of the printed
word that his sermons were delivered, but to the whole of
his huge constituency, at least a million Americans in every
part of the Union, who had heard him recite. Before the
days of broadcasting he had already by sheer vitality and
driving power evolved the technique of making his voice
carry to every corner of the country. No other poet ever
achieved anything quite like it. ' I have put as much
energy into reciting,' he once wrote, ' as a National
League baseball player puts into grand-stands plays.'

It was the passion and sincerity of his conviction that made him so successful. He never rested on his laurels, never commercialised his inspiration as he so easily could have done, and refused to be standardised. To the end life remained for him a crusade and an adventure. Banal, repetitive, bombastic Lindsay often was, because he was an American and could never be at rest, but he was always a poet.

In a very remarkable book, ' The Litany of Washington Street,' Lindsay explained his historical and philosophical view of the United States. He saw American life as following two tendencies, the purely material, arising from the down-drag of the struggle for bare existence in the wilderness, and the spiritual that, springing from the same source, ran counter to it. The first, differentiating America in no way from any other part of the world except in the degree of its intensity, greed and narrow avarice, he typified by the name of Sinclair Lewis's novel, ' Main Street.' But unlike the materialists he did not attach any great importance to it : for the moment it seemed to dominate American life, but it would pass. ' I don't think,' Vachel said once to his friend, Stephen Graham, ' that this money incentive is really a strong one or leads far. That is where I part company with the radicals of this country. They have all founded their faith on the economic theory of history. I'd like to write for them a " romantic theory " of history. I believe in the romantic theory; I do NOT believe in the economic theory.' [1]

The other American tendency Lindsay described as ' Washington Street.' It was ' as far as the human soul may get from the trivial, the puffy, the snappy, the cheap; as far as possible from the world of the smart aleck and the go-getter, the cynic, the liar and the wise guy.' It was a dream of man's spiritual and social equality, stated in the grand manner that America had inherited from its first great President—the aristocrat who made a democracy. ' It has long remained a problem and an almost ineradicable mystery how such a glittering man could be the father of so middle-

---

[1] Stephen Graham, *Tramping with a Poet in the Rockies*, p. 129.

class a country.' But his grand style was still there, and had already taken shape in the tremendous dignity of the sky-scrapers, something entirely of America's own, unknown to any other land or age. It was the same with the American ideal. 'Washington Street is in the grand style from end to end. The grand style has destroyed whole generations of European artists. So I have only sympathy for those who mistrust the grand style. Yet on mature reflection, I think they had better leave the United States; they are going to suffer here. There are so many things in our past and in our present that are grand that, work and expose as busily as the realists may, they will die in the end like ants that try to carry off the White House, and only get away with a little sugar and sand. To abolish the grand style in United States history and in the human imagination because it has been faked by second-raters, is like abolishing all the joy of sun, moon, and stars by a little chatter about mathematical astronomy.' It was all the grander because it was supported by no artificial aristocracy: it rested on the latent spiritual greatness of the ordinary man. ' We've no governing class,' Lindsay once remarked to Stephen Graham. ' We've only got a class that thinks it is the governing class, but it is the most barren in the community. Lincoln's life shows the real truth. Any one who feels he has it in him can rise to the Presidency of the United States.' [1]

It is in this peculiar yet grand manner that Vachel Lindsay sees the United States go by. Even when it is riding in cheap, mass-produced cars there is grandeur in this passage of free men going their own way across a free continent at peace with itself: down the Santa-Fé Trail the autos in rattling humoresque pass westward.

> Listen to the iron-horns, ripping, racking.
> Listen to the quack-horns, slack and clacking.
> Way down the road, trilling like a toad,
> Here comes the *dice*-horn, here comes the *vice*-horn,
> Here comes the *snarl*-horn, *brawl*-horn, *lewd*-horn,
> Followed by the *prude*-horn, bleak and squeaking:—
> (Some of them from Kansas, some of them from Kansas.)

[1] Stephen Graham, *Tramping with a Poet in the Rockies*, p. 204.

And all the while in the hedge the prairie bird sings her song.

> Far away the Rachel-Jane
> Not defeated by the horns
> Sings amidst a hedge of thorns:—
> ' Love and life,
> Eternal youth,—
> Sweet, sweet, sweet, sweet,
> Dew and glory,
> Love and truth,
> Sweet, sweet, sweet, sweet.'
>
> .   .   .   .   .
>
> And then, in an instant, ye modern men,
> Behold the procession once again.
> The United States goes by !

Man free to come and go as he pleases, and the unfenced prairie to redeem his spirit from the bondage of material things, there is the poet's epitome of the American ideal. In an extraordinary poem published in the *London Mercury* of April 1923, Lindsay imagined himself, while tramping in the Rockies with Stephen Graham, encountering a gigantic and romantically-minded mountain cat, who in the gargantuan magnificence of its aspirations personified the whole frontier dream.

> I read the aspens like a book, and every leaf was signed.
> And I climbed above the aspen-grove to read what I could find
> On Mount Clinton Colorado.   I met a mountain-cat.
> I will call him ' Andrew Jackson,' and I mean no harm by that.
> He was growling, and devouring a terrific mountain-rat.
> But when the feast was ended, the mountain-cat was kind,
> And showed a pretty smile, and spoke his mind.
> ' I am dreaming of old Boston,' he said, and wiped his jaws.
> ' I have often HEARD of Boston,' and he folded in his paws.
> ' Boston, Massachusetts—a mountain bold and great.
> I will tell you all about it, if you care to curl and wait.
>
> > If I cannot sing in the aspens' tongue,
> > If I know not what they say,
> > Then I have never gone to school,
> > And have wasted all my day. . . .

THE AMERICAN IDEAL

' In the Boston of my beauty-sleep, when storm-flowers
Are in bloom,
The faithful cats go creeping through the catnip-ferns,
And gloom,
And pounce upon the Boston rats, and drag them to the tomb.
For we are Tom-policemen, vigilant and sure.
We keep the Back Bay ditches and potato cellars pure.
Apples are not bitten into, cheese is let alone.
Sweet corn is left upon the cob, and the beef left on the bone.
Every Sunday morning, the Pilgrims give us codfish balls,
Because we keep the poisonous rats from the Boston halls.'

And then I contradicted him, in a manner firm and flat.
' I have never seen, in the famous Hub, suppression of the rat.'
'*So much the worse for Boston*,' said the whiskery mountain-cat.

And the cat continued his great dream, closing one shrewd
    eye:
' The Tower-of-Babel cactus blazes above the sky.
Fangs and sabres guard the buds and crimson fruits on high.
Yet cactus-eating eagles and black hawks hum through the air,
When the pigeons weep in Copley Square, look up, those wings
    are there,
Proud Yankee birds of prey, overshadowing the land,
Screaming to younger Yankees of the self-same brand,
Whose talk is like the American flag, snapping on the summit
    pole,
Sky-rocket and star-spangled words, round sunflower words,
    they use them whole.
There are no tailors in command, men seem like trees in honest
    leaves.
Their clothes are but their bark and hide, and sod and binding
    for their sheaves.
Men are as the shocks of corn, as natural as alfalfa fields.
And no one yields to purse or badge, only to sweating manhood
    yields.'

Nothing less like Boston in the realm of fact could well
be conceived. Yet the American dream of absolute freedom
persists in very despite of fact.

And the cat purred on, in his great dream, as one who seeks
the noblest ends :—
'Higher than the Back Bay whales, that spout and leap, and bite
their friends,
Higher than those Moby-Dicks, the Boston Lover's-trail ascends,
Higher than the Methodist, or Unitarian spire,
Beyond the range of any fence of boulder or barbed wire,
Telling to each other what the Boston Boys have done,
The lodge-pole pines go towering to the timber-line and sun.
And their whisper stirs love's fury in each pantherish girl-child,
Till she dresses like a columbine, or a bleeding heart gone wild.
Like a hare-bell, golden aster, blue-bell, Indian arrow,
Blue-Jay, squirrel, meadow-lark, loco, mountain-sparrow.
Mayflower, sage brush, dying swan, they court in disarray.
The masquerade in Love's hot name is like a forest-play.
And she is held in worship who adores the noblest boys.

.   .   .   .   .

'In the waterfalls from the sunburnt cliffs, the bold nymphs
leap and shriek,
The wrath of the water makes them fight, its kisses make them
weak.
With shoulders hot with sunburn, with bodies rose and white,
And streaming curls like sunrise rays, or curls like flags of night,
Flowing to their dancing feet, circling them in storm,
And their adorers glory in each lean, Ionic form.
Oh the hearts of women, then set free.   They live the life of old
That chickadees and bobcats sing, the famous Age of Gold . . .
They sleep and star-gaze on the grass, their red-ore camp-fires
shine,
Like heaps of unset rubies spilled on velvet superfine.
And love of man and maid is when the granite weds the snow-
white stream.
The ranch house bursts with babies.   In the wood-lot deep
eyes gleam,
Buffalo children, barking wolves, fuming cinnamon bears.
Human mustangs kick the paint from the breakfast-table chairs.'

And then I contradicted him, in a manner firm and flat.
'I have never heard, in the modest Hub, of a stock ill-bred
as that.'
'*So much the worse for Boston*,' said the lecherous mountain-cat.

257

THE AMERICAN IDEAL

In the last resort, a nation must have a dream at its core or die: there is no other justification for its existence. And it must be its own dream, distinct, peculiar from that of all others. Again and again America has had need of her own flaring, flamboyant dream to save her soul. And she has found it in the recoil of the West, of all things primeval, pure and free, against the dead hand of custom and the rule of the timid and the prudent.

Then I saw the cat there towering, like a cat cut from a hill:—
A prophet-beast of Nature's law, staring with stony will,
Pacing on the icy top, then stretched in drowsy thought,
Then, listening, on tiptoe, to the voice the snow-wind brought,
Tearing at the fire-killed pine trees, kittenish again,
Then speaking like a lion, long made president of men:—
' There are such holy plains and streams, there are such sky-
    arched spaces,
There are life-long trails for private lives, and endless whispering
    places.
Range is so wide there is not room for lust and poison breath
And flesh may walk in Eden, forgetting shame and death.'

And then I contradicted him, in a manner firm and flat:
' I have never heard, in Boston, of anything like that.'
'Boston is peculiar.
Boston is mysterious.
You do not know your Boston,' said the wise, fastidious cat,
And turned again to lick the skull of his prey, the mountain-rat !

And at that, he broke off his wild dream of a perfect human
    race.
And I walked down to the aspen grove where is neither time
    nor place
Nor measurement nor space, except that grass has room
And aspen leaves whisper on forever in their grace.
All day they watch along the banks.   All night the perfume goes
From the mariposa's chalice to the marble mountain-rose,
In the Boston of their beauty-sleep, when storm-flowers
Are in bloom,
In the mystery of their beauty-sleep, when storm-flowers
Are in bloom.

TWO AMERICAN POETS

Lindsay shares with Whitman and the author of the ' Star Spangled Banner ' the distinction of being the singer of American patriotism. The ideal of America, he tells her sons, is open to everyone. The unwanted peoples of the whole world have flocked to her shores, and she has found room for them all. She asks only one thing in return—that they should become hers:—

> Because, gray Europe's rags august
> She tramples in the dust;
> Because we are her fields of corn;
> Because our fires are all reborn.
> From her bosom's deathless embers,
> Flaming
> As she remembers
> The springtime
> And Virginia,
> Our Mother, Pocahontas.
>
> We here renounce our Saxon blood.
> Tomorrow's hopes, an April flood
> Come roaring in. The newest race
> Is born of her resilient grace.
> We here renounce our Teuton pride:
> Our Norse and Slavic boasts have died;
> Italian dreams are swept away,
> And Celtic feuds are lost to-day. . . .
> She sings of lilacs, maples, wheat,
> Her own soil sings beneath her feet,
> Of springtime
> And Virginia,
> Our Mother, Pocahontas.